THE LIBRARY
ST. MARY'S COLLEGE OF MARYLAND
ST. MARY'S CITY, MARYLAND 20686

W9-CMB-303

THE BANYANKOLE

THE SECOND PART OF THE REPORT OF THE MACKIE ETHNOLOGICAL EXPEDITION TO CENTRAL AFRICA

THE BAGESU

AND OTHER TRIBES OF THE UGANDA PROTECTORATE

THE THIRD PART OF THE REPORT OF THE MACKIE ETHNOLOGICAL EXPEDITION TO CENTRAL AFRICA

THE BANYANKOLE

PLATE I

The Mugabe or king

THE BANYANKOLE

THE SECOND PART OF THE REPORT OF
THE MACKIE ETHNOLOGICAL EXPEDITION
TO CENTRAL AFRICA

BY

JOHN ROSCOE, M.A.

Hon. Canon of Norwich and Rector of Ovington, Norfolk
Formerly of the Church Missionary Society

CAMBRIDGE
AT THE UNIVERSITY PRESS
1923

Reprinted by permission of Cambridge University Press
Ⓒ Cambridge University Press

S.B.N.-GB: 576.59255.2
Republished in 1968 by
Gregg Press Limited
1 Westmead
Farnborough Hants
England
Printed in Germany

12-11-78

PREFACE

I HAVE thought it wise to have the notes on this tribe bound as a separate volume, both that the report might be more easily handled, and because the tribe differs considerably from the people of the foregoing report on the Bakitara and calls for special study and consideration.

I have found it advisable in this case to retain the native title of *Mugabe* for the king in deference to the wishes of the officers at work in the country, who dislike the title of king being used for rulers of small African States. I have also used *Nganzi* for the chief minister, and *Bakungu* (sing. *Mukungu*) for chiefs of districts, but on the whole I have followed my usual rule of avoiding the use of native terms requiring constant reference to a vocabulary. I have accepted the local usage in calling the pastoral people *Bahuma* (sing. *Muhuma*) instead of *Bahima*, the Luganda form which I formerly accepted.

Here in Ankole, as in Bunyoro, the information has been obtained at first-hand from men who did not know any English. Though the tribe is older than the Bakitara and milk customs are more strictly followed than in other pastoral tribes, yet their ritual is not so definitely marked as might be expected.

I was unfortunate in arriving in the district when rinderpest was killing the cattle rapidly. This had caused the break-up of many homes, much hardship, and even starvation; I was indeed informed that in one or two cases whole families had committed suicide rather than live upon vegetable diet. Many of the clans and families had wandered far, seeking sustenance, but it was still possible to find a few herds in the country which were untouched by plague.

The tribe is of purer *Bahuma* blood than most pastoral tribes of this region, and even at the present time its members refrain from intermarriage with the serfs who live amongst them and with any tribes who indulge in vegetable food.

The question of the Mugabe's (king's) descent baffled me. It is still an unsettled question whether he was the son of the preceding king or of the king's sister. I am inclined to think that if there has been a change from descent through the female line to descent through the male, it is of recent date, and that formerly the son of a king's sister and not the king's own son succeeded him on the throne.

I am indebted to the same kind helpers as in the work on the Bakitara: Miss Bisset, whose invaluable and indefatigable assistance has enabled me to get on so rapidly; Sir James G. Frazer who has kindly continued to read over my proofs; and my old friend the Rev. W. A. Cox, who had read through the manuscripts before his sudden and greatly regretted death. The loss to the remainder of this work is great, for he was ever ready to examine the manuscripts and his suggestions as to alterations and improvements were of much value.

J. ROSCOE.

OVINGTON, NORFOLK.
   March, 1923.

CONTENTS

CONTENTS

CHAPTER XI. MARRIAGE (*cont.*)

CHAPTER XII. ILLNESS

CHAPTER XIII. DEATH AND INHERITANCE

CHAPTER XIV. WARFARE AND HUNTING

CHAPTER XV. FOLK-LORE

LIST OF PLATES

LIST OF PLATES

MAP

CHAPTER I

ANKOLE, THE COUNTRY AND THE PEOPLE

The Banyankole early invaders of the Lake Region—nomadic life—present constitution of Ankole—the land—the cattle—appearance of the country—the salt district—wild animals—the clans—totemic system—the three great clans and their totems—sub-divisions of the main clans

ONE of the most healthy and interesting portions of the Uganda Protectorate is the district of Ankole. In area it is small, containing, according to the Government returns of 1919, 6131 square miles, while, according to the same returns, the population, including traders and settlers, numbers 149,469. Until recently the people of this region were comparatively unknown, though they were one of the earliest of those tribes who invaded the Lake Region and subdued the small and isolated village communities of negroes who were the original inhabitants of the land. They were of the same stock as the Baganda and the Bakitara or Banyoro, but these tribes and even the pastoral people of Ruanda admit that the Banyankole had settled in the country long before they came there. Evidently their nomadic habits, combined with their complete disregard of everything unconnected with cattle, prevented their making much impression either on the surrounding countries as warriors or on their own country as reformers.

The country in which they settled was well suited for cattle-rearing, and the good climate, excellent pasturage, and plentiful water made it possible for them to continue the nomadic life led by pastoral people, few of whom had any settled dwelling places. Even the Mugabe, by which title the native ruler is now known, had originally only a roughly built bee-hive hut, with a stockade round it forming an enclosure in which cows were kept by night; the ground was always slimy with the animals' droppings, but this and the smell of

the cows were considered wholesome and pleasant. There was
no court-house, for the Mugabe's councils were held under the
shade of some large tree; his main interest in life was guarding
and improving the condition of his large herds; and his food
was milk, which he drank in great quantities, and beer, which
he drank, often to excess, at night.

Ankole, as at present constituted, is much bigger than when
it was an independent state, for the British Government has
added to it Mpororo, Egara, Bweszu and Busongora, small
states which were originally separate kingdoms, entirely
distinct and even antagonistic. The Mugabe of Ankole is now,
under the British Government, ruler of all five states.

In their early times, before outside influence had altered
their outlook, the pastoral people set no value on the land
except for grazing purposes, and the agricultural people, who
cultivated small portions of it, were despised and regarded as
serfs. They could cultivate any land wherever they wished,
but they were expected to do any menial work required by
the pastoral people of the district in which they settled and
to supply them with grain and vegetable food, should they
require it. The pastoral people divided the land up into districts, but these divisions were merely for the purpose of
settling questions which might arise either between agricultural people concerning the boundaries of their plots, or
between herdsmen concerning the use and possession of
watering-places, or between herdsmen and agricultural people,
should the herdsmen allow their cattle to wander over the
fields and destroy the crops. Beyond these cultivated plots,
the country was free to herdsmen, who might pasture their
cattle in any district they pleased.

A man was considered poor or wealthy according to the
number of his cattle, and the places of the chiefs when
assembled before the Mugabe were arranged according to the
size of their herds. All the cattle were regarded as belonging
to the Mugabe, and, though the people to whom he granted
them were at liberty to do as they liked with them within the
country, they might not sell or give them to anyone outside

third totems which differed from each other. Within the clans
the totemic system was of social value, for a man might always
claim the help and support of others who had the same totem
as himself; they might be called upon to help in sickness, to
bury the dead, to give aid to any member of the clan who had
fallen into debt, and, in the case of murder, it was the duty
of every member of the dead man's clan to do his part in
hunting down the murderer and avenging the death.

The tribe was divided into three main clans, each of which
had many sub-divisions. These had, as a rule, the same primary
and at times the same second totem as the principal clan,
but intermarriage was only permitted if they had one distinctive totem. In some cases the totems differed entirely
from those of the clan with which the division claimed relationship. The second totem was not generally regarded as of the
same importance as the primary totem, but, when questions
of relationship arose between clans with the same primary
totem, the second or even the third totem would be named.

The three main clans were:

1. *Abahinda.* This was the royal clan and the totems were
nkima, a small black-faced monkey, and *bulo*, the small millet,
unhusked and uncooked. It was to this clan that the princes
belonged and from it the rulers came. In Karagwe, as in
Ankole, princes were *Bahinda*, in Mpororo and Ruanda they
were *Basambo*, while in Bunyoro, Toro, Koki and Kiziba, they
were *Babito*. The members of the Abahinda clan were not
allowed to work magic or to make medicines. The second
totem was the unhusked raw grain only; when husked and
cooked it might be eaten. It was said that one chief when
hungry had, as was then the habit of the agricultural people,
taken raw grain in the ear and eaten some of it, which was
breaking a custom, for he should not have eaten vegetable food
but have waited until he could obtain milk. Later, his wife
drew his attention to a husk which had clung to his beard
and this annoyed him so much that he made a vow never to
eat unprepared millet again. From that time this was the
second totem of the clan.

2. *Abasambo*. These have as their primary totem *epu*. No one seems to know exactly what this word signifies. It seems to be used as a form of emphatic assertion, either in affirmation or denial, but it is claimed that in this case it represents an unknown animal, like a small gazelle or a large hare, which was captured in Mpororo by certain members of the clan, who quarrelled and fought as to who should take it to the Mugabe. The side which conquered called the animal *epu* and took it as their totem.

The second totem of this clan was a house burnt down; no member of the clan might eat food or salt taken from a burning house, no vessels taken from such a house might be used, and they might not tread upon its site or touch the dust of it. It was said that a man from the original stock of the Basambo who had *epu* as their totem was sent one day to bring out salt and butter from a burning house. Before he got out the roof fell on him and he was burned to death. From this event the clan took their secondary totem.

3. *Abagahe*. Totem, a striped cow, *tubombo*. The milk and the flesh of such a cow were taboo to all members of the clan, with the exception of the owner of the cow.

Sub-divisions of the clan Abahinda with their Totems

CLAN	TOTEMS
1. Ebyanga	*Nkima* (black-faced monkey) and *Bulo* (small millet)

Members of this clan were looked upon as the Mugabe's special friends, and from it he chose his private guards.

2. Enyana	*Nkima* and *Bulo*

This clan had charge of the Mugabe's cows, and from it he chose his chief herdsmen.

3. Abanga	*Nkima* and *Bulo*
4. Engangula	do.
A clan of warriors.	
5. Abataunga	do.
A clan of warriors.	
6. Ebirekeze	do.
A clan of warriors.	
7. Ebyangula	do.

CLAN	TOTEMS
8. Abazozo	*Nkima* and *Bulo*
9. Nkalanga	do.
A clan of princes.	
10. Abalwanyi	do.
11. Abamwango	do.
12. Emanga	do.
13. Obwoma	do.
14. Abazugu	do.
15. Abatagweramu	do.
16. Abatukula maisho	do.
(red-eyed)	
17. Abayangwe	do.

The members of this clan had the task of purifying the Mugabe and painting him with white clay.

18. Abaitira	*Nkima, Bulo* and the breasts of women nursing female children

Any woman of the clan who had a female child took a piece of cow-dung, squeezed a little milk from her breast on it, and handed it to a member of the clan to throw away in the kraal. The members of this clan had much freedom in the royal presence, and might even make jokes there.

19. Abakimbira	*Bulo* and a cow which bore a calf hind feet foremost

The milk of such a cow might not be drunk by the clan until the cow had borne another calf in the usual way. The flesh of the cow was also taboo, should it die or be killed without having borne another calf. Though members of the Bahinda clan, these had not the totem of the black-faced monkey.

20. Abasonga	*Nsenene* (green grasshopper) and *Bulo*

Had not the black-faced monkey. Some members of this clan claimed that they also had as totem a black cow and that only the owner of such a cow might drink its milk or eat its flesh. They claimed that having this third totem they might intermarry with other clans of the Abahinda, but others disputed this.

21. Abaikizi	*Nsenene, Bulo* and food added to a pot in which some was already being cooked

No food might be added to any which was being cooked; if more was required, it must be cooked separately.

22. Abafuma embogo	*Nkima* and *Bulo*
23. Abatalaka	*Nsenene, Bulo* and the breasts of women nursing female children
24. Abungela	*Nkima* and *Bulo*
25. Abafwana	do.

CLAN	TOTEMS

26. Abaigara

This was a clan presented to the Mugabe by his mother, and they became the royal shoemakers.

27. Abaswaswi

The carriers of the royal spear, *Nyamiringa*. When the Mugabe Ntare kita Banyoro was driven from his country by the Banyqro and lost all his cattle, he was in exile for years. Having no cattle, he and his companions were forced to live on honey, roots, seeds and wild fruit until at last a man of the Abaswaswi clan went off to hunt and to spy out the state of the land. He made friends with some of the Banyoro, and dwelt with them until he managed to steal a cow and calf with which he returned to the Mugabe. The latter, much pleased at getting what he considered real food for the first time for months, declared that this man and some member of his clan after him should have the honour of carrying the royal spear. A short time later the medicine-man asked the Mugabe to give him the calf that he might use it to take an augury concerning the Banyoro. The Mugabe went through the usual process of spitting into the calf's mouth and making it swallow the spittle, and next morning the calf was killed and the intestines and lungs examined by the medicine-man who read therefrom a good augury, assuring them that they would return to their own country and recover their lost cattle within a short time. Before long all happened as he had foretold.

28. Abaitweno   ?

From this clan came the men who milked the cows for the use of the Mugabe.

29. Abakungu   ?

These guarded the royal kraal against the danger of grass-fires spreading and setting fire to it.

30. Abamijwa   ?

These guarded the royal kraal against the danger of grass-fires spreading and setting fire to it.

31. Abahangwe   ?

These guarded the royal kraal against the danger of grass-fires spreading and setting fire to it. They also took the clothing from the dead Mugabe, prepared the body for burial, took it to Esanza, and on their return informed the new Mugabe and the people that the Mugabe had been re-born a lion and was alive in the forest.

32. Abayirunto   ?

A man from this clan bathed the king during his coronation ceremonies.

Divisions 1–15 were those from which the Mugabe chose his principal chiefs. Men from the pure Abahinda stock might not marry any women of the Abayangwe or the Abafuma embogo sub-divisions, but were at liberty to intermarry with other sub-divisions.

Sub-divisions of the clan Abasambo with their Totems

CLAN	TOTEMS
1. Abenemurari	Epu and house burnt down

Two chiefs of the Abasambo, Murari and Kukari, who were said to have come from Egypt, wandered as far as Tanganyika and, coming back through Ruanda to Mpororo, they met a woman, Kitami, who governed the country, and one of them married her. They took as their totem Epu and a house burnt down, also a house in which the doorway had been changed from one place to another, and a woman who had had a child by her own father. They claimed descent from Bene, son of Bene Karigira, son of Bene Mafundo, son of Bene Mugambo, son of Abakoroboza, son of Abachuregenyi

2. Abenekiwondwa	Epu and house burnt down
3. Abenebihiri	do.
4. Abenekukari	do.
5. Abenemukonji	do.
6. Abenerugambaje	do.
7. Abenekirenzi	do.
8. Abenemuganga	do.
9. Abawezu	do.
10. Abanyabusana	do.
11. Abanyasi	do.
12. Abasali	do.
13. Abanyika	do.
14. Abatema	do.
15. Abaririra	do.
16. Abanerukima	do.
17. Abanyonzi	do.
18. Abanyaruranyi	do.
19. Abaturagara	do.
20. Abanyamugamba	do.
21. Abenekahaya	do.
22. Abanzira	do.
23. Abasitiaba	Epu and house burnt down and Siti (a red seed used for beads)

They may not handle siti (seeds of the kirikiti?)

CLAN	TOTEMS
24. Abatwe	*Epu* and house burnt down

A division of the Abasitiaba. A father who was old and sick called to his sons in the early morning to go and milk. As it was cold and raining they did not go at once. The old man cursed them for not obeying him and died saying they must not milk cows again. They kept cows but never milked them, though they herded them. They had to call men from other sub-divisions to do the milking, and, should a man refuse without good reason, he was accused to the Mugabe, who deprived him of his cattle.

25. Abaitenya	*Epu*, house burnt down and cow of a yellowish colour

They neither drink the milk nor eat the flesh of a yellow cow.

26. Abasenzia	*Epu* and *Siti*
27. Abami	*Epu* and *Ruhuzumu* (black and white cow)

These separated from the clan because of a fight over milk when a man was killed.

28. Abakungu	*Epu* and house burnt down
29. Abanemucwa	do.
30. Abenebutundu	do.
31. Abasasira	do.
32. Abenenyakizi	do.
33. Abeneguru	do.
34. Abacecezi	do.
35. Abenitanzi	do.
36. Ababyasi	*Epu* and *Karundarego* (a wild creeper)
37. Abatyabe	*Epu* and *Siti*

Belonged to the Basambo but separated owing to a quarrel between two children over some red seeds used as beads, *siti*.

38. Abahambi	?

Claim to belong to Abasambo, who do not acknowledge them. The Basambo will not allow them to sleep in their houses nor to bring their bulls into their kraals. Should one sleep with a Musambo in the open, the Muhambi must wake the other should he wish to turn over. If he did not do so, some disaster would happen to them.

Sub-divisions of the clan Abagahe with their Totems

CLAN	TOTEMS
1. Abalisa	*Lubombo* (a striped cow)
2. Abasinga	Cow with a black stripe
3. Abagina	*Ngobe* (cow, black with white stripes)
4. Abazigaba	*Ngabo* (black and white cow)
5. Abangwi	*Lubombo*

CLAN	TOTEMS
6. Abatorogo	*Lubombo* and *Siti*
7. Abasita	Black cows
8. Abakibiza	*Ngobe*
9. Abalega	do.
10. Abasegi	*Lulimi* (tongues of cows)
11. Abamoli	*Ngabo*
12. Ababito	do.
13. Abenebiraro	*Ngobe*
14. Abanyigana	do.
15. Abenekiimba	do.
16. Abakurungo	do.
17. Abanyara	do.
18. Abenemakuma	do.
19. Abayanzi	do.
20. Abaziro	do.
21. Abataya	do.
22. Abanuma	do.
23. Abanyakafunzo	do.
24. Abamigwa	*Ngobe* and a tail-less cow
25. Abarura	*Ngabo*
26. Abanyimbi	*Ngobe*
27. Abenyitaka	do.
28. Ababuga	do.
29. Abayanja	do.
30. Abaisanza	do.

CHAPTER II

GOVERNMENT

Autocratic rule of the Mugabe—powers and duties of the *Nganzi* or chief minister—pastoral chiefs and the land—the Mugabe's court—guarding the Mugabe—districts and the district chiefs or *Bakungu*—possessions and powers of the *Bakungu*—inferior chiefs—the *Bagalagwa*, chiefs by grants from the Mugabe—employment of herdsmen —agricultural labourers—law and order—right of appeal—causes of strife—fines and confiscations—punishment by detention—taxation of cattle and grain—murder, homicide, and suicide

THE government of the country of Ankole was autocratic and the power was in the hands of the Mugabe or ruler, whose rule was absolute and his decision on any matter final. In order, however, to ease his shoulders of some of the burden of government, he delegated a good deal of his authority to different chiefs, thus creating what might be called the nucleus of a more democratic government while retaining in his own hands the supreme power.

After the Mugabe, the most powerful man in the country was a chief who held the title of *Nganzi*, or "favourite." His office corresponded to that of *Katikiro*, a title which has now been introduced by the Europeans from Buganda, to which country it properly belongs. His power in the land and his influence with the Mugabe were great, and he often acted as the Mugabe's representative and judged cases of appeal from the jurisdiction of the chiefs. One of his duties was to inform the Mugabe when cases of appeal were waiting to be heard. Wherever the Mugabe went, whether on a journey or to war, the *Nganzi* accompanied him; he was the royal confidant and was the only man, with the exception of the Mugabe's personal pages, who had the right to enter the royal presence at any time of the day or night.

The *Nganzi* was always a wealthy man, for he was continually receiving presents of cattle and land from the Mugabe.

PLATE II

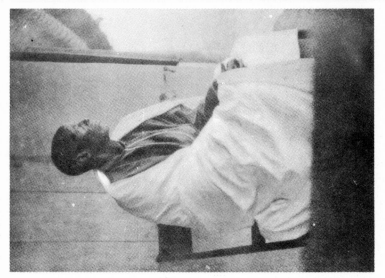

Pastoral (*Muhuma*) chief

PLATE III

The *Nganzi* (principal chief), his wife, daughter and son

Euphorbia tree under which court used to sit

The pastoral chiefs never regarded their land as part of their wealth, for that was always calculated by the number of cows they possessed. Land, however, was indirectly of value, for the agricultural people who resided upon a chief's estates might be called upon to work for him, and they kept him supplied with beer, grain, and vegetable food. Though all the land was open to herdsmen for pasturing their cows, if any dispute arose between herdsmen regarding pasturage, the chief to whom the land belonged could claim the prior right. Such disputes seldom arose except with regard to watering-places. The *Nganzi* had estates in various parts of the country where large numbers of peasants lived and worked for him, and he had great herds of cattle which were pastured all over the land under his herdsmen. He himself always lived in a kraal built in front of the gate of the Mugabe's kraal, for he had to be available whenever the Mugabe wanted him.

When a subject appealed from the decision of any chief to the Mugabe, the latter might order the *Nganzi* or one of his favourite pages to try the case, but disputes concerning cattle in which more than fifty cows were involved, cases where women were accused of deserting their husbands, and other matters of a serious nature had to be brought before him in person. He took no fee for judging a case though, when a fine was imposed, he had the right to take two cows and the *Nganzi* also took two.

The Mugabe's court was not held daily, but the *Nganzi* informed his master whenever a case awaited judgment. The court was held in the open where the Mugabe sat under the shade of a tree. With the exception of those in the forests, the trees of the country were as a rule not large, and the only kind not cut down for building purposes or fire-wood was the tall *Candelabra euphorbia*. Under the shade of one of these, therefore, the royal leopard-skin rug of the Mugabe was generally spread when his court met. He used no seat or stool, but squatted on his haunches in the typical attitude of the cow-people. He usually carried the ordinary walking-stick, a forked stick six to seven feet long, called *Esando*, and his spears and shield were placed near him. The *Nganzi* was in attendance, and behind and at both sides of the Mugabe squatted his pages and his private guard. The important chiefs took their seats near the Mugabe, while the ordinary people squatted a little further off, leaving a path by which those who arrived after the Mugabe had taken his seat might go to greet him.

Only well known and loyal men were allowed to enter the Mugabe's presence armed; such a man simply moved his spear from his right to his left hand, while he shook hands with the Mugabe and greeted him. Men who came from a distance and were not well known or those about whose loyalty there was any doubt had to lay down their weapons some little distance away and approach unarmed. As a further precaution one of the guards would stretch a rod over the path and the stranger had to shake hands with the king across this. Care had always to be taken to guard against an attack on the Mugabe's life, for any man who for one reason or another had been deprived of any of his cows, or a chief who had been deposed, would almost certainly seek to avenge himself on the Mugabe. For this reason any man who had been punished for an offence in either of these ways was generally put to death.

The Mugabe usually sat in court till about noon. During this time he might drink beer, but he did so only on rare occasions and as a rule contented himself with smoking. When he left the meeting he might invite one or two men to accompany him and they would eat and drink beer or milk in the royal kraal while the others dispersed to their homes.

The country was divided into some sixteen districts over each of which there was a chief appointed by the Mugabe. These chiefs were called *Bakungu* (sing. *Mukungu*) or *Abamangi*, and were chosen by each Mugabe on his accession. When one of these chiefs died, the king appointed his successor who was generally, though not necessarily, his heir. The titles belonging to these important chieftaincies were: (1) *Ebyanga*. The holder of this office was usually a prince and nearly always succeeded his father on the throne. He generally gathered round him a large number of friends and adherents who assisted him to secure the throne on his father's death and whom he rewarded by making them important chiefs; (2) *Enyana*. The holder of this office had special responsibility with regard to the Mugabe's cows; (3) *Abanga*; (4) *Engangula*, the holders of which office were warriors; (5) *Abataunga*, the holders of which office were warriors; (6) *Ebirekeze*; (7) *Abaƚenga*; (8) *Nkalanga*, the holder of which office was always a prince; (9) *Abalwanyi*; (10) *Abacwamango*; (11) *Emanga*; (12) *Abazozo*; (13) *Obwoma*; (14) *Abazugu*; (15) *Abatagwerana*; (16) *Abataremwa*.

The *Bakungu* chiefs were always pastoral people and had under them as serfs many agricultural people who dwelt on their land, took charge of their goats, sheep and dogs, and supplied them with grain and beer for their food and drink at such times as they might not, for one reason or another, drink milk. The Mugabe always gave a *Mukungu* chief a present of from one to three hundred cows which became his personal property and were used for the food of the chief and his household. Though these cows were a gift to the man and he regarded them, as well as any others he might possess, as his own property, the Mugabe might deprive him of them all if he saw reason to do so, and no man could sell or exchange cows outside the tribe without the king's permission. It is said that there was once a time when men could do as they liked with all the cows they possessed, but in later times the Mugabe considered himself the owner of all cows in the country. The herds of a *Mukungu* might graze in any part of his district, or, like all cattle-owners, he might send them to any other part of the country.

The authority of a *Mukungu* in his own district was limited, for he had no control over the movements of the subordinate chiefs and other people who might take up their residence or pasture their cows there. All the land was free to cattle-owners who might settle where they liked and move when they liked, and the duties of the district-chief were to settle cases of strife between different owners or their herdsmen, to keep watch over any herds of the Mugabe's cows which were in his district, and to see that the men in charge of them treated the cows properly and did not get into trouble with other herdsmen. There was no animosity between the *Mukungu* and the subordinate chiefs in his district, but the latter were quite independent and only acknowledged him as their superior when some dispute arose among them and required authoritative settlement.

In very recent times, that is, under British authority, one or two of the agricultural people have risen to importance and have been made district-chiefs, but before the influence of western civilisation began to make itself felt such a thing was unknown.

The manner of life of one of these important *Bakungu* chiefs differed in no way from that of the ordinary cow-owner, for he lived in his kraal with a number of his cows about him while the rest of his herds wandered about the country under the care of his herdsmen.

In every district there were a number of inferior chiefs who were subordinate to the *Mukungu* of that district but were, as already explained, quite independent of him, except as regarded their relations with each other. The *Mukungu* himself often conferred chieftainships on friends and relatives who would then settle in his district under the same conditions as the other *Bahuma* or pastoral people who might choose to take up their abode there. These men either brought with them a number of serfs who cultivated the land and provided other labour or they found agricultural people settled there who willingly became their serfs. In addition there were a number of chiefs who were known as *Bagalagwa*. These were men who had been pages in the service of the Mugabe and who had grown too old for such posts. To such men the Mugabe would give estates, cows and serfs. The *Bagalagwa* in each district were under one of themselves and he, in difficult cases, appealed to the *Mukungu* of that district, who in his turn might refer the matter to the Mugabe. In matters which concerned a number of cows greater than fifty the case had to go direct to the Mugabe and any person who concealed a case was fined, the fine going either to the *Mukungu* or, if the case was important, to the Mugabe.

The pastoral chiefs seldom lived in one place for more than two or at most three years, for it was considered necessary to move frequently to keep the cattle free from disease. They would also move if anyone died in the kraal, but in such a case, though they might move even into another district, it was more usual to settle only a short distance away from the original kraal.

Those pastoral people who owned large herds of cows employed as herdsmen men of the pastoral stock who either possessed no cows or had not enough to support a wife and family. Such a man would become the servant of some rich cow-owner, who supplied him with a number of cows for his own use and for the support of his wife. These cows the herdsman regarded as his own and the real owner had no right to the milk from them, though he might, if he needed it, ask his herdsman to supply him with some, a request which the herdsman was quite at liberty to refuse. The herdsman thus got the milk from these cows, and his own cows, if he had any, got the use of the bull of his master's herd and of the salt provided for his master's cows, while the only return he had to make was to herd his master's cows.

These herdsmen were quite free to leave their masters without any warning. If some request, perhaps of a young bull for meat or a cow-hide for clothing, was refused, a herdsman would show his displeasure by absenting himself from the kraal. If his master showed no signs of willingness to come to an agreement, he would return to fetch his wife and they would depart to place themselves under some other master, leaving their former one to manage as best he could.

Each cow-owner had also attached to him a large number of agricultural workers, a *Mukungu* having from one to three hundred of these serfs. The land was all in the Mugabe's hands and he granted portions to the chiefs for their serfs to cultivate. The herdsmen were forbidden to trespass with their cows on such cultivated land. The chief might bring his serfs with him when he moved to a new part of the country, or he might find agricultural workers already settled there. These serfs were free to leave their masters at any time but they never attempted to set up establishments for themselves and live independently unless they had the direct permission and sanction of the Mugabe, who might for some special reason grant a portion of land to one of them as his own estate. In addition to supplying their pastoral masters with grain and beer, they looked after their dogs, goats and sheep, and did their building and other labour for them.

The chief of a kraal settled all matters within the kraal unless there was any serious disturbance resulting in a fight, in which case he had to appeal to the district-chief. Should the fact that he had tried to keep such a case secret come to light he had to pay the fine of a bull, which went to the *Mukungu* or the Mugabe according to the seriousness of the case.

The *Mukungu* chiefs were thus responsible for keeping the peace in their own districts, but a large amount of bribery and corruption went on. A dissatisfied client, however, was at liberty to appeal from these smaller courts, if indeed they could be called courts, to the Mugabe, and any case involving a number of cows greater than fifty had to go to the higher court.

The most frequent causes of strife were connected with the cows. One set of herdsmen would attempt to drive another herd away from the watering-place where they were drinking or to deprive them of their salt water, and a free fight would ensue. Fights also arose when one man considered himself defrauded. If a man killed a cow and distributed the meat, he might use force to get the payment promised by those who had bought it, instead of taking the correct course of suing them for debt in the courts. There were also sometimes cases when a man had promised à woman relative in marriage and, having received part of the marriage fee, refused to fulfil his side of the bargain.

When a case was brought before the district-chief, both accused and accuser had to bring a cow as the fee, and the chief as a rule kept both cows, though in some cases one might be given to the owner of the kraal from which the injured man came. If anyone had been hurt in a quarrel, the *Mukungu* usually brought the case to the notice of the Mugabe. Should the injury have been caused by stone-throwing, the Mugabe took one cow from the offender, or, if both parties had suffered injuries, he took one cow from each. If the fight had been more serious and spears had been used, all the cattle of both parties were confiscated and held until the case had been tried. An injured man seldom received any compensation, though, in very rare cases, the Mugabe might order a fine of one cow to be paid to a man who had been seriously hurt. If a man died from his injuries, his relatives received a number of cows according to the Mugabe's decision, and two cows out of every ten of such a fine were paid to the Mugabe, the *Nganzi*, or the *Mukungu*, as the case might be. This proportion of the fine was the only payment taken by the Mugabe when cases came to his court.

There was no place of detention for people who had committed a crime nor was this used as a form of punishment, though sometimes in a serious case a man might be put in stocks, consisting of logs of wood into which one or both feet were thrust through holes cut in the logs. Such detention, however, was only practised in the case of doomed men and was very rare, for such men were generally put to death at once and there was no necessity for detention.

A criminal who had escaped to some distant place and was caught there, might be tied with a rope when being brought back, but even that was considered to be too degrading to the accused.

The chief method of punishment was by fine, and, should an accused man not appear to answer the charge against him, he lost his case and was deprived of all his possessions.

TAXATION

The chiefs had no right to levy a tax upon the people in their districts. Every year the Mugabe sent his men into each district to collect a number of cows. The messengers had power to take as many cows as they thought fit, but the usual proportion was two cows from a herd of one hundred and one from a herd of fifty. Herds under fifty paid no tax, so that two or three herdsmen who had joined together to set up an independent kraal were free of tax until their herd amounted to over fifty cows.

Twice each month a district-chief had to send beer and millet to the royal kraal for the use of the Mugabe's household, and the Mugabe's own peasants took beer and grain to him daily. Though a peasant always supplied his master with grain and beer, there was no stipulated amount and he was free to refuse if his store was running short.

MURDER

A murderer had to go about his work very cleverly if he was to escape the penalty of his deed, for it was the business of the whole clan of a murdered man to discover and kill the murderer. Murders were thus not very common and few murderers escaped detection. It was not necessary, however, to discover in all cases the actual criminal, for, if it was found that he had escaped into safety, the members of the injured clan attempted to capture and kill any member of the murderer's clan, irrespective of age or sex, for any life would pay for a life and satisfy the ghost.

It was, however, preferable to find the actual murderer, and, as soon as the deed was discovered, the chief of the district was informed and a search instituted among the dwellers in that district for the culprit. A suspected man against whom there was no real proof might be watched for some time until he betrayed himself by a chance word or act. If, however, the search was unavailing, a diviner would be set to work to discover by an augury the name of the guilty man. When such a step was taken, the fear of magic, added to the dread of the vengeance of the ghost, usually led the murderer to reveal himself.

The clan of a murdered man rarely made any appeal to the Mugabe; if they did, it was generally for a spear with which to kill the murderer. Sometimes, however, if the clan of the murderer was very powerful and revenge was impossible or might have serious consequences, the weaker clan would appeal to the Mugabe in order to get a peaceful settlement and compensation. The Mugabe might give a powerful clan three months in which to produce the person of the murderer, and the case would then be tried.

It was not necessary for the Mugabe himself to be present at such a trial, but some member of the Bayangwe clan had to be there. When the trial took place, the relatives of the murderer brought a cow and a sheep to the place. These were killed and the Mugabe or his representative called for six men from each side and stood between them while they dipped their fingers in a vessel containing the blood of the animals and swore to be friendly. Then the fine was paid and the matter ended. From the fine paid by the murderer's clan, two or three cows went to the king and, in addition to the fine, the murderer or his clan gave a cow in milk and its calf to the father of the murdered man. This method of settling the matter was called *Kirabo*.

Sometimes, however, a more formal procedure was gone through at the trial. The murderer's clan brought a sheep and a bull, and both clans mustered in force and stood on opposite sides of some open space while the Mugabe stood between them. A branch of the sacred tree *kirikiti* was planted beside him and one of the drums which, as described in chapter IV, were attendants on the sacred drums, was placed there. Each party then rubbed a little butter on the tree as a sign that they wanted peace, and declared to the Mugabe their desire to settle the case amicably. The Mugabe next summoned a man from the offender's clan and bade him pluck a little wool from the sheep and hand it to a member of the injured clan, who put it on the tree and proceeded to go through the same process, handing the wool to the former man, who put it also on the tree. A pot of beer was now handed to the man from the offender's clan who drank and passed it to the other to drink. A pipe was next handed to the former who smoked and passed it to the other and both puffed the smoke over the tree. The bull was killed and the blood caught and brought to the two men, who smeared each other's hands with it and swore friendship. The meat of the bull was cooked in the open and all the people partook of it as a sign of the renewal of friendship. The Mugabe then beat the drum, announced that they were reconciled, and swore to stand by the injured party should the covenant be broken by either. When things were not thus settled, the king generally took the whole of the murderer's property; but if the clans were reconciled, he imposed a fine, sometimes amounting to one hundred cows, of which some twenty went to him and the rest to the injured party. Should the fine be forty cows, the Mugabe took six of them. After this the murderer might return to his home and fear no further trouble from the other clan. No murderer might sleep on a bed, but had to lie on the floor until the case was tried and settled.

If a man killed another accidentally, he escaped to some place of safety until he could explain his conduct and arrange matters. The dead man's clan asked for compensation, and the Mugabe heard the case in open court and fixed the amount of the fine.

A suicide for whose deed no reason could be found was buried in waste land, but if a man or woman committed suicide for grief at the death of a relative they were buried with much honour, for it was looked upon as a laudable act. In almost all cases suicides were buried like other people and the usual mourning ceremonies were gone through.

CHAPTER III

RELIGION AND BELIEF

Ruhanga, the creator—divine dynasty of kings—fetishes and shrines of different gods—story of Kyomya and the drums—the earthquake god—importance of the ghosts—family ghosts and offerings—foreign ghosts—re-birth of the dead—spirits of rulers enter lions—offerings to the Mugabe's ancestors—medicine-men and methods of taking auguries—fetishes and amulets—rain-making—blood-brotherhood—dreams

THERE was little in the way of formulated religion, for, though there were gods who were acknowledged as superior beings, there were no priests, the duties usually performed by such men being left to mediums and medicine-men, and there were no temples and only a few sacrifices, which were performed by the medicine-men.

The creator was Ruhanga, who was thought to have lived in the sky. He was known as Creator and Powerful One, but no prayers were offered to him though his name was used in ejaculations such as "Tata Ruhanga," an exclamation used in joy at the birth of a child and accompanied by clapping the hands. Another ejaculation in which the name was used was "Ruhanga akutambire!" "May god heal you!"

Ruhanga created a man Rugabe and his wife Nyamate and set them to people the earth. They were not ordinary mortals, for they had no mother but were both created by Ruhanga. They had a son, Isimbwa, who was the first of a dynasty of kings who ruled the country and who did not die, but became the gods of the people. These deified kings had no temples, but there were certain men and women who claimed to be their mediums and agents and to be able to cure sickness and help the people. The list of these early kings was given as follows:

Isimbwa, son of Rugabe—Ndahaura—Wamara—Ruhinda—Nkubayazurama—Owanyira—Rugamba na Mazu—Nyabugaro—Kasasira—Rumongi—Mirindi—Ntare kita Banyoro—Macwa.

Another list which was also given differed from the first:

Kazoba — Wamara — Kagoro — Ndahaura — Mugenyi — Kyomya — Twona — Ryangombe — Nyakiriro — Kiro — Mugasa — Timbwe —Karuzi—Kalinzi.

Each of the principal gods had his special fetish and the guardians of these lived in the Mugabe's kraal. The most popular deity was Kagoro, and his medium carried his emblem about to kraals where help was needed. Wherever it went, a cow was given and a shrine built to the god.

Kazoba had a special shrine in the country of the clan Baisanza, whose members went there to ask for favours, taking to him cattle and beer.

Mugasa was a royal deity and was also specially concerned with this clan Baisanza. If anyone else wished to consult this god, he had to approach him through an appointed member of the clan who might intercede for him.

When any person applied to Nyakiriro, he had to present him with one or two copper bracelets and a cow.

Wamara was said to be the god of plenty and fertility, and when a woman had twins, the elder was dedicated to him and the other to Kagoro. After the birth the mother presented a cow to each of these gods. These were kept alive and only women might drink the milk from them. This was done to preserve the husband, the children, and the herds from death.

The mother of Kyomya was said to have been a princess and the sister of Wamara. Wamara married her and they had one son, Kyomya. Later Wamara sent the woman away but kept the son, who became a trader and wandered to Bukoba with salt, coffee-berries, cats, and other goods. When he returned to Ankole, he became herdsman to a cow-man named Kyana who, in addition to herding, made him fetch fire-wood. Soon the wife of Kyana began to suspect that Kyomya was not an ordinary mortal and she and her husband laid all kinds of traps for him, but he evaded them all. At last one day while he was getting fire-wood, Kyomya discovered the sacred drums which his father Wamara had received from the moon and which Kyana had stolen. He flicked his fingers and the drums came to him, and a few days later he left Kyana to take the drums back to his father at Ruwanda in Ankole near Kabula. After that he left the world and became a god.

The earthquake god was originally called Omusisi, but of recent years some people have claimed to be the mediums of an earthquake god called Nabinge. This is probably the name used for Omusisi by another branch of the pastoral people, from whom it has now been introduced into Ankole. These priests built a hut and hung about in it objects which rattled and made a noise when shaken. When anyone came to consult them, the priests made a noise like the rumbling of an earthquake and shook the hut until it seemed as if it were falling down. This so terrified the applicants that they willingly made offerings to the sham mediums in order to ward off the danger which threatened.

At the time when Ruhanga created the first man and woman, he also created a peasant man and woman to be their servants and these were the ancestors of the serfs.

The really important supernatural beings were the ghosts. These had their abode in another world which was, however, of little importance, for they spent most of their time hovering round the living, helping them or visiting their displeasure upon them according to the treatment they received from their surviving relatives and friends, and punishing any infringements of clan law and custom. They were never seen but their presence was felt, for the wind which blew amongst the trees and grass of the grazing-grounds showed the presence of ghosts of the cow-people, while those of peasants were heard rustling amongst the grain or in the plantain trees. It was to these ghosts rather than to the great gods that the people turned for help and to them they made offerings and prayers.

All classes of the people from the Mugabe downwards had shrines for the family ghosts, and cows were dedicated to them. These were kept alive and the milk from them was daily placed on a special stand devoted to the ghost, where it remained for some time until the ghost had taken its meal of the essence, after which the remainder was drunk by the owner of the house and those of his children who lived with him. On the side of the bed furthest from the door in the hut was the sacred place where milk for the ghost of the owner's father was placed. The special pot for it was called *kyenzimu*. If the owner's mother was dead, a pot for her ghost, called *ekyenshugi*, might also be placed there.

It was only the ghosts of men who were universally feared, but women feared the ghosts of women, for they were sometimes dangerous to women of their own clan and to children. If a woman's ghost was the cause of sickness among children, the mother would persuade her husband to give milk to pacify the ghost. Another method of laying such a ghost was for the woman to go to cross-roads, build a shrine, and offer a little beer and grain. If this did not have the desired effect, the woman persuaded her husband to accompany her to her own clan where they offered a goat, or, in extreme cases, even a cow to the ghost.

Even the poorer herdsmen had their little shrines for ghosts and dedicated the milk from certain cows to their departed relatives, the owner of the shrine drinking the milk afterwards. When the departed intimated in some way that he desired to have a meal, the owner of the shrine brought either a fat cow or a bull, which was secured near the shrine during the night. In the early morning it was killed and the owner of the shrine and his clan-brothers ate the meat near the shrine.

When the ghost of a man, who had come from another country and died, was causing trouble to any member of a clan, a bull was taken either to the hills overlooking the country from which the man came or to the path by which he came. The animal was dedicated to the ghost and they called upon it to accept the offering, after which they killed the bull and ate or gave away all the flesh. The bones were burned to dust, for nothing might be left or taken back.

It was not easy to discover the actual belief of the people with regard to the final state of the ghosts, but it seemed that they were supposed to be re-born in their grandchildren. This

was not precisely stated, but people said that certain graves
might safely be left untended, with only a tree to mark the
spot, though as long as the ghost was disembodied, the grave
had to be distinguished and a shrine kept near it for offerings.
Children were called by the names of former members of the
clan because it was thought that the ghosts would then take
an interest in them and help them.

There were no ghosts of trees or animals, for only human
beings were thought to have spirits which became ghosts.

The ghosts of kings, however, did not remain spirits but
entered into lions. When a lion became dangerous, a medicine-
man had to be consulted before any steps could be taken to
get rid of it. This man had to discover by augury whether the
attacks were merely the act of a ravenous animal seeking
prey or whether they were a sign that the Mugabe had
neglected to make such offerings as would satisfy the spirits
of his ancestors. In the Mugabe's kraal there was a place
called *Kagondo* which was devoted to the shrines of past
rulers, and there frequent offerings were made and milk from
dedicated cows was placed daily for a time before being drunk
by the special cow-men who herded these cows and by the
men who guarded the shrines.

When an offering was required, a cow past bearing or a bull
was brought in the evening to a place near the shrine, where
a rope was tied to its leg. The other end of the rope was buried
in a hole about a foot deep and the earth was beaten down
hard so that the animal was secured. It was left there during
the night for the ghost to examine and accept it, and a guard
from the royal clan, Bayangwe, kept watch over it. In the
early morning the Mugabe came and offered the animal to
the ghost, saying, "This cow I give to you; in return pray
cause me no more trouble." An offering of this kind was made
when the Mugabe felt ill and an augury proved that the illness
was caused by the ghost of one of his ancestors. Animals for
food were killed by being poleaxed just behind the horns, the
axe being driven well into the skull, but a cow for a sacrifice
was killed by cutting its throat. The blood was allowed to

run on the ground near the shrine and the meat was eaten
by the Mugabe and the members of the royal clan on the spot.
Sometimes it happened that the meat lasted several days
and a fresh set of relatives of the Mugabe were called to eat
it each day, for none of it might be taken away, and all must
be cooked and eaten near the spot where the animal was
killed. The head of the animal was eaten by the special men
who looked after the fire-wood.

When one of the cows which had been dedicated to the
ghosts was killed, the herdsmen of the herd from which that
animal was taken received some of the meat, their share being
cut from the back without any bones. No bones might be
broken in killing the animal or afterwards in cutting up the
meat, and all that was not eaten had to be consumed by fire
so that nothing was left.

MEDICINE-MEN

Ghosts and magic were the causes commonly assigned to
illness and the first duty of a medicine-man who had been
called in to a case was to discover by augury the cause, for
upon this the treatment depended. The methods employed
in dealing with cases of illness will be more fully dealt with
in the chapter on Illness, p. 134.

Medicine-men, however, were consulted in other matters
and auguries were taken in all kinds of difficulties. The
Mugabe, or any of the people who could afford to pay large
fees, summoned a diviner, who examined the entrails of
cattle, sheep, or fowls, or used some other of what were considered the superior methods of taking the augury.

One diviner, who was specially called in to discover the
cause of any illness of the Mugabe, used two sticks and an
insect called *ntondo*. He fixed one stick upright in the ground
and placed the other in a slanting position against it. On the
sloping stick he put an insect and made a noise as if spitting
upon it until it began to move; then he repeated to it the
names of royal ancestors who might be the cause of the illness.
If the insect turned towards him, he knew that the name was

not that of the ghost responsible for the Mugabe's state of health, and he tried name after name until the insect walked up the stick, thus declaring that the ancestor last named was the cause of the illness. Offerings were then made, as already described, to the ghost of that ancestor at his shrine in the Mugabe's kraal.

In another case a number of holes, shaped like troughs for watering cattle but not so big, were made. The Mugabe or the chief concerned was given a little of certain herbs finely powdered on which he spat to bless them and whispered to them his wishes. The diviner enclosed this powder in balls of clay and dropped one in each water hole. He took butter and oiled his hands well and then broke up the balls of clay in the water and sprinkled more of the powder on it. From the forms taken by this powder he gave his augury. If it was good, some of the water was put on the breast, shoulders, and forehead of the enquirer, to whom the blessing was thus conveyed.

Another test was known as the butter test; when a diviner was going to use this, he filled six to ten cooking-pots with water and put them on the fire. When the water boiled, the medicine-man took a bunch of herbs, *ezubwi*, dipped it in the boiling water and squeezed it into each pot until the water was discoloured. A piece of butter was handed to the enquirer who whispered his wishes over it and the medicine-man then dropped a bit of it into each pot. According to the way in which the butter melted and spread in the water, he gave his verdict. Should a fly or other insect fall into the pots during the process the test was invalid and they had to begin afresh. If the augury was good, the enquirer was anointed with the water from the pots.

These superior medicine-men also worked auguries with animals. A fowl, goat, sheep, or bull, according to the importance of the case, was killed and the medicine-man examined the markings on the intestines and on the lungs, which he stretched, in order to discern the markings better, by inserting his finger into them. When the Mugabe wished to go to war he appealed to some of these medicine-men to tell him whether the expedition would be successful, and the chief medicine-man always accompanied the army and took auguries at intervals during the course of the campaign.

The poorer people could not afford to consult these higher medicine-men, who were known as *Bafumu*, but they applied to those of a lower class, *Omulaguzi*, who took auguries by scattering seeds or by throwing sticks into water, or other such methods. One man used a number of bits of stick, which had to be six, twelve, or fourteen. He made a pretence of spitting on them and declared to them the cause which required the augury. He then threw them into a pot of water and gave the augury from their position.

Another medicine-man took a cup of millet and six, twelve, or fourteen stones or lumps of mud over which he made a pretence of spitting while telling them the problem which required solution. He threw the millet and the stones or mud on to a skin and, watching the position in which they fell, read therefrom the augury.

FETISHES AND AMULETS

There were few fetishes used, the chief of them being the royal fetishes known as *Mirimbo*, which were horns filled by certain medicine-men with herbs and other ingredients. The maker pronounced incantations over these before he filled in the ends. Claws and teeth of animals, and even hollow roots and pieces of bamboo, were used as receptacles for medicine said to be blessed by some particular god. The object thus filled was sold by the medicine-man and was said to contain the essence of the god and to be of value in battle or against wild beasts or in other dangers.

Amulets were made by different medicine-men and medicine-women as charms against a variety of evils. There was a special kind, called *ngisa* or *mpeka*, which was made by women-doctors (*Omusuzi*) to be worn by women who desired to have children. These women-doctors made amulets for women only, while the medicine-men (*Bafumu*) dealt both with men and

women. The remnant of any herb which had proved efficacious
in illness was often made into an amulet to guard against a
recurrence of the same disease. Amulets were also used as
charms against fever, snake-bite, attack from wild beasts,
eye diseases, swellings on the body and other troubles.

In time of war, women wearing fetishes went round a
kirikiti tree rubbing it upwards with butter with their hands
and praying to it to guard some individual in the battle.

RAIN-MAKING

The rain-makers of Ankole belonged entirely to the serf
class and were called *Abaizi be nzura*. Their fetishes were
horns of antelope and male sheep and were filled with herbs
and such ingredients as they considered suitable for their
purpose.

When the people wanted rain they took a black sheep to
the rain-maker, who killed it, allowing the blood to flow
on his fetish. He then built a shrine in which he put the
fetish and he and his clients ate a sacred meal of the flesh
of the sheep there. Beside this shrine he also pronounced his
incantations and prayers for rain. From this time until the
rain fell the rain-maker had to practise sexual abstinence,
for indulgence would render his charms ineffective.

All kinds of gifts might be brought to the rain-maker by
the people who came to ask for rain. The Mugabe always sent
a cow and others brought hoes, millet, or sheep. If the rain-
maker considered that the pay offered was inadequate, the
chief of the district might take from the people by force what
was necessary to pay him.

If the rain did not come and the people showed their
annoyance by troubling the rain-maker, he might become
angry and, by redoubling his efforts, bring not only rain but
hail and thunder.

These rain-makers had the power to stop rain by their
fetishes, and they also blew through whistles to raise a wind
which might carry off the clouds and cause the rain to
cease.

There was also another man, Kuamula, who could stop rain, but he was looked upon as an evil person and not regarded in the same light as a legitimate rain-maker. He made a bundle of dried and rotten *kirikiti* twigs, pieces of the trees *luwawo*, *bubohaboha* and *namanya-ku-nenakasi*, and earth, and tied this to a reed which he fastened to a post planted in the ground in some secluded spot. Another stick to which he tied meat was put in a sloping position against this post and under it he lit a fire, saying, "I want sun so that my fire may burn and cook my meat. Let there be no rain to extinguish it." This brought drought and famine, unless the people paid him large sums to remove his spells.

BLOOD-BROTHERHOOD

When two men formed a friendship more than ordinarily close and wished to cement it publicly, they went through a ceremony before witnesses.

One man went to stay the night with the other and in the early morning, before the cows were milked, they came into the kraal and sat on the ground facing each other, while the witnesses, chief among whom was the sister of the man who was host, stood around.

Between the two men were laid a coffee-berry, some leaves from the *kirikiti* tree, and a sharp knife or an arrow such as was used for bleeding the cows. The arrow was preferred for the purpose, and a razor might never be used.

Each man in turn took the arrow, pinched up the flesh near his navel and made a few scratches until he drew a little blood which he caught in the palm of his hand. Each took half the coffee bean, rubbed it in the blood, and placed one or two leaves of the *kirikiti* tree between the fingers of that hand. He then with his other hand took hold of his companion's hand and took the half bean from it with his lips. The host took the arrow and rubbed it against the thumb-nail of the right hand of the other man as though he was cutting it, put it on his head as though shaving the hair, and passed it round his body and down to his right foot as though to cut the nail of his great toe. The other man then took the arrow and went through the same performance. During the process the man performing the action swore to be true and loyal to the other and his family, saying, "Let me die if I fail to be a true brother." The sister took hold of the right wrist of each and said that they must not part from each other. Each presented her with a bark-cloth or two bracelets before they separated.

DREAMS

When a man dreamt that he was dead, it meant that some relative or friend, possibly at a distance, was dead.

When a man dreamt that he had received a present, he expected either to receive one himself or to hear of some relative having done so.

When the Mugabe dreamt an unpleasant dream, he sent for medicine-men, who might drive off the evil by making him smell a drug which made him sneeze, or by giving him a certain root to chew. When he had dreamt of evil attacking him or the land, the medicine-man brought a pot of water from which the Mugabe took a sip and spat it out five times. A bunch of herbs, *mwetengo* and *mbuza*, was given to him and he passed them over his head, saying, "Let the evil pass away," spat on them and sent them from his presence.

When he dreamt about war, he called the leading chiefs to him and explained the situation and together they decided whether they should take action.

CHAPTER IV

RULERS OF ANKOLE. PART I

Difficulty in obtaining names of rulers—importance of the Mugabe's sister—possible matrilineal succession—list of rulers—relations with neighbouring kings—royal intermarriage—the Mugabe's kraal—the milk—the cows—the entrance—the houses—cooks and brewers—moving the royal kraal—life of the Mugabe—hunting—the court—pages—drinking milk—washing—meals—evening meetings—the Mugabe's bed—the royal drums—the hut—contents of the hut—the chief drums—attendants of the drums—offerings to the drums—spear and staff of the drums—repairing drums—sacrifices to the drums—the drums and war—the Mugabe's cows—herdsmen

WHEN I first visited Ankole more than twelve years ago, it was impossible to obtain from the people any information as to the names of their previous rulers, and the names of the mothers of the rulers were totally unknown. On making enquiries on this, my second visit, I found them prepared with a list of kings, but on neither occasion was I able to obtain the names of any of the kings' wives, brothers or sisters. It seems that contact with other tribes, especially with the Baganda and the Bakitara, aroused a desire to have a genealogy of the royal family, and a list of kings was prepared for the purpose.

It was quite evident that there never was a queen, and that the wives of the Mugabe, or king, never had any official position or took any prominent place in the kingdom. The Mugabe's sister, however, was an important person, though she was not called queen nor was she a wife of the Mugabe. She married whom she pleased and, though the Mugabe would try to induce her to marry some man of his choice, she was not compelled to follow his wishes. The sister of the present Mugabe refused to marry the man he chose for her, even though he attempted to enforce his wishes and was so angry at her refusal that for a long time he would not see her. This as well as many other customs, especially those connected with inheritance and the purification ceremonies, points to the probable existence in former times of a custom of matrilineal succession, which, however, the present generation refuses to acknowledge, as they consider such a regime inferior to the patrilineal system which obtains in the surrounding countries, and thus dread the scorn of their neighbours.

Another reason for the difficulty experienced in obtaining any of the names of past kings was that the name of a king was never again mentioned after his death and, moreover, if it corresponded with some word in ordinary use, that word was dropped out of the language. Thus, when the last Mugabe, Ntare, died, the name for a lion, which was *ntare*, was altered to *ekichunchu*.

The list of rulers which I received on my recent visit was as follows:

1. Nyamhanga	2. Rugabe	3. Isimbwa
4. Ndahaura	5. Wamara	6. Ruhinda
7. Nkubayarurama	8. Nyeika or Owanyira	9. Rugamba na Mazu
10. Nyabugaro	11. Kasasira	12. Rumongi
13. Mirindi	14. Ntare kita Bunyoro	15. Macwa

16. Kahaya I, in whose reign cattle increased so greatly in the country that a poor man had at least fifty and a rich man's herds ran into thousands. Though rinderpest has now killed thousands of the cattle, yet there are still more in the country than there were at the time when plague last visited them, nearly thirty years ago

17. Lwebishengaze   18. Gasiyonga (mother, Bukandu)
19. Mutambukwa (mother, Bawomura)
20. Ntare, whose mother, Kiloga, was a Munyoro princess
21. Kahaya II (mother, Nkasi of the Basambo)

The old title of the ruler, which is still used as a title of respect, was *Mukama*, but as this was also the title of the ruler of Kitara (or Bunyoro), the British, for the purpose of differentiation, introduced the official title of *Mugabe*.

In the old days, the kingdom was only a small one, but the present district of Ankole includes four other kingdoms, Mpororo, Egara, Bweszu and Busongora. In the past the kings of these countries were always at enmity and none of them ever visited the countries of the others except in war. One of the early British Government officials ordered a king of Egara to come to Ankóle. The king at first refused, but, when pressure was brought to bear, he came, as it seemed, willingly. When, however, he reached a hill from which he could see the houses of the Ankole king, he quickly drew a a knife, ripped his stomach across, and fell dead.

Though the kings of the different countries might not meet, it seems to have been quite common for their sons and daughters to intermarry, and when the countries were not actually at war, the people generally went freely from one to another to trade. The traders of Ankole, however, might go into Mpororo only in secret, though they might go openly into any of the other kingdoms. At one time princes of Ankole only married in their own clan, but under king Kahaya I it became usual for them to marry girls from the royal families of other countries.

The kings were thought by the people to have come from heaven and to be the ancestors of all their people, whom they ruled by divine authority. The Mugabe had the power of life and death over all his subjects, and it was believed that his people held their property solely through his clemency, for he was the owner of all the land and all the cattle.

THE MUGABE'S KRAAL

The Mugabe's kraal stood in the midst of the dwellings of his chiefs and retainers which formed the capital, *Orurembo*, the royal kraal itself being known as *Kikari kyo Mukama*.

The Mugabe's kraal differed from that of his chiefs only in size, for, as it enclosed many houses for wives and attendants, it covered a very large expanse of ground. The site was changed at least every second year and often every year, for it was thought that fresh ground was necessary to keep the cows clean and free from pests.

The kraal, which was in shape more oval than round, measured about a quarter of a mile across at its broadest part, and was built on a hill or rising ground. In the surrounding fence there was one main entrance, leading into a large open space which was used for cows, though the special cows of the Mugabe, which numbered one hundred, were not kept there but in two kraals outside the enclosure, fifty in each kraal, and only the cows of wives and resident attendants were kept in the royal kraal.

The cows of the Mugabe were looked after by the royal herdsmen, who carried two large pots of milk to the Mugabe every morning and evening. There was no royal milk-house for his milk, but it was carried from house to house wherever he happened to be, and the pots were strung up on a stick some eight feet long, such as was used by the cow-men for carrying milk-pots from kraals in the country to their masters; this was fastened at each end to the rafters so that it hung horizontally, and the milk-pots were slung upon it.

The cows inside the royal kraal all belonged to the Mugabe's wives and those attendants who were permanent residents. Each house of any importance in the royal kraal had its own courtyard where the cows came by night and where there were houses for the herdsmen and for the calves. The houses of the Mugabe's wives were built at various places within the enclosure and the king had the right to sleep in any house he might choose. Each wife had a number of cows given to her and she had her own herdsmen who looked after them and brought them for the night into the court of her house, where they slept in the open.

The main gate was the only entrance by which visitors were permitted to enter the Mugabe's kraal, but the special servants could enter by two smaller gates, which were placed at the sides of the kraal so that water running down the hill might not flow in by them. Only special guests might enter directly into the Mugabe's presence, others had to wait outside the main entrance while the gate-keeper announced their arrival to the Mugabe. The gate was kept fastened and the visitor had to wait outside, where there were waiting-rooms, while the gate-keeper asked for an interview and returned with the Mugabe's answer. The visitor might be told to wait longer or might even be denied admission altogether. When the main entrance was closed for the night, admission could only be obtained through a hut at one side in which there were always watchmen.

Inside the main entrance was a large open space for cows in which there was the fire, *nkomi*, the main fire of the kraal. To the left was a large hut for the special herdsmen, a number of small huts, and the usual dung-heap on which the daily sweepings of the kraal were piled. On the right of the open space was a second fence dividing it from the private houses of the Mugabe.

Inside this fence was first the house, *Rwemihunda*, and with it five other huts were connected by covered passages. The second was called *Kiniga*, and in it the pages of the Mugabe lived in order to be always within hearing of the summons of the Mugabe wherever he might be. In the third house, *Kageri kamu*, lived two specially favoured wives who took the names of *Enkunwakazi* and *Musongori*. The fourth house, *Watumwoha*, was for women from among whom the Mugabe chose one when he went on any journey or to war. When he went to war a special kraal was built for him and to it he took a young girl, called *Ekinyasunzu*, who made his bed, managed his private matters, and acted as his wife for the time. If on his return she was found to be with child, she was taken to a special house and cared for until the child was born. She was not necessarily a pastoral woman and was not given the rank of one of the Mugabe's wives, for she never covered her head like a married woman, but in other respects she was treated as one of his wives and any child she might give birth to was counted as a prince. In this house also were two wives with the titles *Ntagasya Mukama* and *Karabaraba*, the latter being the wife who sat near the Mugabe at evening meetings and upon whom he leant when he felt tired. She also at such times carried any messages he might wish to send.

The next house, *Buganzi*, was a general house for wives, and *Kabagiriri* was a house for wives who had given birth to children. There were also in the kraal about a hundred houses for wives and their attendants and women of inferior station.

The Mugabe went to any of the houses as it might please him and his pages carried the royal milk-pots and slung them over the pots of the wife with whom he meant to spend the night. Each house was provided with a rod suspended from the roof over the platform where the wife kept her milk-pots, and the pages slung the royal pots on this rod. Two pots were brought to the Mugabe after each milking and he drank milk as a rule four times during the day and four times during the night, drinking twice from each pot.

The quarters of the cooks were also in this part of the kraal, but were divided from the wives' huts by a fence which prevented the Mugabe from seeing what was going on beyond it as he moved about among his wives. When the Mugabe ordered food to be cooked for guests it was carried by a path round the outer part of the enclosure so as not to offend the royal eyes or nose. The chief cooks were named *Obwoma* and *Orwekubo* and, like the fire-wood bearers and water-drawers, they were of the agricultural class.

The brewers lived outside at the back of the royal kraal and daily sent some of the best beer they had into the kraal for the Mugabe's use. There was a hut in the inner part of the kraal where the beer for the daily consumption of the Mugabe was kept and to which the *Bakungu* chiefs also sent beer and grain twice monthly.

The royal kraal was completely surrounded by dwellings, for the brewers, wood-cutters and water-drawers had their huts at the back, the kraals of the leading chiefs lay round the sides, and the *Nganzi* or chief minister had his kraal in front of the gateway. These people acted as general guardians of the Mugabe to prevent any foe from approaching and finding him unprepared.

Whenever the Mugabe wished to move the site of his kraal he consulted the royal medicine-man as to the advisability of the change and as to the choice of a new site. A bull, which had to be entirely black, was brought to the Mugabe, who whispered into its ear, "Stop evil from coming to me, to my children or to my country," and spat into its mouth.

The assistants then threw the animal down and held it while the Mugabe stepped over it and stuck his spear into the ground on the other side. The medicine-man killed the bull and examined its lungs and intestines and he and his companions ate the meat on the spot where it was killed, for none of it might be carried away.

If all was well the new kraal was built, and at the end of six months the medicine-man came again with a fowl and held its beak open until the Mugabe spat into its throat. This fowl was buried alive in the gateway of the new kraal where both people and cattle passed over it, and thus evil was kept from entering and injuring the Mugabe.

As each new house was built either for the Mugabe or anyone else, it was dedicated by having a fowl buried alive in the doorway, while a second fowl was buried at the side of the mound used as the bed so that the owner might step on the place as he went to or left the bed. A special fetish was hung over the door. This consisted of a swallow, which was cut open from the underside of its beak to its tail and dried. The body when ready was stuffed with the herbs *omubuza*, *mwetengo* and *musingo*, bound together at the breast and tail, and suspended over the door to keep evil out and render harmless any magic which might be directed against the inmates.

The fire from which all the fires in a new kraal were started was brought from the Abaitira clan.

The Life and Duties of the Mugabe

There were no restrictions laid upon the movements of the Mugabe, though he had to be careful not to hurt himself or cause loss of blood. He might move about the country as he liked and often accompanied the royal herdsmen to the pasturage and stayed with the cattle until he felt tired, when he returned to the kraal for a meal and rest. He was generally fond of hunting and might arrange a day's sport. If the place of the hunt was at some distance from the royal kraal he would be carried there, in order to arrive fresh for the sport.

and the porridge being brought in separate wooden dishes. He ate the meat with a wooden two-pronged fork and the porridge with a wooden spoon. A bull or fatted cow was daily killed for food for the inmates of the royal kraal, and the Mugabe's meat was taken from this animal, for he was not restricted to special cows but might eat beef from any. He might, however, only eat the meat from the shoulder, which was cut up into small pieces and cooked for him, while the rest was used for the household and guests. The food was brought to him by pages, and, with the exception of a favourite wife who was in attendance to do anything he might require, no one else might approach while he was eating.

The Mugabe might invite some of his chiefs to a meal after sitting in court but they were served in the courtyard apart from him, though he might send to any specially favoured guest some of the meat from his own table. None of his wives might touch his meat or his milk vessels and any meat that was left over when he had finished had to be eaten by some of his pages. He sometimes sent milk to his private advisers (*Batabazi*) and it was carried to them by a boy and a girl who held office only during their minority. As soon as they were adolescent they were sent off to marry and the office was given to others.

After his midday meal the Mugabe generally went to rest until evening when a large number of chiefs assembled at the royal kraal to talk over general matters and drink beer. During these gatherings the Mugabe sat in a special house where three short posts were arranged so that he might sit between two of them, resting his arms on them, while he leaned against the third. A special wife sat by his side to make another prop for him to lean on if he so desired. In later times, when the idea of chairs with backs instead of stools began to penetrate the country, a low curved wall of reeds was built between the two side posts so that the Mugabe might sit between the posts and lean back against it. He sometimes used a wooden stool to sit upon and in the house he sometimes sat upon the bed, but as a rule he squatted like an ordinary cow-man.

After this evening meeting the Mugabe might have another meal of beef and beer and before going to bed he might drink some of the evening milk. It often happened, however, that he, as well as some of the chiefs, drank so much beer at the meeting that they had to be carried away. The servants who accompanied their masters were responsible for them and had to see them safely deposited in bed. The Mugabe was never said to be drunk; the servants said *Kusinda* (he sighed).

The Mugabe never moved about in his own kraal or elsewhere without some weapon and rarely without a guard, but he seldom lost his temper during the daily gatherings, though he was known sometimes to strike a chief or servant in wrath, whereupon the pages at once put the offender to death. In the evening, however, when he had partaken too freely of beer he often gave way to violent fits of rage, especially when among his wives, and in these he would strike people and break things until he could be got to bed to sleep it off.

It was never known outside the Mugabe's part of the kraal in what house he intended to sleep. If he felt inclined to do so he made a round of the kraal to see the cattle, and then entered the house of the wife with whom he meant to spend the night. One or two pages followed him and the milk-pots were brought and hung up over the platform on which the wife kept her pots. The wife prepared the bed, in which the Mugabe slept between well-buttered bark-cloths. This secrecy was observed lest the Mugabe might be attacked during the night by anyone who wished to kill him. It was said that there had been cases when a prince killed the Mugabe by night in order to secure the tnrone.

THE ROYAL DRUMS

At a little distance from the royal kraal was a small enclosure in which stood the hut of the royal drums. These were the only drums in the country, for, unlike most African peoples, the Banyankole did not make constant use of drums

PLATE IV

Dressing a cow-skin

PLATE V

Sacred drums in their house with offering of milk before them

but got their music from a primitive harp, shaped like a tortoise shell, which was played by women, while the serfs used water-pots containing varying quantities of water, so that they sounded different notes when struck on the mouths with pads attached to sticks two feet long.

At one time these royal drums had their hut on another hill to the north of the River Ruiri, for a stream of water had to flow between them and the Mugabe's residence. When, however, the Mugabe became a Christian, he had the drums brought to his own hill, where a special hut was built for them. Their hut was always domed and might have no point or pinnacle; inside there was a stand or bed (*Emitagara*) on which lay two drums, known as *Bagendenswa* and *Nakasaizha*. These were the chief drums, and they were never beaten except by the Mugabe at his coronation. On the left side of the stand lay *Kabembula*, and beside it a small drum, *Mpulo*, which was beaten by the guardian at each new moon and when the other drums were taken out. The other drums, which lay on the floor, were called *Luseshi*, *Gazo*, *Enzeru*, *Eigulu*, *Mpondi*, *Kikaro* and *Nabahangwi*. At the back of the hut behind the bed lay a quantity of material for repairing these drums, and this had to be carefully guarded for it might not be used for any other purpose. To the left of the hut was a bag, *Ensegu*, in which were the instruments necessary for taking an augury should it be needed, and beside it lay some whistles and an iron rod (*Nalusalu*) upon which the tools for making the drums were sharpened, for this might not be done upon a stone. In front of the bed or stand was a row of milk-pots belonging to the drums, in which the daily offerings of milk were put.

The chief drums were the two which lay upon the bed. These were covered with white skins with a black strip across them, making them look like a pair of great eyes in the gloom of the hut, for they lay on their sides facing the low doorway through which the only light came. A sacred herd of cows yielded a supply of milk which was daily offered to these drums in the pots which stood in front of them. It was placed there in the morning and remained until nine or ten o'clock, by which time the drum-spirits had taken the essence and the remainder might be drunk by the guardians. The same ceremony was transacted after the evening milking. The guardians of the drums were called *Barurura* and might be chosen from any tribe or clan of the cow-people. There was also a woman, *Mulanga* of the Abarura clan, who was known as the "wife of the drums," and whose duty it was to look after the milk, the churning, and the covering of the drums. Another woman from the Abasinga clan looked after the fire in the drum-house, which had always to be kept burning because the drum-spirits required warmth.

Offerings of cattle or beer were made to the drums by chiefs when a son had been born to them or when they had received promotion to some office or had been successful in some expedition and earned the commendation of the Mugabe. The Mugabe also made an annual offering of cows to the drums, so that they possessed a large herd; those offered to *Bagendenswa* had to be red or white and those for *Nakasaizha* black. These cows were sacred and the Mugabe alone might order one to be killed; no one but the guardians might eat the meat of an animal thus killed and the skin was kept for repairing the drums. It was from these cows that the milk was taken which was daily offered to the drums, and from the surplus milk butter was made for smearing on them and for other uses connected with them, such as preparing the cow-skins for covering them.

The drums had also their sacred spear, *Nyamiringa*, and a staff, *Karembe*, which were kept in the hut. When a princess was married, the chief guardian of the drums took the spear and stuck it in the ground at the head of the bed upon which the bride was lying. In the morning when he went to fetch the spear, the husband had to give him a cow, for the princess was a daughter of the drums who must therefore receive a marriage gift for her. The staff was also taken to a royal wedding and the bridegroom had to make it a suitable present in cattle.

The man who repaired the drums bore the title *Ebigirema*; he might not make any other drums nor allow any of his materials to be used for other purposes. The cow from which the skin for re-covering a drum was taken was always black, white, or red, according to the drum for which it was required. It was first offered to the drum in the shrine and afterwards killed near the door. The skin was dressed with butter and the worker trod and stamped upon it until it was soft and supple, when it was taken with the drum to the forest Muzairi. While still supple with butter, it was moistened with water and stretched on the drum where it shrank while drying. Four sheep were then killed and given as remuneration to the men who assisted in the repairing of the drum.

There was a pad on which each of the drums was carried to the forest, and this was also made from the skin of a black, white, or red cow which had a calf alive and well. The two special drums when on the stand rested on pads made of calf-skin. The calf was first presented to the drums and was then killed near them, and the skin was softened by being stamped upon and treated with butter. The meat of the calf was given to the guardians.

When the drums were being covered with new skins, which was always done at the accession of a new Mugabe, a boy, old enough to herd cows and very fat, was killed, and his blood was caught and mixed with that of a cow. Papyrus specially brought from the river was burned to ashes and these were made into balls with the blood and rubbed upon the drums. Some say that the boy's throat was cut and the blood allowed to flow into the drums. This, however, has not been done for three reigns and it was impossible to discover what actually did happen and what fetishes were concealed in the drums. One or two people expressed the idea that the smearing of the drums with blood, which was done at other times as well as at the coronation, was to remind the people that the Mugabe had power to kill, but this statement was not generally made.

Whenever the drums were moved for any purpose, the chief guardian beat a greeting to them on one of the small drums and his assistants clapped their hands before them and talked to them to prevent their being annoyed at being moved and thus put to inconvenience. They were never taken into the royal kraal, though the Mugabe might go to them.

Sometimes the guardian of the drums stated to the Mugabe that they required meat, whereupon the Mugabe ordered a cow to be brought from the herd of the drums. It was kept for one night near the house of the drums with other cows, and in the morning it was taken before the drums where the guardian presented it to them, saying, " This is the cow which the Mugabe consents to your having. Now let him live in peace with his neighbours, drive illness away from him and make him powerful!" The cow was then killed, the blood being caught and kept for smearing on the drums.

When the Mugabe intended to go to war, a special ceremony with the drums was enacted. He sent to his chief cow-man for a rope or thong (*mboha*) which had been used for tying the legs of restive cows when being milked, a little hair from the penis-sheath of a bull, and a little clay from the place where a cow had trodden and left the impression of its foot. The Mugabe in person took these offerings to the drums, and was preceded by the royal spear-bearer with the two royal spears, which he stuck in the ground before the drums. The guardian then raised the two drums and the Mugabe placed the things which he had brought underneath them. This was supposed to ensure the safety of the Mugabe and the success of the expedition. On his return the Mugabe made a special offering to the drums of fifteen cows, three of which had to be of the special colours of the drums, black, white and red.

The drums also formed a kind of sanctuary, for, if a man feared that for some reason he was going to be deprived of his property by the Mugabe, he would try to make his way to the drums and, if he reached them, he could not be despoiled. So, too, if a man who was to be put to death succeeded in escaping to the drums, he was safe and became their perpetual servant.

THE MUGABE'S COWS

The cattle of the Mugabe were distributed over all the country under special herdsmen. They were divided into herds according to their colour, each herd being kept strictly separate from the others so that the bulls of one herd were never able to come to the cows of another.

The Mugabe appointed men to be the herdsmen of his cows, giving each man as a rule a hundred cows and leaving him to choose his own assistants. The chief herdsmen were known by different names according to the colour of their herds, in most cases by a name denoting that colour:

Emamba, black

Ebisa, white

Enchere, yellowish white

Empogo, black with red

Embubi, black and white

Emiroko, red and white head with patches of white on red body

Enkungu, hornless of any colour

Engazo, red

Ebitare, very pure white

Misina, brown

Mayenzi, red with black

Bugondo, red and white

Emiremba, red legs with white or black body

These men were responsible to the Mugabe only, but the chiefs of the different districts had to keep a general watch over the Mugabe's herds and settle any disputes among herdsmen. The herd from which the special milk for the Mugabe and his household was brought was kept in two kraals just outside the royal kraal, fifty cows being in each. The two herdsmen in charge of this herd were special favourites of the Mugabe, and new men were appointed to these posts at the accession of a new Mugabe, though he might retain the herdsmen appointed to the ordinary herds by his predecessor.

Though private individuals looked upon their herds as their own property, the Mugabe had the right to take cattle from any herd whenever he so desired, even in addition to the regular taxation of the herds.

CHAPTER V

RULERS OF ANKOLE. PART II

Illness of the Mugabe—treatment for grey hair—finding the cause of illness by augury—interview with sons and chiefs—the royal poison—announcing the death—mourning—preparing the body—the royal tombs at Esanza—re-birth of the Mugabe as a lion—return of the messengers—mourning—accession—purificatory ceremony—contesting the accession—lighting the fires—accession ceremonies at Ibanda—the new capital—wives of the Mugabe

ILLNESS AND DEATH

NO Mugabe ever allowed himself to grow old: he had to put an end to his life before his powers, either mental or physical, began to deteriorate. It was even thought undesirable that the Mugabe should look old, and treatment was applied to prevent his hair from growing grey. A bird, *kinyankwanzi*, was caught and killed, the body being dried and burnt to ashes, which were mixed with butter. This mixture was prepared by the medicine-man, who pronounced some magic incantations over it, and, when the night was darkest before the new moon appeared, the Mugabe smeared his head with it. The bird, *kinyankwanzi*, was sacred and, if any unauthorised person killed one, he was deprived of all his possessions.

When the Mugabe felt unwell, but the illness was not considered serious, he sent a message to the *Nganzi* who then asked the diviner to discover what ghost was the cause of the trouble. This he did by a test with the insect *ntondo* and two sticks, in the manner already described (*v.* Religion, Chap. III). When the insect, by climbing towards the second stick, had announced the name of the ancestor whose ghost was the cause, the *Nganzi* returned to inform the Mugabe, who made an offering at the shrine which was sacred to that ghost.

If the Mugabe felt slightly unwell in the morning, he had all his fetishes brought to him and spat upon each of them before proceeding to his ordinary duties. If, however, he felt seriously ill, he did not appear in public and was said to be *kwesima*, taking rest, for no one dared to say that the Mugabe was ill.

No Mugabe ever went on living when he felt that his powers were failing him through either serious illness or old age. As soon as he felt his strength diminishing he knew it was time to end his life, and he called together his chiefs and also his sons, who never came to see him except on this occasion. At this interview he made no reference to his intentions but talked of affairs of the state. Either then or at some earlier time he nominated the son whom he wished to succeed him as Mugabe.

When all was ready, he summoned the royal medicine-man and asked for the king's poison. This was always kept in readiness in the shell of a crocodile's egg. The white of the egg was dried and powdered and mixed with the dried nerve from the pointed end of an elephant's tusk and some other ingredients, the exact mixture being kept strictly secret. This had only to be mixed with a little water or beer to be ready for use, and when the Mugabe drank it he fell dead in a few moments.

There was no formal announcement of the death, but the inmates of the royal kraal made a noise like the crying of jackals. The news was carried through the country by word of mouth, and the expression used to announce the death was *kutasya*, to return, the word used for the coming back of the cattle to the kraal at night.

All the fires in the royal kraal and in all the kraals of the Mugabe's herds were extinguished as soon as the news of the death reached them, and all goats and dogs in or near any royal kraal were killed, for they were supposed to retain the evil of death. For this reason people, on hearing of the death, at once hurried their animals to some distant place. Every fully-grown bull in the royal herds had its scrotum tied to prevent its mating with the cows. The royal drums were covered and were not seen until the new Mugabe was appointed.

All work ceased in the land and the blades of all weapons had to be wrapped up in grass or fibre; even an axe might not be used for cutting fire-wood, which had to be broken by hand. Every man, woman, and child in the country had the head shaved as a sign of national mourning, and were rubbed with a bunch of the herb they called *mwetengo*, which was considered to possess special powers of removing impurities which, if left, would cause illness and even death. This herb was used for many purificatory purposes. When people ate meat from an animal which had died of some disease, they rubbed some of the leaves of this in water and rinsed their mouths two or three times to remove all danger. Also a man who had been imprisoned, or rather detained in the stocks, rubbed his body over with it after his release to remove any evil influence before he rejoined his family.

Any man who was engaged had to go and marry his bride on the day of the death, or, if she was too far away or too young to be married, he had to send her a belt of the strap he used for binding the legs of restive cows when they were being milked; this she had to wear round her waist as though she had been confined. Should he neglect this precaution he lost his bride; the engagement was at an end, and he had to look for another wife.

Princes and princesses put on bark-cloth garments and did not wear their cow-hide robes or ornaments of any kind.

The chief wife, assisted by the Mugabe's sister, was in charge of the preparations inside the royal kraal, and special men of the Abahangwe clan were called in to arrange the body for removal to its resting-place and to guard it until all was ready. All ornaments were removed from the body and it was washed with water. The legs were bent up into the squatting posture favoured by cow-men. The right arm was placed under the head and the left arm laid on the breast.

A cow, which had to be perfectly white and in good condition and must have one healthy calf, and a white sheep were brought in the evening when the cattle returned from pasture. The cow was milked and a little of the milk was

poured into the dead man's mouth while the rest was kept
for use later. Both animals were killed by having their
throats cut and the skins were prepared for use by the men
of the royal kraal, who first dried them in the sun, then
stamped upon them and treated them with butter until they
were soft and supple[1]. The blood of the animals was supposed
to be allowed to run on the ground but the men of the kraal
often caught it and drank it. The preparation of the skins took
two days, during which a special hut was built at the edge
of the Esanza forest and the body remained in the royal kraal.

The body was laid on the cow-skin, and the sheep-skin,
formed into a kind of bag, was placed on the lower part of
the stomach. Some small millet (*bulo*) and the remainder of
the milk from the cow was put in the sheep-skin and the cow-
skin was folded over all and tightly stitched. Another account
stated that the millet was put on the dead man's stomach,
the milk poured over it, and the sheep-skin laid on the top,
after which the body, thus prepared, was wrapped in the
cow-skin. The meat of the cow was eaten by the men of the
Abahangwe clan who were in charge of the body, while the
sheep was given to the servants who helped in the preparations.

The place for royal tombs was on the edge of a forest at
Esanza on the Koki side of Ankole, a journey generally of
about thirty miles from the royal kraal. Some thirty or forty
men of the royal clan set out on the morning of the third day
after the death and bore the body to Ibara where they slept
one night, killing a bull for food. On the following day they
went on to Esanza where the body was handed over to the
priests. The messengers waited at the edge of the forest where
they built huts. While they were waiting they had the right
to help themselves to cattle from any herd, and they lived
on milk, beef and beer.

---

[1] A former account given in *The Northern Bantu* states: "In the evening
of the second day a large cow is killed and the raw hide is wrapped around
the body and stitched together, and the corpse is taken to a sacred forest
called Esanza. The ox may not be killed in the ordinary way by having its
throat cut, but is thrown down by a number of men who quickly twist its
head round and break its neck."

The priests carried the body from the border of the forest to the hut which had been prepared for it. Inside this there was a stand like a bedstead with posts fixed in the ground and side-pieces and cross-pieces resting on them. The body was placed on this bed and the cow-skin was cut open so as to expose it. Under the bedstead was a large wooden vessel to catch any fluids which might come from the body, and the priests and one at least of the men who had come from the royal court remained in the hut day and night. The body was turned daily from one side to the other for a month, or longer if necessary.

As decomposition set in, the body swelled, which was called being pregnant. Later it burst and the juices which dropped into the vessel beneath were kept for further use. A red cow which had her first calf, both cow and calf being in good health, was brought and milked and the milk was mixed with the fluids from the body. The vessel with this mixture was placed on the bed, and again the guards kept watch until the mixture became a mass of grubs.

The priest then selected a large grub which he declared to be the Mugabe re-born. He took it into the forest and shortly returned with a lion cub into which he affirmed the grub had turned and which was, therefore, the Mugabe in a new condition. A white bull was killed and the blood given to the cub to drink, and the men who had brought the body waited to see that it was healthy and thriving. When the next new moon appeared the messengers set out to return to the capital and announce the re-birth of the Mugabe.

The disposal of the body of the late Mugabe was a point of little importance. Some said that it was buried in the forest and no further notice taken of it, while others asserted that it was simply left on the bed in the hut which, being uncared for, soon fell down. The lion cub, however, was tended until it was old enough to run wild, when it was turned into the forest.

Each year the Mugabe sent two cows for milk and two for meat to the spirit of his father. The two for meat were taken and killed in the forest for food for the lion and the milk from the others was used by the priests. The messengers who took the animals to the forest were rewarded on their return with a cow.

Until the messengers who had taken the body to the forest returned to the capital there was no mourning, though no work was done and no weapons were used. All the people in the royal kraal, having shaved their heads and rubbed the purificatory herb *mwetengo* over their bodies to remove the evil of death, then quietly awaited the news of the re-birth. The Mugabe's widows took off all their ornaments and gave them away. Some of them strangled themselves when they heard of the death, others who had children left the royal kraal and went to live with their sons or daughters, while young widows generally remained to become the wives of the new Mugabe.

When the messengers arrived with the news of the re-birth of the Mugabe, mourning began and the people raised cries as of jackals and hyaenas which continued all that night. The people in the royal kraal had their heads shaved again and rubbed over with the herb *mwetengo*. The water they had used was then thrown away on some waste land where no one was likely to pass over it.

ACCESSION

Next morning a boy was chosen whose parents were both living and well and who was himself in good health. He went to the royal well where he drew water and filled either a wooden vessel like a beer-trough or a clay trough such as was used for watering cows. The Mugabe's cattle were brought before the royal kraal and the princes and princesses and crowds of people assembled there.

At cock-crow the prince who had been nominated by the Mugabe as his successor was brought forward and given the dead Mugabe's shoes. The Mugabe's stool, which was a solid block of wood carved roughly into the shape of a stool, was placed on the royal mat, and the prince sat upon it while the late Mugabe's brother, or, according to some accounts, the *Nganzi*, proclaimed him as the chosen ruler. According to one account, the *Nganzi* then lectured the new Mugabe on his duties, after which each of the principal chiefs admonished him and praised the dead ruler. The Mugabe, meanwhile, said nothing but stared steadily on the ground, and all the other princes kept silence.

The Mugabe's stool was placed near the vessel of water which had been brought from the royal well and in which white clay had been mixed. A chosen sister of the new Mugabe then approached and was given two bunches of the sacred herbs, *nyawera, ehoza, muliera, omugorora* and *mulokola*. Dipping these in the water, she sprinkled first the new Mugabe, touching him on the knees, shoulders and forehead, then the royal family and the people and cattle; lastly, she sprinkled the liquid towards the four quarters of the earth to purify the land. Herds which were at a distance were purified by a special messenger who was sent round the country with the herbs and some of the water. All vessels belonging to the late Mugabe were also brought out and purified after any that had flaws in them or were decorated with wire had been destroyed. When the work of purification had been done, the princess claimed a certain portion of the royal herds as her own.

According to some accounts the Mugabe then rose and sprinkled the people and land, and, if any prince desired to contest the accession, he also rose and did the same before departing to raise an army and fight for the throne.

The guardians of the royal spears, stool, shoes, drums, drum-sticks, fetishes, and tobacco pipes then brought these things to the new Mugabe for him to touch, and the Mugabe rose and, uncovering the royal drums, tapped a few beats on them, and declared himself to be the eldest son and the legal heir. He then dismissed the people, promising to rule wisely and agreeing to all that the chiefs had said to him. He again declared himself Mugabe and told the other princes to submit to his rule.

If the princes did not intend to contest the accession, they departed to their homes and returned in a few days to do homage, bringing with them presents of cows. Should any of them, however, wish to fight, they departed and raised an army and civil war was proclaimed. When one prince decided to fight, the others either joined one of the contending parties or took advantage of the state of affairs to raise an army themselves and try to gain the throne. The prince who had been proclaimed Mugabe did not go to war in person but sent his representative, and the war went on until only one of the claimants was left alive. Should a rebellious prince succeed in killing his opponents, including the prince who was on the throne, he appointed his favourite sister to the office of Mugabe's sister in place of the sister formerly appointed, but it was not necessary to repeat the purification ceremony and he went on to the further ceremonies of accession.

When the fighting was over and the Mugabe established on his throne, his first task was to order the fires in all the royal kraals to be re-lit. This was done with fire brought by men of the Abaitira clan and not with fire-sticks.

Up to this time the residence of the new Mugabe had been in his father's kraal in the old capital, but he now left it and took a journey to Ibanda to a place Kizongo on the river Kigabiro. In this river there was a pool in which the Mugabe was bathed by a man of the clan Abayirunto. On coming out of the water he was smeared over with white clay and a woman, *Nabuzana*, handed him a fetish, *Omuwambo*, which was decorated with beads, cowry-shells and wild plantain seeds, and covered with a strip of bark-cloth which was twisted round it. A band of cow-hide on which were stitched beads, cowry-shells and plantain seeds, was placed on his head and a spear and staff such as herdsmen carried were handed to him. The staff was made from the sacred tree *kirikiti*, or, as they called it, *Murinzi*. On his shoulders was put the dress of a herdsman, a skin taken from a young bull, and he was then taken to a small kraal named *Bwakahaya*, where a white barren cow, two white cows in milk, and a white sheep awaited him. He milked the two cows, which afterwards returned with him to the capital, while the other cow and the sheep were killed and the meat eaten by the guardians of this kraal.

The Mugabe was then taken to a large stone, *Kitura,* on an adjoining hill where the diviner killed a cow and took the augury to discover where the new capital should be built. They went to the indicated site where a temporary dwelling was prepared for the Mugabe until his permanent kraal could be made ready. On their arrival the servants brought a staff and a pot of white clay with which the forehead of the Mugabe was smeared. The royal drums were brought and smeared with the clay and the Mugabe beat them and was again proclaimed ruler. A chief was chosen and sent throughout the country bearing a drum to proclaim the new Mugabe.

The Mugabe then appointed his mother and sister to their offices and chose his new chiefs and the headmen over his cows. He generally appointed new chiefs to all the principal chieftainships, but retained the former chiefs as his advisers. All the chiefs came to do him homage and bring presents.

It was usual for the cow-people to begin married life at an early age so that a prince when he came to the throne was probably already in possession of two or three wives, for he might take any girl he desired, simply sending his messengers to bring her to him. As they brought her they took cows from anyone to feed her and the prince later sent her parents a number of cows to compensate them for the loss of the usual marriage-fee, and, if the girl was already betrothed, he also sent a gift to the man.

When a prince came to the throne he selected one or more of his wives to be favourites, but this did not give their children the prior right to the throne, for any prince might fight for it. The Mugabe might marry women from either Basambo or Bagahe clans and he might take his own sisters to wife, though such alliances were not recognised and he never married the sister whom he appointed to the office of Mugabe's sister.

CHAPTER VI

THE MUGABE'S MOTHER AND SISTER

The Mugabe's mother—her power—illness—drinking the royal poison—preparing the body—tomb at Kabigirira—re-birth as a leopard—coming of the heir—the Mugabe's sister—her marriage—rights of her children—illness and death—tomb at Kabangiginya—re-birth as a python—sister of Ntare—death of princes and princesses

THE MUGABE'S MOTHER

WHEN a new Mugabe was established on his throne, he at once raised his mother to the rank of Mugabe's mother. She had her kraal at a little distance from the royal kraal and over her own estates and among her own people she had supreme power and appointed her own friends and relatives to be her chiefs. The Mugabe visited her when he would, and she might visit him at any time.

When the Mugabe's mother fell ill, she was tended by some of her maids, but, should the illness prove serious, the Mugabe was sent for and came to see her, bringing with him the royal medicine-man. The Mugabe alone went in to see the patient, and, should he consider the illness serious, he communicated with the medicine-man, who mixed the royal poison and gave it to him. He handed this to his mother, who drank it and died at once.

The maids in attendance washed the body and prepared it for burial like that of the king, except that the left arm and not the right was placed under her head and the body was wrapped in bark-cloths before being stitched in the cow-skin. A white cow in perfect condition, with its first calf, was brought from her herds and killed by having its throat cut. The servants prepared the skin, making it quite soft, and the body, wrapped in bark-cloths, was laid on it and stitched up tightly.

During the night the inmates of the kraal kept up a constant howling as of hyaenas, and early next morning the body was conveyed to the forest Kabigirira, near Esanza, where a hut with a bed was prepared as for the Mugabe. The messengers waited while the special priests turned the body from side to side, as in the case of the Mugabe, until the stomach burst, when the fluids were caught and mixed with milk. The pot with the mixture was kept until it became full of grubs when one of them was taken into the forest and was said to become a leopard. The messengers who had taken the body returned home with the information that the Mugabe's mother had become a leopard, after which the women wailed for another night.

In the morning her successor was selected by the Mugabe from the same clan and she inherited the title with all her predecessor's cattle, goods, and estates. The Mugabe and his sister went to purify her, after which she purified the Mugabe and churned in her house to ensure a plentiful supply of butter.

As in the case of the Mugabe, all the full grown bulls of the herds had their scrotums tied during the mourning and were then killed, new bulls being introduced into the herds.

THE MUGABE'S SISTER

The sister who was chosen by the Mugabe to purify him on his accession became an important person, for she was regarded as responsible for his welfare. She took the title of *Munyanya Mukama* and was given estates in which her power was absolute. She was not queen but was the most important woman in the country. Her kraal was built near that of the Mugabe and she kept always in close touch with him.

The regulations for the marriage of the Mugabe's sister differed from those followed in the other pastoral tribes where princesses were not allowed to marry any but their half-brothers. The Mugabe's sister married anyone she wished,

PLATE VI

Sister of the king (Mugabe) with her husband and child

PLATE VII

Decorations on the walls of a princess's house

and, though the Mugabe might exert his influence to get her
to marry a man of his choice, she was quite at liberty to
refuse. For some generations it has been the custom for this
lady to marry a prince from one of the neighbouring countries,
who thereupon came to live with her in Ankole. Before this
became usual, she, like other princesses, married some important chief of her own country. The custom of marrying
a prince from another country was extraordinary considering
the deadly enmity that prevailed between the rulers of neighbouring lands, and there seems to be some confusion as to the
law of inheritance with regard to the children of such a
marriage.

If the wife died before her husband, he evidently returned
to his own country, but he might only take with him the
cattle which he possessed in his own right and none that had
belonged to his wife. If there were children, they took a
portion of the property of their mother, but most of it went
to the princess who was appointed by the Mugabe to succeed
her and who was regarded as her heir. The sons of such a
marriage, however, were said to belong to the father, and,
if they inherited property from him, they went to his country,
whereas, if they inherited property from their mother, they
could not take it out of her country.

When the Mugabe's sister fell ill, she was treated in the
ordinary manner and was never given the royal poison. If
she died her body was wrapped in bark-cloths and carried
to Kabangiginya, part of the royal burial-ground at Esanza,
where the same rites were enacted as in the case of the king,
and she was said to be re-born in the form of a python which
lived in the royal forest. The messengers returned and informed her people and they mourned until the Mugabe sent
her heir, when the mourning ceased. If the dead princess had
a child, this child purified the sister who was chosen to be the
heir; if not another sister performed the office.

When the Mugabe died, the principal sister might strangle
herself, or she might retire into private life. The sister of the
Mugabe Ntare married a prince of Mpororo. When Ntare

died this sister gathered some twenty of his wives and told them to go into a hut. She then broke the drum and spear of her brother, and, joining the women in the hut, told them to hang themselves, after which she did the same. No one objected as it was looked upon as the right thing to do.

Princes and princesses were also treated at death with a certain amount of ceremonial observance, and purificatory rites were performed. They were buried in the royal forest and were supposed to be re-born in the form of pythons.

CHAPTER VII

PASTORAL LIFE

Nomadic life of herdsmen—the kraals—houses—fires—the day's work
—the fetish *Amaleka*—milking—herding and watering cows—the
calves—cleaning the kraal—drawing water—cleaning milk-pots—
churning—butter and butter-milk—uses of urine—milk regulations—cows of the ghosts—eating beef—women and milk—taboos on
milk—domestic animals—sheep and goats—fowls—dogs—clothing—
hair—slaves—currency—counting—seasons and time—the stars—
music and dancing—salutations

THE cow-men paid little attention to districts or their
boundaries when grazing cattle, for they regarded all the
land as free to the herds though it was forbidden to trespass
on land which had been granted to any member of the
agricultural class for cultivation. Anyone, too, might burn
off grass in any place, and this was regularly done twice a
year, in January, when the millet was ripe, and again in June.
Herdsmen were nomadic, wandering over the country with
the cows as they thought best for themselves and for the
health of the animals. When they found a favourable place,
they made a rough zareba, known as a *kiraro*, which had three
or four grass huts built in the fence at some distance from each
other. To this centre the cattle returned each night, and here
the herdsmen remained until the pasturage for several miles
round was exhausted. A new centre was then chosen and the
men built the fence and their shelters anew. In the dry season
they would probably remain only a few weeks in one place,
but during the rains, when grass was more abundant, they
built better huts and remained in one place somewhat longer.
The number of cows to be found in one of these kraals
was generally one hundred, so that the common name for
a herd was *egana* or hundred. One bull, that is, one full-grown
animal in good condition, was allowed to each herd of one
hundred.

Chiefs and wealthy men seldom if ever wandered about the country with the cows. They built themselves permanent dwellings in kraals near the capital or in their districts and divided their cattle into herds of one hundred, putting a herdsman over each with men under him. These herdsmen were pastoral men, for no member of the agricultural classes was ever employed where the cows were concerned. Sometimes a kraal would be formed by several poorer cow-men who would unite their cows into one herd and share the work of the kraal, for it was impossible for one man, even if he had only a few cows, to herd them, keep his kraal clean, look after the calves, and do the many other things necessary. Two or three men would therefore combine and arrange the work of the kraal as did the herdsmen of the larger herds, taking it in turns to go out to pasture the cows or to stay at home to look after the kraal and the calves. It was also necessary for some to be on the alert at night in case of an attack by wild animals, so that at least four or five herdsmen were required for a herd of one hundred cows.

As a kraal was generally only a temporary habitation, little attention was paid to comfort, the most important part of the erection being the fence, which had to be fairly strong as a protection against wild beasts. The kraal was nearly round in shape, huts being built at intervals and the spaces between them filled with branches or thorny bushes. The kraal might face in any direction, but if it was on the side of a hill, the gate would be made on the higher side, facing up the hill.

The huts were built with their doorways facing inwards to the centre of the kraal, and that of the chief herdsman was always on the far side directly opposite the gate and facing towards it. The huts were bee-hive in shape and were built with no regard for comfort, the sole aim being to get protection from the weather with as little trouble in building as possible. Slender trees or strong branches were fixed in the ground to form a circle of the required diameter, leaving a space for the doorway, and the tops of these were bent inwards and tied together to form the apex. Over this frame-

work of stout ribs and at right angles to them were secured
reeds or coarse grass stems, and on the top of these was laid
a grass thatch. Inside the hut of the ordinary hired herdsman
there was seldom any attempt at furniture, for a man simply
laid his cow-skin rug, if he had one, on the ground and slept
there without covering. There were no doors, for the men
had to be able to see the cows and to rush out to their help
in case of danger.

The chief man in the kraal generally had a better hut but
the principle of building was the same and the poorest
materials were used, timber being always difficult to obtain.
His hut was bigger than the others and inside, especially if
the kraal was to be in use for some time, platforms of earth
were built for beds to raise the person above the floor-level.
The owner's bed was about a foot high and four feet wide by
eight long; grass was spread upon it and the man slept upon
a cow-skin laid over the grass, covering himself with bark-
cloths. Near his bed was a light reed screen behind which his
daughters slept. Next this, a little further round in the hut,
was the sacred spot, a platform about a foot high and four
feet wide by six long; this was covered with grass and on it
the milk-pots and fetishes were kept. Beyond this again was
the sleeping place for the sons, who might either sleep on the
floor or have a platform like the parents, and at the foot of
their place was the fire. The head of such a house generally
sat on the floor about the middle of his bed, while his wife
sat on his right near the opening to the daughters' quarters.
The children sat on the other side of the hut and visitors near
the doorway.

Near the principal hut was the dung-heap, *Lubungo*, on
which the refuse of the kraal was daily swept. In the centre
of the kraal was the great fire, *nkomi*, which might never die
out unless the owner of the kraal died. The fuel used for it
was dried cow-dung, and, when a blaze was wanted, grass from
the calves' huts was thrown on it. Grass fires were lit at
different places in the kraal when the cows were to be milked,
both to give light to the milkmen and to keep flies from

tormenting the cows. When the men went to a new kraal, fire from this central fire was carried to the new place to light the central fire there.

By the doorways of certain of the huts were small huts for the calves, in which they were secured by night both for their protection and to prevent their taking all the milk from their dams. These calf-huts had to be swept out daily and fresh grass put in, the old grass being used for burning on the fires. The cows had no shelter but spent the night in the open in the kraal.

There did not seem to be much ritual connected with the building of one of these kraals, but, when they entered a new one, the headman milked a cow that had had two calves, both of which were alive and well. He drank milk from this cow before anyone else might drink any milk in the kraal. This was *Ya kuza omusozi*, "to give luck," like that of the cow from which the milk was taken. On the night when he entered his new house, the owner had to have sexual intercourse with his wife.

A day's routine in a kraal began with the first signs of dawn. It was customary to keep fowls in a kraal, for the men trusted to the cock to wake them at daybreak. At cock-crow the fire in the centre was stirred up and grass thrown on it, while other fires were lit at different points in the kraal. The cows were brought up to these fires and were taught to stand near them ready for the milkmen.

While the men were thus preparing for the milking, some of the women set to work to churn, while others cleaned any milk-pots that had not been cleaned the night before. The wife of each man who had cows then placed her pots in rows inside the door of the hut and with them a fetish, *Amaleka*, which usually lay with them on the milk platform. This fetish was made by an elderly medicine-woman and was composed of a little hair from each cow in the herd, mixed with certain herbs and cow-dung and made into a ball. It was often enclosed in a bark-cloth or cow-skin cover to preserve it from damage, for it was in daily use.

The owner of the cows or the man in charge of the herd usually squatted near the door of his hut to watch the milking. Each cow was brought in turn up to the fire and a boy or assistant allowed its calf to suck a little until the milk flowed freely. The calf was then pulled away and held in front of the cow while the milkman milked as much as he thought desirable. The cow was turned out of the kraal to graze by the gate with its calf, while another was brought and milked. Each pot as it was filled was handed to the wife who held it over the fetish for a moment and then put it amongst the others ready for distribution when the milking was done. As a rule each cow had a separate pot, but if there were two cows both giving little milk, one pot might be used for the two. As long as these milk-pots were standing in the doorway of the hut, it was a sacred place.

When the milking was done, the milk was distributed to the family and the members of the kraal. Those men who were going out with the cattle drank as much as they could at once, for it was their only meal until night. Those who were to be working in the kraal might reserve some to be drunk later, when they had finished the heavy work of cleaning up the place, and the children's milk might be kept for them during the day, but no one ever drank milk from the morning milking after four in the afternoon. Any that was left then was either put into the churn or given to the dogs. In the evening as a rule the milk was drunk immediately after the milking.

The men of the kraal took turns in taking the cows to pasture and those left at home had many tasks to perform in the kraal. Three men, or two men and one boy, were generally needed to go out with a herd of one hundred cows and by seven o'clock they would be ready to start. The calves were then separated from their dams and the cows were driven away, grazing as they went. The men in charge followed the cattle about, directing them by word of mouth and keeping guard over them lest any wild beast should attack them. The cows wandered sometimes as far as twenty miles in a day and during the dry season they had to be watered twice a day, usually between nine and ten in the morning and again between three and five in the afternoon. In the rainy season, however, it was only necessary to water them in the afternoon, as the moisture in the grass was sufficient for their needs. The cows were trained to obey an order and the watering of a large herd showed the wonderful control the men had over them. Sometimes it was possible for the cows to go down to the water and drink, but at other times the water had to be drawn from deep wells and poured into troughs which were dug some twelve feet long and eighteen inches wide and deep and lined with clay. This work was done by the men who were left in the kraal and the troughs were ready for the cows when they arrived. A certain number were allowed to go at a time to drink while the rest had to wait until their turn came. They were so accustomed to being called by name and to obeying orders that they waited patiently until they were told to come and drink.

If a bull fell into a well while drinking, it might not mate with cows again, but had to be killed.

About half-past six, as the sun set, the cows were brought back into the kraal for the night and were milked again. After the evening milking they remained in the kraal and got neither food nor water during the night. At no time did they get artificial food and no attempt was made to improve the milk supply. If the pasturage happened to be poor, the cows had to suffer. There were, however, certain seasons of the year when cattle-flies were especially troublesome and so irritated the animals that they could not feed during the day; at such times the herdsmen would take them out to pasture for two or three hours during the night.

When the cows went off in the morning to the pasture, the calves were either driven back into the kraal or remained outside in charge of special men or of women or children. The calves, while still young, were only allowed to go out for an hour or two in the morning and again in the late afternoon when the sun was not hot, but the older calves went out for longer periods. As a rule these were looked after by children, but, if there were no children in the kraal, the work might be done by women or by some of the men.

The first task of the men who were left in the kraal was to sweep up the droppings made by the cows during the night and tidy the place. The sweeping was done with the soles of the feet and with the hands, and when they had finished they washed their hands and feet with water. Herdsmen did not usually bathe with water, as it was supposed to have an injurious effect on the milk. It was therefore more usual to smear the body over with moist white clay, which was allowed to dry and was then rubbed off and butter rubbed on. Before milking for the Mugabe, however, the men washed their hands with water, or preferably with cows' urine.

The dung which was swept up was put on the heap at one side of the kraal while some was dried and heaped upon the central fire. The huts of the calves had also to be swept out and the old grass collected for future use as fuel while new grass was brought and spread. Fire-wood had also to be brought in for the fires in the huts, which were kept burning constantly and were not allowed to go out during the night. Some of the men had to carry milk and butter to the owner of the herd if he was at a distance from the kraal. Then, if the water had to be drawn from wells or pits for the cows, some of the men had to go and dig the troughs and fill them and also to bring water for washing the milk-vessels.

A pastoral woman might never go to draw water, for, if she fell into the water, her husband might never treat her as his wife again. If he did so he would die, unless he belonged to the Abasambo clan, when he might send for a doctor to give her medicine to cause sickness, after which she might go to him again.

If the wife of a cow-man fell from her husband's bed, she might not return to him until she had been given medicine to make her sick.

The work of the women in a kraal was to look after the milk, the milk-pots, and the churning, but, if there were no women, this had to be done by some of the men or boys. After the milk had been drunk in the morning, the pots were handed back to the woman in charge who, with her maids, washed them, using generally water and a little earth. If any pot was thought to be sour, urine from a cow was boiled and the pot was washed out with this and afterwards with water. Grass was sometimes burned in the pots to sweeten them. The clean pots were put in the sun to dry and were then fumigated over a little pottery furnace in which a special kind of scented grass was burned. The milk-pot was inverted over the chimney of this furnace and the smoke fanned into it, which gave the milk a flavour much appreciated by the cow-people. The pots when dried and ready were all returned to their place in the hut until the time of the evening milking, after which they were merely washed out with water and replaced on their stand, ready for the morning.

Churning was done in the early morning before the heat of the day. A large bottle-necked gourd which was used as a churn (*kisabo*) stood beside the milk-pots and each day the wife poured what milk she could spare into this. When it was ready for churning, the neck of the gourd was plugged with a tuft of grass, and the person churning, generally a daughter or a servant, rocked it to and fro on her lap until the butter separated. The liquid was filtered through spear-grass (*mutete*) to secure all the butter, which was put on a large wooden plate, *kiteraterero*, big enough for the worker to wash it and work it up with the hand to cleanse it from the remains of the milk. It was then put into the vessel (*ensimbo*) in which it was kept.

Butter was used for smearing upon the body and for rubbing into skins and bark-cloths used for clothing, to keep them soft. When used for food, the butter was mixed with salt, and the meat, plantain, or millet-porridge was dipped into it. Butter was also largely used for barter, and weapons and other commodities were purchased with it.

The butter-milk was generally drunk by women and children, for few men, and those only of the lower class, would

PLATE VIII

Milk-pots and gourd churn, a set for one family

PLATE IX

Milkman carrying milk

drink it. Any that could be spared was given to the dogs. Men, however, were fond of clotted milk, which was prepared by pouring milk into a vessel called *kirera* in which a little sour milk had been left. This caused the milk which had been poured in to turn sour very quickly and it became clotted. Before being drunk it was stirred up and the clots broken.

Cows' urine was used for many different purposes. Women drank it mixed with certain herbs as a medicine during pregnancy and also used it for cleaning any milk vessels that were thought to be sour. Cow-skin garments were washed in it to keep them free from vermin, and butter was rubbed on them afterwards to soften them. The people also used it to wash their heads, rinsing them afterwards in fresh water to get rid of the smell and to prevent the urine from getting into the eyes and making them smart.

The staple food of a cow-man was milk, but there were occasions when to drink milk would be harmful to the cows and he had therefore to refrain. If a cow died either from illness or accident, the men of the kraal would eat the meat and drink beer that night, leaving the milk for the women and children and for churning. A man had to allow time for the meat to digest and pass from the upper part of the stomach before he drank milk again, lest this should come in contact with the meat; if, therefore, he ate meat at night he would not drink milk until after the morning milking. Sometimes, too, when milk was scarce, some members of the family would take millet or plantain porridge in the evening and drink no milk until morning. Even the Mugabe, who was allowed many liberties not permitted to ordinary men, was not allowed to drink milk and eat meat at the same meal.

It was a wife's duty to see that the milk was properly distributed after each milking. Certain of the cows were dedicated to ghosts and the milk from these had always to be kept separate from the ordinary milk. The ghost of the former owner of the herd had always his special cow or cows in milk and the vessels containing the milk from them were placed on a particular spot behind the present owner's bed for a time, after which the owner and his children alone might drink it. Even the wife might not partake, for she was of a different clan from her husband and the ghost. There were many other occasions on which the milk from certain cows was taboo to certain people and the wife had to see that such milk was kept separate and given to the right persons. She kept separate pots for these special purposes and after the milking was done, distributed the milk to members of the family and to the herdsmen. Some of the milk was drunk at once by the men, while other members of the family and the owner would often set some aside to be drunk later.

A sick man was permitted to drink milk, but as a rule one cow would be set aside to supply him and he would not be allowed to drink milk from any other until he was well again. Though milk might not be boiled, hot water might be added to it when it was to be used for a sick man. If a man ate potatoes or beans, he had not only to fast twelve hours but had also to take a purgative to ensure that all contaminating matter had left his system before he drank milk again.

Though children were allowed to eat hares, the only meat a herdsman might eat was that of cows or buffaloes, but these he might eat even from an animal which had died of some disease. If there was any doubt about the meat being fit for human consumption, the man drank or rinsed out his mouth with water and certain herbs (*mwetengo* or *muhukyi*), a precaution which was considered sufficient to remove all danger and to render even loathsome meat wholesome.

Milk was never sold and was as a rule given only to pastoral people to drink. It might never be put into any iron vessel, nor boiled, nor put into hot water, for this would have a deleterious effect on the cows and might cause the milk to cease, thus depriving the people and the calves of their food.

Women lived as much as possible on milk, but there were many taboos which they had to observe. A wife might never drink milk from cows which were sacred to her husband's ancestors, for of this only the husband and his children might partake; the wife, being of a different clan, was forbidden to do so. A woman while menstruating might not drink milk for four days, for, if she did so, the cow's udder would swell and its milk cease, and the animal might become barren. If, however, her husband or father could supply her with milk from a cow which was past bearing, she might safely drink that. A wife continued to sleep with her husband and to look after the milk-pots and churn while menstruating, and there was no idea of danger to anything but the cows. The wife of a herdsman might not touch butter or butter-pots from ten in the morning until four in the afternoon, for, if she did so, the cows would bear bull-calves only.

When a cow had been with the bull, the milk was taboo to all grown men and women for four days and was drunk by boys and girls. When a cow had a calf, the calf was allowed to drink all the milk from its dam at two or three milkings after its birth; after that, the milk had to be drunk by a small boy or girl, preferably the son or daughter of the owner, until the navel cord fell from the calf, when the milk became common. When a cow bore twins, only the owner and any unmarried children who might be living at home might drink the milk, and, if the cow bore twins a second time, the milk was given away to strangers, which was supposed to prevent the cow from bearing a third set of twins.

A cow which was sacred to the ghost of the owner's father might never be milked by a son of the owner. The man who milked it brought the milk-pot to the owner, who placed it by the bed on the side furthest from the fire. When it had been there some three hours, the owner and any unmarried children who lived at home drank it. The only other person who might partake was a friend or relative of the owner who had spent the night with him and slept on the same bed. When such a cow died, only the owner and members of his household might eat the meat.

Milk was never used as a sign of any pledge or of the ending of any quarrel: this was always done over beer.

DOMESTIC ANIMALS

In addition to the large herds of cattle which were the most important factor in their lives, the pastoral people possessed goats and sheep, which they gave to the agricultural people to look after for them. A few sheep were sometimes kept in the kraal and herded with the cows, for a ghost might, through a medicine-man, demand that a sheep be kept in the herd to ensure to both man and beast immunity from illness. This animal was not sacred and when it died anyone might eat the flesh and another was brought to take its place. Most of the sheep, however, were cared for by the peasants, and goats were never kept in the kraals.

Sheep were widely used among the pastoral people on ceremonial occasions such as marriages and funerals, and both sheep and goats were used for sacrificial purposes and for the taking of auguries in cases of illness and trouble. When a ghost had to be exorcised, a goat or a sheep was usually again required either to sacrifice, alive or dead, to the ghost, or to pay the medicine-man, and they were also used for barter and for making small presents to friends or visitors when the owner did not wish to part with a cow or a calf.

Fowls were kept in the kraal because a cock was needed to warn the inmates in the morning when it was time to arise and prepare to milk the cows; they were also often demanded by medicine-men for the purpose of auguries. Pastoral people, however, never ate either fowls or eggs and they never sold fowls, though they might give them away.

A fowl over which some incantations had been pronounced was often killed and hung over the door of a hut to ward off some evil, or it might be buried alive in the doorway or near the bed for the same purpose. If a woman was heard to imitate the crowing of a cock, her husband divorced her and no man would marry her.

Some dogs were kept in the kraal, for they were useful as scavengers and cleared up any food, bones, and so forth left about the kraal by the children. Even the Mugabe kept a few favourite dogs always near him, but the majority were

PLATE **X**

Peasant girl with hair cut in ridges

PLATE XI

Fat women who sit to dance
The performance is with the arms and upper part of the body

looked after by the peasants and were used for hunting. They were kindly treated and never driven away, but their food was scanty, though any milk that was left over and was not required for churning was given to them.

When a dog had puppies, a cow was bled and the dog was given blood to drink in addition to milk, and offal was given to it for food. Puppies, if not wanted, might not be destroyed before their eyes were open. Dogs were never sold but might be given away to friends. Should a woman kill a dog, her husband divorced her at once and no man would marry her, for she might never again cook for any man.

When the Mugabe died, the dogs and goats found in the vicinity of any royal kraal were killed; when the news of the death was heard, people who wished to save their animals had to send them away to a distance before the search parties could find them.

CLOTHING

Children of both sexes went entirely naked until they reached the age of puberty. At this age a boy was presented by his father with a bow and a quiver of arrows and he began to wear the full dress of a man, which consisted only of a small cow- or calf-skin (*engyisho*) over the shoulders, and sometimes a skin-apron (*entuiga*). These skins were shaped and fringed according to the owner's fancy, and princes and chiefs often had their shoulder capes made up of strips of cow-, leopard- and antelope-skins, or of cow-skins of different colours. The hair was left on the skins, which were stitched together with sinews of animals, usually of cows. It was more usual, however, to use the leopard- and antelope-skins for rugs than for clothing.

Girls at the age of eight or nine began to wear on the head a kind of grass veil like a mat (*enyagamo*) some two feet square, made of lengths of straw stitched side by side. When a girl reached marriageable age, she wore the full dress of a woman, which consisted of a large robe of skins wrapped round the body under the arms and secured with a belt, and another large cow-skin or sometimes a bark-cloth covering her head and falling to her feet, often trailing a yard or more on the ground. The whole person was thus covered, only the eyes being visible through a small opening left so that the woman could see.

The wives of the Mugabe and princesses usually had their robes made of different coloured skins dressed with the hair on and then cut into strips some four inches wide and stitched together, the effect of black, white, and red strips being much admired.

It was only in the presence of her husband, her father, and her brothers that a woman might go without the head-covering. She might sleep with a friend of her husband, but must cover her head and might never allow her face to be seen by him in the open.

The cow-men often dressed the skins for clothes themselves, but the agricultural people were the recognised skin-dressers.

Ornaments were worn and admired by both sexes. Boys and men wore bracelets and sometimes necklets, made generally from the stiff hairs of elephants' tails, though the necklets were regarded as more particularly a woman's ornament. A girl wore no ornaments until she was to be married, when her father presented her with some. The ornaments of women were necklets (*ekidungu*), anklets (*enverere*), and bracelets (*olugaga*) and were usually made of fine twisted wire, though some were of solid iron or brass.

HAIR

The hair of the pastoral people was not in tightly curled tufts like that of the negroes, but it was always wavy and never straight. It was usual to shave the head once a month, but all the hair was not shaved off. A man whose father was alive left one tuft like a bit of pencil as a sign that he was living, and one for the Mugabe, and sometimes one for his own children. If the Mugabe, or the man's father, or one of his children died, one tuft was shaved off. These were not always the same tufts, for each time the head was shaved, the old tufts were taken off and new tufts left.

A girl's or woman's head was shaved in patterns, sometimes in broad lines from ear to ear, sometimes in a spiral with a circular patch on the top. New patches, which were called *kikara,* were left each time and the old taken off. A patch was always left on the top for her husband or, if she was unmarried, for her father, and one on the side for the Mugabe. If the husband or father, or the Mugabe died, the corresponding patch was shaved off. When a woman grew old and white hairs appeared, she wore a wig, made from her own hair which she had saved for this purpose, to hide them.

There was no rule about hair being shaved by any special person, but, when a girl was about to be married, her mother shaved the hair from all parts of her body and cut her nails and threw the clippings on the floor of the hut. From the time of marriage both men and women shaved all the hair from their bodies, leaving none but the head patches.

There was not so much fear of hair falling into the hands of evilly disposed persons as in some parts of the country, but it was generally put into some part of a field or on some waste ground, or a man might have it concealed in the roof of his hut, but, if he left the place, he did not trouble to remove it. The hair and nail-parings of the Mugabe were preserved until he died, when they were put in his grave.

A woman who grew a beard was looked upon with the greatest horror and was called *Ekunguzi,* a term of scorn. Should she marry and her husband discover that she had hair on her face, he was horrified and made her pluck it all out, and stow the hairs away in a gourd for safety. Should one hair be lost, it was believed that either her husband or her child would die. If such a woman belonged to the Abaririra clan, she was taken by members of her clan and bound hand and foot, purifying herbs were tied to her neck and she was drowned.

SLAVES

Many of the people owned slaves who were bought and sold like goods. If a man gave a slave a wife and a child was born to them, this child was the property of the owner of the slaves, who, however, could not sell it but had to keep it in the family.

There were many degrees of service from the bought slaves up to the messengers of the Mugabe:

Muhuku = a bought slave who might be used for menial tasks.

Mwambale = servants in personal attendance on their masters.

Mwiru = peasants, who cultivated and were to a certain extent independent, though under pastoral masters.

Musumba = herdsmen who milked and were of the pastoral class.

Bagalagwa = personal servants of the Mugabe who, after they finished their term of service, were given cows and land.

Banyiginya = the highest class. These were princes, but the Mugabe might use them as special messengers for confidential work.

CURRENCY

The cow was the standard by which all prices were regulated. A male slave could be bought for a cow and a bull, while a female slave cost two cows or a cow and a cow-calf.

A bull might be sold for six or eight goats or for a sheep and a ram, or a hoe might be given with the sheep in the place of the ram.

Household utensils were made by the serfs of the agricultural class, to which the smiths also belonged. The pastoral people paid butter and skins for these and for salt, while meat was given for spears, arrows and canoes.

COUNTING

The pastoral people were accustomed to count and to deal with very large numbers, for the herds amounted to thousands and even tens of thousands. They also used a system of sign-counting, using the fingers of one or both hands. They had, however, no means of indicating dates, unless some outstanding event marked the time.

1. *Emwe*, indicated by extending the index-finger
2. *Ebiri*, two first fingers extended and the others bent inwards into the palm of the hand
3. *Isatu*, index-finger bent inwards and held by the thumb and the other fingers extended

4. *Ina*, four fingers extended while the index-finger is flicked from the thumb against the inside of the second finger

5. *Itano*, fist closed over the thumb, first finger on the joint of the thumb

6. *Mukaga*, three first fingers extended and the little finger bent inwards and held by the thumb

7. *Musanzu*, second finger bent inwards and held by the thumb and others extended

8. *Munana*, index-finger bent in under the third and flicked against the second

9. *Mwenda*, second finger on each hand bent in and held by the thumbs and the hands shaken. This number is sometimes called *Isaga*

10. *Ikumi*, both fists closed with the thumbs folded under the fingers

11. *Ikumi, limwe,* or *nemwe*	12. *Ikumi ne biri*
13. *Ikumi ne isatu*	14. *Ikumi ne ina*
20. *Makumi abiri*	30. *Makumi asatu*
40. *Makumi ana*	50. *Makumi atano*
60. *Makumi mukaga*	70. *Makumi musanzu*
80. *Makumi munana*	90. *Makumi isaga*
100. *Igana*	200. *Magana abiri*

10,000. *Magana ikumi*

SEASONS AND TIME

The year was divided into four seasons, beginning with *Akaanda*. This lasted about two months when the sun was hot and the weather good for the cattle. Then came *Kaswa*, three or four months of rainy weather; after which there were some four months of sun and heat, called *Kyanda*, followed by *Empangukano*, two months of rain.

The month was reckoned from the appearance of one new moon to the appearance of the next. This period was divided into two: *Okwezi*, fifteen days when the moon was of use for seeing, and *Omwirima*, fifteen days with little or no light from the moon. One of the royal drums was always sounded when the new moon appeared, to warn the people.

They now divide the year into twelve months according to the western custom:

January = *Biruru*. The month of the millet harvest when the weather was dry but with occasional showers of rain.

February = *Kata*. A dry month with hot sun. The ˌmall millet already reaped was stored and the large millet sown.

March = *Katumba*. A month of heavy rains when beans were sown and potatoes planted.

April = *Nyaikoma*. A rainy month. Guards had to be set upon the growing millet.

May = *Kyabehezi*. The harvest of the large millet. A little rain.

June = *Nyairurwe*. A little rain, often drought and winds.

July = *Kichulansi*. Very hot sun. Some rain. The runners of the sweet potatoes planted.

August = *Kamena*. The rains began to fall and the heat of the sun was less. Small millet sown.

September = *Nyakanga*. A little rain.

October = *Kaswa*. A rainy month. Flying ants and edible grass-hoppers appear. The small millet needed weeding.

November = *Musenene*. Heavy rains.

December = *Muzimbezi*. A little rain.

The divisions of the day were:

5– 6 a.m. = *Kasese*	6–9 a.m. = *Amasyo gasetuka*
9–12 a.m. = *Gasugera*	1–2 p.m. = *Ehangwe*
2– 3 p.m. = *Amasyo neganyuwa*	3–5 p.m. = *Amanyo gakuka*
5– 6 p.m. = *Amasyo omhwebazyo*	7–9 p.m. = *Ente zataha*
10–12 p.m. = *Ente zahaga*	12 p.m.–3 a.m. = *Etumbi*
3– 5 a.m. = *Enkoko zazaga*	

Some of the hours through the day have also definite names:

11 a.m. = *bagya omu birago*	3 p.m. = *ente zairira amaka*
12 a.m. = *bagya ha kwesera*	4 p.m. = *enyana zataha*
1 p.m. = *ente zakuka*	5 p.m. = *batweka omu makome*
2 p.m. = *abesezi baruga ha maziba*	6 p.m. = *ente zataha*

Dawn is *omuseke muguguguta* and cock-crow is *enkoko yasubi'ra*. If a cock crows in the night they call it *enkoko yatera ekiro*, and, if it crows in the afternoon, it is *enkoko yaba'ra izoba*. Sunset is *marengi* or *nahuni*.

STARS, ETC.

Kakaga = the Pleiades	*Nyamuziga* = first star of evening
Kalinga = Orion's foot	*Okwezi omu kyera* = full moon
Abasatu = Orion's belt	*Okwezi kwalinga* = old moon
Enganzi = evening star	*Okwezi kutahira* = new moon
Nyakinyunyuzi = morning star	*Omuletza oruhemba* = comet
Rumalanku = Venus?	*Ekibunda* = eclipse

MUSIC AND DANCING

There was little attempt at music among the pastoral people. The women, who were too fat to dance, sat together inside the kraal and one of them played a harp and sang while the others moved their bodies and arms, making a buzzing noise between their lips; the men outside joined in and danced, swaying their bodies to the rhythm and jumping into the air. An account of the dancing among the agricultural people, where both men and women danced standing in the ordinary way, will be found in the description given later of agricultural life.

GREETINGS AND SALUTATIONS

In the morning they said "*Orairegye?*" which might be translated, "How have you spent the night?" and the answer was the same—"*Orairegye.*" Later in the day they said "*Osibiregye?*" "How have you spent the day?" and the reply was "*Nsibiregye*" or "*Nsibire kirunge,*" "I have spent it well." This greeting and answer were used in order to keep the omens good even if a person were known to be ill, in which case the further question was asked, "*Orairota endwara?*" "How is your illness or pain?"

When equals met after an absence, one asked, "*Kaizhe buhorogye?*" and the other answered, "*Kaizhe buhoro,*" and both repeated this many times. It was customary to shake hands and often the question, "*Mugumire?*" was asked, to which the answer was "*Tugumire.*" These might be translated, "are you without fear at home?" and the answer was "we are quite free."

Anyone meeting an elder had to wait for the elder to say to him "*Mphoro,*" to which he replied, "*Eh.*" Even the Mugabe would wait for his senior relatives to say this to him. A child might greet its elders with "*Erirege,*" an expression of uncertain meaning, to which the reply was "*Eh.*"

CHAPTER VIII

THE COWS

Long-horned cows—colours—birth of calves—navel cord of a calf—rearing calves—precautions against in-breeding—treatment of cows to make them accept calves and give milk—dewlap—the horns—sickness in the herd—medicine-men—lightning—bleeding cows—cow diseases—death of cows—charity—killing cows—cooking meat—salt for the cows

THE cattle peculiar to Ankole were long-horned, well-built animals something of the Hereford type. They were noted throughout the Lake region, for the length of their horns was often so great that the tips were four or five feet apart. Few of them, however, gave much milk, and the milk-man would take from each about a quart, leaving the rest for the calf. Little, if any, attempt was ever made to improve either the milk supply or the quality of the meat, for their aims were to increase their numbers and to have as large a proportion as possible of cow-calves.

Cows were known by different names according to their colours and the following is a list of the names used. As these, however, had in many cases to be accepted from the natives without seeing the actual type of animal indicated, and as natives always find a difficulty in naming or describing colours, the accuracy of the list cannot be vouched for. It will serve, however, to show how the cows were clearly differentiated and how a name constituted a description which enabled a herdsman to pick out from his herd any animal required:

Kahogo, dark red
Kozi, black
Katare, pure white
Kagondo, red and white
Kasecha, yellow with black stripes
Kahuru, black and white
Katango, black with some white markings
Kakara, mixed colours, not red or black
Kasina, brown

Kagazo, light red
Kasa, white with some red or black
Kagobi, black and yellow
Kagabo, black or red with white on the sides
Kashaiga, yellowish-white
Kayenzi, red with some black markings
Karemba, red legs with white or black body
Omurara, black with white stripe

Twelve months was said to be the time required by a cow between the birth of one calf and the birth of the next, and the cow was not milked after the sixth or seventh month of gestation.

It was quite common for cows to calve when out grazing, though herdsmen generally kept watch, keeping count of the period by the moons, and, if they thought the time was near, they would leave the cow to pasture near the kraal and not allow her to wander far. If, however, one had her calf while grazing, a herdsman remained to watch her lest she should be left behind as the herd moved on, and be lost. When the calf was born, this man carried it back to the kraal and the cow followed him.

If a cow calved in the pasture, the after-birth was left for the wild beasts to eat, but, if the birth took place in the kraal, dogs were called to eat it, unless there was some taboo on the cow or she bore twins, in which cases the after-birth was buried in the dung-heap in the kraal lest the calves should die. If there was a case of cross-birth, a medicine-man was called in and invariably succeeded in turning the calf and bringing about true presentation. The fee given to him for such a service was one sheep.

The cow-men did not like a cow to bear twins, chiefly because the calves were not so strong as when there was only one. If an animal had twins the milk was drunk only by the owner and his unmarried children. Should the same cow bear twins a second time, the milk was given away to prevent the thing happening again.

When a young cow bore her first calf the herdsman went to the old cow, the mother of this young one, and milked a little milk from her on to a tuft of grass (*ezubwe*). He gave this grass to the young cow to eat and, taking another tuft, milked a little milk from her on to this and gave it to the old cow, her dam, to eat. This was supposed to make the calf grow and prevent its dam and the old cow from falling ill.

The navel cord of a calf was carefully watched, and, if it split before falling off, the strands were counted   An even number of strands was a good omen, indicating that many calves would be born, but an odd number was bad. The umbilical cord was tied together with a strip of bark-cloth so that, when it was dry, all the strands fell away together. It was then wrapped in a ball of cow-dung and preserved. A cord which fell off without splitting was thrown away.

When milking time came, the calf was first allowed to suck for a few moments and was then held before its dam while she was being milked, for they said she could withhold her milk should the calf not be there. If the calf died, its skin was dried and held before the cow; sometimes a cow became quite attached to the dried skin and refused to be milked if it was not there. At other times a cow whose calf had died would be taught to allow the calf of another cow to suck from her, in which case the calf was used at milking time for both cows.

For the first month of its life, a calf was kept in its hut and only allowed out at milking times. Fresh grass was put in the hut every day and at the end of about a month the calf would begin to eat the grass, after which it was allowed to browse for a short time in the cool of the morning and in the evening near the kraal, where it could be watched from the gate. Later it went out with the other calves for longer periods. Until it was seven months old, it was called *Nyana* (calf), but then it was said to *kyukire* (change) and was considered old enough to accompany the herds as they went to pasture. It still sucked from its dam, but this was prevented during the day by smearing the teats with dung. By the time it was a year old, it no longer sucked from the dam, for she, being again with calf, would not permit it to do so. Shortly after this the heifer would probably become pregnant and, when it did so, it was regarded as a full-grown cow. When it was old enough to go with the bull, it was called *erusi* (marriageable), and when it had been with the bull it was *kibanga*. When it had borne its first calf it was called *ezigazire*, after the second calf, *esubire*, after the third, *ezigiza*, and then no more attention was paid to its age and a good cow went on bearing until she had had as many as twenty calves.

PLATE XII

Chief medicine-man of the cows singing his incantations
to heal a herd of sick cows

PLATE XIII

Chief medicine-man of the cows

When too old to bear, a cow was called *kichula* or *ngumba*, while a young barren cow was *mberera*. A young bull was called *ekimasa*, and, when old enough to serve cows, it was called *engundu*.

Herdsmen were careful to exchange young bulls to guard against in-breeding and they particularly guarded against a young animal gendering with its own dam. Should this happen, the calf born was called *matembani*, which denoted a calf born within forbidden degrees of consanguinity, and it was never allowed to bear calves. A calf which was born malformed, especially if it was sexless, was called *mbangulane*, which meant that it was worthless.

Cows of the long-horn breed had usually a mark on the small hump and a cow which was born without this mark was regarded as sacred; only the owner and his family might drink milk from it.

Should a cow bear a calf and refuse to allow it to suck, a medicine-man was sent for to treat it. He took the herbs *ekinyangazi ne kibyakurata* and *musogasoga*, powdered them, and mixed them with salt and hot water; this mixture was poured up the cow's nose and some was put upon the calf, which was brought before the dam. The effect usually was that the cow licked the calf and then, accepting it, allowed it to suck from her. If this was unsuccessful the medicine-man went to a shrine and prayed: "The ghost of my father, help me," and tried again. He also made a new fetish which he tied on the cow's horn to induce her to accept her calf. For this service the medicine-man demanded a pot of beer, and, should the owner of the cow refuse to pay this, the man cursed the cow and the calf died. A calf was seldom reared by artificial feeding, though the method was known and on rare occasions used. If the dam finally refused the calf, a foster-mother was sought, but, if one could not be found, the calf was killed and eaten.

If a cow was not giving as much milk as the herdsman considered she should give, he gathered the herbs *omuwhoko* and *ekikamisa wa gali*. These he dried over a fire and rubbed them to powder, then, with the addition of water, he made them into a ball, full of water and the juice of the herbs. He thrust his hand with the herb ball into the uterus of the cow and squeezed the juice from it. This irritated the passage and caused the milk to flow. The effect on the milk lasted three or four days and the process might have to be repeated. The men said that it did not usually injure the cow, though some affirmed that, if repeated often, it made her barren. This method was at times resorted to to make a cow accept a foster-calf or when she refused her own calf, and the man, after passing his hand into the uterus, wiped it on the calf's back, which caused the cow to lick it and allow it to suck. This process was called to *kuwatika* a cow.

When a cow had not enough milk to nourish her calf, the herdsman often took away the calf and gave it to a cow which had a bull-calf, killing the bull-calf and leaving the first cow to cease giving milk and to bear again.

When a cow, after having a calf, did not again become pregnant as soon as they expected, the owner milked her only once a day. If this had not the desired effect, he took some of the herb *mpara*, chewed it, and squirted the juice from his mouth into and round the uterus; this set up irritation and caused the cow to seek the bull at once. The process was called to *okuhagirana* the cow.

A cow which developed the loose folds of skin below its throat, known as dewlap, was regarded as a blessing to the owner. As this developed and the flesh reached the ground, it was tied up to prevent it from dragging in the dust. Such an animal might not be put to death in the ordinary way by spearing it in the head but had to have its neck broken by strong men who twisted its head round sharply. Only the owner of the kraal and his family might eat the flesh.

When a cow with one horn turned up and one down had a calf, a knife or a spear was heated and a mark burned on one of the horns. This was regarded as a decoration and other burns were sometimes made on cows for the same purpose.

When a cow's horns turned down and grew so long as to

PLATE XIV

The chief medicine-man of the cows performing his incantations to heal a sick herd

PLATE XV

Chief medicine-man of the cows

get in its way and hinder its walking and grazing, the owner took a bit of stick to the Mugabe and told him what had happened. The Mugabe, taking the stick, spat on it and handed it back to the owner, who took it to the cow and tapped the horns with it. The horns were then cut off close to the head with a hot knife or axe. To stop the bleeding and heal the wounds they were seared with a heated spear, and a medicine of the herbs *miseka* and *mugasa*, powdered and mixed with flour of millet, was sprinkled on the wounds. The cow soon recovered from the operation and was none the worse.

When a cow with straight horns was given to goring its companions, the herdsman burned a notch on each horn and bent the tips back so that the horns were blunt.

In each district there were cow-doctors or medicine-men who were called to assist the herdsmen when anything went wrong with the cows. They knew the different herbs to use for illnesses, and they were also said to know drugs which would make cows bear cow-calves. They were paid for their work with sheep or goats.

If sickness broke out among the cattle in a kraal, the owner called in a cow-doctor and asked him to discover by augury the cause of the illness and the remedy. In the evening a bull or an old cow that was past bearing was given to the medicine-man, who tied a bunch of herbs round its neck, took it outside, and drove it round the kraal. If the illness was affecting more than one kraal in the vicinity, he took the same animal to each and drove it round outside them, keeping it on the move the whole night. At daybreak he brought the cow to the entrance of the kraal and killed it there, cutting its throat and catching the blood in a vessel. He took a bunch of the herbs *nyawera* and *mugosola* and either sprinkled all the members of the kraal with the blood or touched them with it on their foreheads, arms and legs. The cattle were then sprinkled and first the people and then the cows went out of the kraal, jumping over the body of the dead cow as it lay in the gateway. The medicine-man took the bunch of herbs from the cow's neck and tied them over the gateway so that the cows passed under them when they entered in the evening, and the disease was thus prevented from returning to the kraal. He removed the carcase, for the meat was his, and no member of the kraal might eat of it, for to do so would be to cause the disease to return. Often, in addition to this magic, the cows would be treated with herbal medicine given in water.

There was a special medicine-man who was called in when lightning had struck men or cows. He had a whistle which he blew during a storm to make the lightning pass over without doing damage. Should a man or a cow be struck and killed, people brought either hoes or sticks and beat them over the body to cause the lightning to come out and the spirit to return. When lightning killed some of a herd of cows, the rest of the herd was kept in the place and the owner was sent for. He spent the night there fasting; no one might spit, no fire might be lighted, and no stranger passing the spot could go on but had to stay the night. On the next morning the special medicine-man arrived. His first duty was to discover by divination the cause which had led to this disaster and none of the cows could be milked until this was known and an appiopriate gift had been made to the god of thunder to pacify him. When this had been done, the herd was driven home to the kraal, the cows were milked and the calves fed and then they went out to pasture as usual. The medicine-man was given two cows as his fee and the owner might thereafter again drink milk and kill or sell his cows. The ceremony was called *kangkula* or purifying the herd. Should one of the cows bear a malformed calf during this time it was taken to the Lake Karagwe and thrown in as an offering to the offended spirit who resided there. A pot of water was drawn from the lake and brought to the owner who sprinkled some on his family and washed himself with it. The owner was not allowed to drink milk from the cow which bore a malformed calf under these circumstances, though, when one was born under ordinary circumstances, he alone might drink the milk of the dam or eat the flesh of the calf.

Cows were often bled, usually for medicinal purposes. This was done by tying a string round the cow's neck to make the veins swell; an arrow, with a guard to prevent it from going too far, was then shot into the vein and the amount of blood required was taken.

COW DISEASES

Ezwa. Foot and mouth disease. The medicine-man, or one of the principal men in the kraal, bled the cows in the morning and, when they had gone to pasture, he poured the blood on the central fire. When it had congealed and dried, he scraped it up and put it into small bundles of dried elephant-grass to be used as torches. In the evening when the cows returned, the torches were lighted and men went out of the kraal and carried them amongst the cattle, calling on the disease to release the cows and go. The cows were then driven into the kraal, their feet were washed with hot water from a special pot, *oluhega*, and those whose mouths were too sore to allow them to feed were fed with grass plucked for them by the men. Cows seldom died of this complaint but were isolated and treated as described above and eventually recovered.

The medicine-man pronounced a charm to prevent the illness from spreading, and amulets were hung round the cows' necks. The inmates of the kraal were forbidden to eat salt, men might not go to their wives, no stranger might enter the kraal, and no girl from it might visit friends in another kraal.

Amasyihu. A disease which attacked calves. The head and face broke out into sores and the calf died, as they said, "of a rotten liver." No treatment was used, but the animal was left to get well or die.

Obuzimba. The cow's body swelled as though it was becoming very fat, its glands and throat also swelled and it usually died in three or four days. The herdsmen sometimes treated this by blistering, but as a rule the disease was left to run its course.

Obusaghi. If a jackal fell into a water-hole and was drowned, any cows which drank the water died.

Muzuzu. The cow was taken with a shivering fit and died at once. No cure was known.

Omulaso. This disease lasted a month, after which the animal died; the meat might not be eaten.

Kyiha. A lung and heart trouble contagious and fatal.

Kabube. An illness which affected the joints so that the animal wanted to lie down. If it was forced to walk about it recovered.

Kukonagire. A calf's sickness. It affected the legs and at times the body swelled. No treatment was known: the sickness ran its course and was frequently fatal.

Omuhindu. The ears cracked and bled, and the hair of the animal stood on end, but the animal usually recovered if a little care was taken of it.

Mulyamu. Rinderpest. A disease only known in recent years. No cure.

Kipumpula. Swellings on the thighs, shoulders and backbone.

The flies which tormented cows were called *Engoha*, but those which brought disease were *Mbalabala* and *Nkubikisi*.

When a cow was suffering from constipation or from retention of the urine, the herdsman made a fetish of hippopotamus skin and a tuft of hippopotamus hair and walked among the cows waving this over them. He then took it to the suffering cow and pushed it into her uterus, which caused the urine to flow.

When a cow died, the owner mourned five days for it and refrained from sexual intercourse with his wife. On the sixth day he squeezed the juice from the herb *mwonyo* into a pot and he and his wife, sitting together, stirred the juice with their left hands, put some in their mouths, and spat it out three times to purify themselves and the kraal. The man then had sexual intercourse with his wife. This was to prevent other cows from dying in the same way.

If the only cow of a poor herdsman died, he visited the members of his clan and begged from them, often getting two or three cows in the place of his lost one. The poor were

PLATE XVI

Peasant girl in goat-skin dress

PLATE XVII

Elderly peasant

always looked after by their relatives, and, should a man who
was able to help refuse his aid to a poor brother, he was
marked and no one came to mourn at his funeral. The effect
of this was believed to be that he suffered loss of friends in
the other world, to which he was sent without the usual
lamentations.

It was considered wrong to kill cows which were still able
to bear, and the ordinary herdsmen, though they ate the
meat of any cow that died, never killed cows except on very
special occasions such as marriages or funerals. When it was
necessary to kill an animal, they chose a cow too old to bear
or a bull that was not required. The animal was killed by
spearing or striking it with an axe on the head just behind
the horns, a method which did not waste much of the blood,
for it remained in the meat. The killing was always done outside the kraal where the men assembled to eat the meat,
cutting it up into small squares and roasting it over a fire
round which they sat. Some meat would be handed in to the
kraal to ⁺he women, who either ate it themselves or cooked
it for their husbands. Among the wealthy cow-people the
cooking was always done by slaves, but in the poorer classes
wives cooked for their husbands, though water and fire-wood
were brought to them by the men.

Meat was cut into small pieces and either roasted on spits
or boiled and served in wooden bowls or closely woven wicker
vessels. If it was boiled, millet was sometimes served with it,
though the grain was never cooked with the meat but boiled
in water separately.

When an animal was killed for the Mugabe's use, any blood
that flowed was caught and drunk by the servants of the
Mugabe. The skin of the cow, unless the Mugabe gave special
orders, went to the royal skin-dresser and was prepared for
the use of the Mugabe's wives, and the head was given to the
fire-wood carriers. The cook, who was always of an agricultural
clan, divided the animal. The Mugabe might only eat meat
from the shoulder, one leg went to his wives, any given to the
herdsmen had to be taken from the back without bones, and

the rest was cooked for the Mugabe's guests and other members of his household.

When a chief killed a cow, he followed the royal custom in dividing it, though he was not restricted to any special part for himself. When the Mugabe or a chief gave his men a cow to kill for their own food, they had always to return the heart and tongue to the owner, for they were forbidden to eat these parts.

SALT FOR THE COWS

It was considered essential to the health of the cattle that they should have salt once each month, and the carrying of salt was one of the tasks which a cow-man might undertake. Like building a kraal or a house, it was work done for the sake of the cattle and therefore not derogatory to his dignity. All sorts of things from goats and sheep to household utensils were taken to barter for the salt. When a man had left his home to go to one of the salt-markets, his wife might not have sexual relations with any man nor even cross the doorstep when a man was on it or shake hands with a man. When the man returned with the salt he took it to his house, and that night he had to sleep on the floor near the fire and keep apart from his wife and other women until the salt had been given to the cows, which was done the next day.

In the morning, after the cows had gone out to pasture and the kraal had been swept, the owner had the loads placed in a line before him in the kraal. A pot of milk was brought and he drank and puffed a little over each bundle. He then took a pot of butter and rubbed a little on each bundle. One of the logs used for filling up the gateway, a thong for tying the legs of restive cows during milking, and a bunch of purificatory herbs were brought and laid to smoulder on the central fire.

When it was time for the cows to come home in the evening, the salt was taken to the watering-place where large troughs were made and lined with clay and filled with water. The salt was added to the water, and when the animals had finished drinking they were driven home. As they entered the kraal, a boy stood at one side of the entrance and a girl at the other, each holding a pot of water and a bunch of the herb *nyawera*, with which they sprinkled the cows as they entered, saying, "Grow fat, give much milk, and have many calves." This ensured the best results and no evil effects from the drinking of the salt water.

CHAPTER IX

AGRICULTURE AND INDUSTRIES

The agricultural people—clothing—ornaments—music and dancing—
ownership of land—care of land—cultivation of millet—care of the
crops—harvest—storing grain—grinding corn—other crops—tobacco
—brewing millet and plantain beer—building huts—furniture—potters—carpenters—smiths—smelting—the smith's anvil and hammer

THE agricultural people of the lake region were probably
early inhabitants of the land, who were subdued by
immigrating hordes of pastoral people. These did not exter-
minate the conquered races but made them their serfs to do
the work which their cow customs forbade them to do for
themselves. The agricultural people were not slaves, for they
were free to move about the country as they would and to
leave one master and join another at their own will. They
were, however, generally attached to certain districts and,
when once settled, they seldom cared to move.

For clothing boys and men of the agricultural people wore
one goat- or calf-skin, passing under the left arm and tied
on the right shoulder. This hung down to the thigh or even
to the knees but was open down the right side, no attempt
being made to hide the person. The skins were usually roughly
dressed and the more wealthy members of the agricultural
class had them carefully prepared.

Girls, when children, often ran about naked or wore a skin
like that of the boys, but it was tied on the left shoulder and
passed under the right arm. As they grew up the size of the
skin was increased and it was more carefully dressed and
softened. The hair was either shaved off or worn inside next
the body. When married, a woman wore three or four skins
stitched together and fastened with a belt round her waist,
which was the sign of a married woman.

After marriage a woman wore ornaments of which the most
important were the anklets, without which no married

woman's dress was complete. She also wore bracelets and
neck ornaments of wire or elephant-tail hairs and beads. The
wire anklets and bracelets were made and fixed on by the
smith, who was given fourteen or more goats by the husband
for his work. In addition to this he invariably took for himself one of the ornaments he had made, and incantations were
pronounced over it to remove from all of them any evil that
might be attached to them.

The serfs were fond of dancing, in which both men and
women indulged, though they danced apart and generally
at different times. The drums used to accompany the dancing
were ordinary water-pots which were filled to different levels
with water. The drummers were armed with sticks to which
pads of reeds, rather larger than the mouths of the pots, were
attached with fibre. With these the men beat on the mouths
of the pots, producing a sound not unlike that of drums, while
others sang, danced, and gesticulated in time to the music.

Girls and young women wearing skin-aprons stood round
the drums, some of them with flat rattles. These were made
of hollow reeds which formed cases some ten inches long by
half an inch wide and were filled with seeds. Ten or more of
these cases were secured side by side in a frame, and this
was shaken up and down in time to the music. Others
accompanied the rhythm by singing and beating their hands
on their skin-aprons in front, which made a dull sound.

Certain tracts of land were given by the Mugabe to chiefs
and they could permit peasants to cultivate plots on that
land, but as a rule a peasant could cultivate any piece of land
he liked and there were no restrictions on his breaking up new
land except previous occupation. A man had merely to dig
a little or even to pluck some grass from the plot he meant
to dig, take it home, and tie it to the roof of his house as a
sign of possession. After that, should any man seek to cultivate
that land, the first comer informed him of his ownership. If
the intruder went away all was well, but, if he objected, there
was a fight and the original claimant, if worsted, might appeal
to the district-chief. Even if the first owner had left the land

for some years, he had the right, if he had dug it, to return and occupy it. An intruder, even if he had made improvements and enlarged the plot, could not claim the land if the first owner came back and lit a fire as a sign that he had returned. If there was trouble, the matter was brought before the district-chief and settled by ordeal. The disputants were given each a plantain root to eat, and this made the fraudulent claimant ill, while the true owner felt no bad effects. The man thus proved to be in the wrong might be fined anything from two goats or a sheep to as many as twenty goats.

When a man started to dig his field, the first sod cut had to be carried home and kept there until harvest, to ensure a good crop and success.

No attempt was ever made to fertilise land, for such an idea was entirely foreign to the minds of the people. Land was plentiful and if one field ceased to yield to the satisfaction of the owner, all he had to do was to break up fresh ground, leaving the old field for a time, or perhaps entirely. After a few years, when nature had to some extent restored the necessary properties to the soil, or when, as the native said, the ground was rested, he might try the old site again. If it then repaid his efforts, he might continue to cultivate it for a time, but, if not, he would probably forsake it entirely.

Artificial irrigation was unknown and crops were only grown in the wet season, though there were rare instances when a man would choose a plot of low-lying land near a river and raise a crop during the dry season. Such rare cases prove that it was not ignorance of the possibilities of the land but rather indolence which prevented the people from having fresh vegetable food all the year round. After harvest they dried and stored sufficient grain to keep them in food until the rains came and made it possible to grow a fresh crop.

The main crop was the small millet commonly called *bulo*, which was sown in August and September in ground that had been carefully hoed and prepared. When a man was going to sow his first seed for the season he made his preparations at 3 a.m. and wakened his family with the first streaks of dawn,

PLATE XVIII

Scare-crow in cornfield

A post in the scare-crow telegraph line
showing resonant objects

PLATE XIX

Water-pots used as drums

Dancing to the rhythm of the water-pot drums

for they had to be awake while he went to sow. If on the way to the field he met a person he disliked, he turned back and refrained from sowing seed that day; during the time of the sowing husband and wife had to be careful to have sexual relations only with each other, lest the seed should fail to germinate and the weeds grow.

When the plants were a few inches high they were thinned out and those pulled up were carried home, where they were eaten either uncooked and seasoned with salt or boiled. The rains made the crops grow rapidly, and in January, after six months' growth, the millet ripened. As the grain filled out flocks of birds visited the fields and it was necessary to employ scare-crows to drive these off. Children were employed in most villages for this purpose, and they had to be specially on the alert in the early morning and again in the evening, tor at these times the birds were particularly active. These young people often showed much ingenuity in their devices to save labour. Figures were made of grass and armed with sticks so that in the distance they resembled living persons waving sticks. At other places poles eight to ten feet long were firmly fixed at intervals in the ground; from the tops of these were hung large snail-shells, thin blades of iron, and other articles and the poles were connected by a cord which led to some tree or hillock, where an observer sat and jerked the string from time to time so that all the things tied to the poles rattled. At the same time the watchers shouted and used clappers of flat boards which made a noise loud enough to be distinctly heard over the field. In some places men and women built huts in their fields and lived there from the time the fresh shoots appeared until harvest, to protect the crops from wild pigs and other nocturnal visitors that might destroy them.

Only the family might eat of the first-fruits of the crop and the grindstones might not be used by anyone else after the corn was ground until the first-fruits had been eaten. Should either the man or his wife give any of the food away before this, the other would die. For this family meal the grain need not be ground and cooked, for even to eat a little of it un-cooked would remove this taboo.

When the harvest was ready, the wife went one day alone to the field and picked two kinds of grass, the seeds of which had burrs and stuck to the clothing. These she made into a kind of pad and laid it in the field, putting a stone upon it. She then gathered two small sheaves of the grain and placed them so that they stood over the pad. This was supposed to bring a plentiful harvest.

Next morning the man and his wife came together to reap the grain as soon as the dew had dried off it. They were careful to leave a patch for the husband's mother, who came herself and cut it and carried it home. Should they neglect this observance, the seed from that particular field would be useless the following year.

The reaping was a long and tedious business, for the grain was cut head by head with some six inches of stem and tied into small bundles. These were put in baskets and carried to a spot in the field where they were heaped together in a pile. A hole was made in the centre of the heap to allow the moisture to escape as the grain dried, and the heap was left four or five days to ripen by the heat generated. The heap was covered by night with plantain or other leaves to protect it against the heavy dews or rain, and it became very hot so that the grain matured quickly. If it was desired to hasten the ripening process, a pit some two feet deep was dug and the grain put in and covered over so that the heat generated ripened it in two or three days.

When the artificial ripening process was completed, the ears were spread out in the sun on the threshing-floor to dry and the grain either fell out or was beaten out with a short stick as the head of corn was held in the hand, the grain falling on the threshing-floor, which was merely a flat place swept clean of dust and often smeared over with cow-dung. This work was done by the women, who also winnowed the grain by pouring it from a flat basket held up as high as the head, so that the wind carried away the chaff.

PLATE XX

Large grain basket

PLATE XXI

Potters

The granaries were large baskets four or five feet high, smeared with cow-dung outside and inside and raised about two feet above the ground on stones or stakes. They were covered with detachable thatched roofs which could be raised to take out the grain. The first grain had to be put in by the man, who got into the store to do it. If he was away, his wife had to await his return, because, if she stored the grain before he put in the first basketful, he would die when he ate it. When required for use the grain was ground between stones to a coarse flour and made into stiff porridge.

Each hut had a slab of stone either under the eaves or near the door, which was used as the grindstone. It was generally two feet long by one foot wide, and a second stone four or five inches long and four wide, with a flat surface, was used to rub the grain to flour. The lower stone was raised a few inches from the ground with one side a little higher than the other, to allow the flour, as it was ground, to fall down into a basket placed to catch it. The woman who ground knelt at the higher end of the big stone with a basket of grain by her side and, taking a handful at a time from this, she rubbed it to flour between the stones. Naturally such flour contained a certain amount of grit so that porridge made from it was liable to make anyone ill whose system was not accustomed to such rough diet.

The time of harvest was a season for rejoicing, not only because there was an abundance of food but also because at this time they had freedom from the strain of necessary work and good supplies of grain for brewing beer. This season was thus the natural time for marriages, dances, and other festivities, and the people looked forward to it as an opportunity for relaxation and indulgence in beer-drinking. They cast all cares aside and gave themselves up to a time of merriment.

As long as his store lasted the peasant took grain from time to time to his pastoral master. There was no stated amount, but he took small supplies until he found his store getting low, when he took a large basketful, and this was understood by the master to indicate the last supply for the season.

This small millet was the only kind of food which was stored for supplying future needs, but they grew three other kinds of millet which were used more especially for brewing. Plantains and sweet potatoes were used to eke out the supply of millet. Peas, beans, ground-nuts and marrows were grown as additions to this food and were used as a relish in place of meat, which was seldom to be got, while maize was also cultivated, though it was looked upon as a luxury to be eaten between meals and they never considered it a part of their diet.

Tobacco was largely grown, for it was used both by pastoral and agricultural people. Men and old women smoked it and many young women chewed it. A few plants were grown near the hut on the dust-heap where the sweepings from the hut, which included the dung from goats and sheep and the dust from the wood-fire, were thrown. The dust-heap was thus a fertile spot and tobacco plants always thrived there and produced very good leaves. Peasants rarely attempted to prepare the leaves, which were merely dried in the sun and rubbed to small pieces and dust before being smoked.

The story of the introduction of tobacco into the country is as follows. During the reign of Ruhinda of Ankole, the king of Karagwe, also called Ruhinda, sent a medicine-man with six bags of tobacco, saying that it was medicine which would make Ruhinda of Ankole well and strong. The two kings were friends, so Ruhinda tried the tobacco, and, finding it soothing, went on and became a smoker. Later the chiefs learned about this and some of them took to smoking. When the medicine-man found his stock running out, he sowed two plots and grew more, showing the people how to prepare it before he returned to his own country.

BREWING

The people of Ankole were very fond of drink and brewed beer whenever it was possible. To make millet-beer, the millet was first put into water for four days so that it began to sprout. It was then spread on mats in the sun to dry and mixed with an equal amount of dry grain. The whole of this was ground to flour between stones, mixed with boiling water and boiled. After standing four days, it was again boiled, by which time the amount was reduced to one-fourth of the original. To this more grain, which had been wetted and allowed to sprout, was added and the whole stood in pots for two days and was then boiled again with the addition of water and more unprepared millet. This was poured into pots, and from a large pot, in which some of the first boiling had been left, a little was added to each pot, making in the end about ten times the original amount. This was left for a night and was then filtered through papyrus fibre. The result was a thick liquid which was ready for use.

While the beer was being prepared, the man engaged in the brewing might not touch butter or have relations with any women except his own wife.

To make plantain-beer, the plantains, of the kind known as the male or beer-making plantain, were cut when fully grown but not ripe and put over a slow fire of millet-chaff or cow-dung in a shallow pit for three days to make them fully ripe. They were then pulped in a large wooden trough like a bath. A quantity of millet which had been prepared as malt in the way described above was mixed with the juice and the whole covered for two days until it fermented, after which it was filtered and was ready for use.

If the beer was made from the first plantains cut from a new garden, the owner had to drink it himself to ensure the success of the plantation.

BUILDING

Every youth was expected to assist in building huts either for his own family or for friends, so that by the time he reached the age when he required a hut for himself he was quite competent to make it.

From the time a man started to collect materials for a new house he had to avoid all women other than his wife, who on her part had to observe the same taboo and admit only her husband to her bed. Should one or the other offend in this matter, the materials which had been collected were useless and might only be used as fire-wood. If the guilt was concealed and the building proceeded with, the man would die.

The huts built by these peasants were of the bee-hive shape, and in size were seldom more than eighteen feet in diameter and ten feet high at the apex, many of the huts being much smaller than this. Six or seven poles of light timber supported the structure and over these was woven a framework of basketry like an inverted round hamper, millet stems bound together with strips of cord from papyrus stems being largely used for this. Papyrus stems were often interlaced with the millet stems to strengthen the structure, and the whole was overlaid with a thick covering of grass. The floor was simply the ground, which was smoothed by hoeing it over and beating it hard with sticks. The fire-place was composed of three large stones placed in a triangle so that a pot might rest upon them; should a second pot be required two more stones were placed to form, with one of the first three, a second triangle, the space beneath the pot being sufficient to allow fire-wood to be thrust under it.

Little furniture was used, but among the more progressive there might be a bedstead composed of four stakes, eighteen inches long, with forked tops. These stakes were imbedded in the floor and in the forks were side, head and foot pieces, to which laths of papyrus stems were secured. On these was spread a layer of grass or a cow-skin on which the owner and his wife lay, covered with any clothing they might have or with a bark-cloth or cow-skin if they were of the more prosperous members of the community. A few water-pots, several cooking-pots of various sizes, and two or three baskets were all the utensils required, and a hoe or perhaps two, one or two knives, the man's spears and shield, and a few fetishes completed the whole of their possessions. In all cases the furniture, bed-clothes and utensils depended upon the abilities and exertions of the couple themselves, for the more progressive would take the trouble to have better and more

PLATE XXII

Carpenters making milk-pots

PLATE XXIII

Milk-vessels and washing-bowls of wood

comfortable surroundings, which would be lacking in the case of the indolent or incompetent. The live stock of a prosperous peasant would be a few goats and sheep which by night were tethered to pegs in the floor near the walls of the hut.

When the house was finished, should a sparrow enter it before the man took possession, or if any man slept in it with the owner's wife before the owner himself did so, he would never live in it. If one of his children was the first person to fall down near it, or if some person carrying millet spilt some near the house, it was a bad omen. To avoid these dangers, they brought a child belonging to some other family and made it fall down near the house, and someone brought a grind-stone and turned it up against the house, letting a little flour fall from it.

POTTERY

The potter went out to the nearest swamp to get his own clay when he wanted it. He brought the lump of clay home and put it in a small pit, covering it to keep it from drying hard, and left it for seven days. When about to make pots, he ground up some broken pots and mixed the dust with the new clay, adding some juice of the herb *mwetengo* to keep the pots from breaking. He worked up the clay to a stiff putty on a cow-skin, and started to mould the pot by making the bottom in a shallow hole or in the bottom of a broken pot. He then made the clay into long rolls and built up the sides of the pot with these, smoothing the clay as he built them up with the curved shell of a gourd which he moistened frequently in a pot of water by his side. The pot while in course of being made was called *ntango*, and when it was drying before being fired, a process which took some six to nine days, it was called *musingo*.

The potters of Ankole never attained to the skill of those of Kitara, for there were few men or women who devoted much time to the art. Each family had its man or woman who made pots, and it was a rare thing for pots to be carried to any recognised market-place for sale. The Mugabe alone had a few more skilled potters who supplied his needs, so that there was no competition and no incentive to improve the pottery. There were some milk-pots of a graceful shape, with long slender necks, but the sides were thick and the clay was brittle and not so well worked as in those made by the Bakitara. The water- and cooking-pots were thick unpretentious vessels and no attempt was made to beautify them.

CARPENTERS

The Ankole carpenters were superior to the other artisans, though they rarely advanced from the well-known shapes of vessels used by their forefathers. They were a body of men belonging to the serf class, whose fathers had somehow learned the art of wood-working and passed on the knowledge to their children, who took up the work they laid down in old age or at death. The Mugabe had a number of carpenters who were his special workmen and lived in places allotted to them by him. All the needs of the royal household were supplied by them.

The wooden vessels in common use were milk-pots, butter-pots, meat-dishes, water- and washing-pots and troughs for making beer, and the carpenters also made stools. Milk-pots were made from a tree called *musa*, large pails for drawing water from *kirikiti*, and meat-dishes and washing-pots from *emituba* and *mzika*, while for stools they used *emituba*.

The tools used by the carpenters were long gouges, adzes, and scrapers, and they might never sell their tools even to pay fines, for to do so would cause them certain ruin.

The carpenter, when he required timber for his work, went out himself to cut his tree; if on his way he met a man whom he disliked or who had a grudge against him, he returned home, for he knew he would not find a suitable tree that day. When he found the right tree in the forest he felled it, using a small hatchet formed of an iron blade tapered like a wedge and fixed in a strong haft two feet long. This was his only instrument for cutting the tree into short logs, for he possessed no saws and did not know the use of them. It took him three days to cut the chunk of wood he required for a pot, and he carried it home and buried it under chips in his house to season before he began to shape it. The period allowed for seasoning the timber varied according to the man's requirements, but most timber was used before it was fully seasoned. Three days were then required for the making, one day to, shape the pot and two to hollow it out and finish it.

When a man wanted to make a new beer-bath, he brewed a quantity of beer and asked six carpenters and thirty or more friends to come and help him. They went with him to find and fell the tree and cut off the length required for the bath, and when this had been done they drank the beer and feasted on a goat. Until the carpenters had made the bath, the owner might not sleep with his wife, and this taboo continued until beer had been made in it. His wife also had to observe strict continency. The first beer made in a new bath might not be sold but had to be drunk by the owner and his family or friends.

SMITHS

The smiths, like the carpenters, belonged to the serf community, but they did not attain to the skill of the carpenters in their work. They formed a single class, for the men who did the smelting were also the men who worked the metal up into the required articles. The smiths went to the hills to fetch their own iron-stone and, as they used that which lay near the surface in abundance, they seldom had to dig more than one or at most two feet to get the kind they wanted. This was broken up into bits about the size of walnuts, tied up in bundles of grass and carried to the place where the smelting was to be done. Their charcoal was prepared from the small trees and scrub which grew in the neighbourhood.

During the time spent in smelting, the men had to be careful not to have sexual relations with anyone but their own wives. No man might step over the wood of which he was making his charcoal, and, should he be seated on the door-step of his hut, no one might enter or leave until he rose.

No woman who was menstruating might come near him. These taboos were in force until the iron had been smelted and the smith had made a hoe from it.

When the wood and iron were ready, a hole was dug some two or three feet deep and two feet in diameter, and lined with clay, the clay walls being continued to some three feet above the ground. When dry this furnace was filled with layers of dry reeds and grass, charcoal and iron-stone. An arched top or dome, with a hole four or five inches across in the centre, was built over the top of the furnace. Round this were arranged the bellows, probably three pairs of them, consisting of round earthen pots, open at the top, with a nozzle on one side. Over the top of the pot a goat-skin was fastened loosely enough to be moved up and down by a stick fixed to its middle. The nozzles of each pair of bellows entered an earthenware pipe which opened into the furnace, and each pair was worked by one man who sat between them and used one hand to each.

The smelting was begun at six o'clock in the morning and the fire was kept burning until two o'clock in the afternoon, the charcoal being added when necessary through the hole in the top of the furnace. After the fire had been allowed to die down, the iron was left to cool for some six days before being dug out. Any that was not thought to be properly smelted and clean was smelted again, but the clean metal was cut up into blocks of the sizes required for spears, hoes, knives and other implements, and the smith carried these off to his own home.

The tools of a smith were not many. His anvil was a large stone and the hammer a bit of iron, six or eight inches long rounded and tapered slightly for the hand-grip. He might possess a pair of tongs, but more usually he pointed the iron on which he was working and forced it into a piece of wood, or, splitting the wood, he slipped the iron in and bound the wood together. His furnace was a shallow hole into which he put charcoal and inserted the nozzles of bellows like those he used for smelting, though here one pair sufficed.

Should the smith require a new anvil he went about among the hills to find a suitable stone. On the night before he went

PLATE XXIV

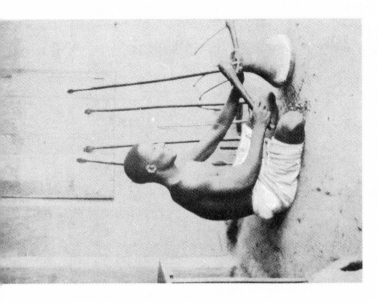

Carpenter, showing his tools and method of
hollowing a wooden milk-pot

Smiths with bellows and furnace

PLATE XXV

Carpenters making pails and hand washing-bowls

Smith working on a stone anvil

out he had to keep apart from all women except his chief wife, and next morning he went out, fasting, with some other men whom he had engaged, to find a stone. When it was found, the men carried it home for him, and he called his relatives to participate in a feast which he made as a recompense for the bearers of the stone. A hole was then made in the ground where the anvil was to stand; millet and certain purificatory herbs were put into the hole and the anvil set on them, whereupon it was ready for use without any further ceremony.

When the smith wished to make a new hammer he began by collecting a large quantity of food to make a feast, for which he killed not less than two and sometimes as many as six goats, and invited some twenty of his fellow-craftsmen to come and help him. The iron for the hammer was already smelted and had been brought to the house without cleaning off any of the fibre in which it had been wrapped and which still clung to it. The men began to work at nine o'clock in the evening and finished the hammer about eight o'clock next morning. Then a pit deep enough to hold three or four gallons was dug and filled with water, and the smith's wife, his father and mother, and his grandparents were summoned from a hut in which they were waiting. The father and grandfather took the hot hammer and put it into the water to harden it, passing sacred herbs over it as it lay in the water, to purify and bless it. The hammer was then carried into the house and the feast was prepared and eaten. Any fibre which had clung to the metal was brought and put at the head of the man's bed, while the hammer was laid at the foot, and the man lay with his wife on the bed to complete the work.

After two or three days, the smith took the hammer and made a knife or a hoe from some of the smelting of iron from which the hammer had been made. This he gave to some member of his family to show that the hammer was a good tool.

As in the case of the carpenters, the Mugabe commanded the services of the most skilful smiths for any work he required. He paid no wages, but made presents of goats or sheep to these artisans, who were never allowed to suffer from any of their transactions with him.

CHAPTER X

BIRTH

Importance of sons—taboos during pregnancy—treatment of a pregnant woman—the midwife—birth—the after-birth—the fire in the hut—eight days of seclusion—birth among peasants—the umbilical cord—the return of an absent husband—feeding of infants—naming children—cutting teeth—learning to walk and to talk—marriage arrangements—games—training of boys and girls—taboos during menstruation—twins—care of an insane woman in pregnancy—treatment of a woman whose children die in infancy—treatment of a wife who bears only girl children—taboo on a wife who leaves her husband

IT was the desire of every woman to marry and have children, for an unmarried woman had no position or standing in the community and a man would never be satisfied with a childless wife. Sons were especially desired, for a son inherited his father's property, and, should the husband die, the very existence of the widow depended on her son. Among poor people without property it was the usual custom for a son to provide for his parents in their old age, and among better class people it was not at all uncommon for a father who felt himself growing old to hand over his property to his son, who would then provide for him while he lived out the remainder of his life free from responsibility. The most important reason, however, for desiring a son was that it was the duty of a son to perform the funeral rites after his father's death and to see that all the necessary observances were paid, so that the ghost might take its proper position in the other world. If no one attended to this matter, the poor ghost was despised by its ghostly clan-fellows and other ghosts completely ignored it.

There were very few women who did not bear children, for the sexual freedom which a woman enjoyed after marriage made it almost certain that she would bear children unless, indeed, she was barren, which very seldom occurred. Owing to the tender age at which a woman was married, it might be some years before she began to bear children, but cases of girls becoming mothers at twelve and thirteen years of age were not infrequent.

When a woman found that she was pregnant she did not make any change in her usual diet, though she would eat beef in preference to grain, if milk was scarce. In some clans certain kinds of salt were forbidden to women in this condition. She remained with her husband but was careful to allow no other man to have sexual relations with her. At the end of two months her husband gave her a strip of lizard-skin called *ngonge* or *luzaro*, which she tied round her waist and wore until the child was born. On it she hung small bits of stick, two inches long and as thick as a pencil, together with a few cowry-shells, which were supposed to ensure a healthy child. This served as a sign to other men that only her husband, her father, and her uterine brothers might touch her. Until he had given his wife this amulet to wear, the husband might not go to war or undertake any journey, and a woman never left home after she had conceived unless the medicine-man ordered her to go away.

The husband's mother or some other woman who was versed in medicines made a mixture of herbs for the wife to drink to keep her bowels in order and to make the baby strong and healthy. The mixture was composed of the herbs *ekikoni nyabitu* and *omugabogabo*, which were dried, powdered, and boiled in cow's urine. Salt was added and a little of this was drunk in milk once a week, or more often if necessary. Another purgative used was *zizi* or *efuha*, prepared in the same way as the first.

Once during the period of pregnancy, a woman was made to drink the first milk from a cow that had just calved. This was usually left to the calf and women did not care to drink it. The husband's father, however, would insist upon it, and, if she refused, he might use force to make her take it because of its value to the child she had conceived.

A woman with child might not tread upon cow-dung, especially from a sick cow. She had to wear sandals to prevent contact with the dung while she moved about the kraal.

About the eighth month of pregnancy the husband sent to his father-in-law to ask him for some seeds called *empeka* and *birunga*. These were threaded on string like beads and made into a circlet which was worn on the head by the expectant mother to ensure a safe birth. During labour these were taken off the mother and put on to the neck of the churn until the child was born, when they were put upon its wrist as a charm. They believed that a woman always conceived during the increasing moon, and a child, to be lucky, must not be born during the days when the moon was waning or invisible.

The woman was waited upon by her mother-in-law, or, should she be dead or for any reason unable to come, the woman's own mother would come to attend her. When the birth took place, one or two other women were present, but the responsibility rested upon the mother-in-law, who acted as midwife. Some women preferred to remain on their beds, but as a rule the midwife took the cord of a net used for carrying milk-pots and secured it to a rafter near the door, spreading a carpet of newly gathered grass below it; upon this the woman squatted, holding the rope, while the midwife sat behind her, supporting her, until the child was born. There was seldom any difficulty, and even in a case of cross-birth the women were generally able to force back the child and turn it so as to get correct presentation and save both mother and child. Death during child-birth was almost un-known.

When the child was born the midwife cut the cord with an ordinary knife or a strip of reed from the roof and handed the child to one of the assistants, while she attended to the mother. Among the pastoral people each child was supplied with a nurse who took charge of it from birth. The child was washed with urine from a little girl of some five or six years old, the circlet of seeds which the mother had worn on her head was tied on its wrist and it was wrapped in a bark-cloth. Among the serfs, the child was washed with water and made to drink either milk or plantain-wine out of a cup made from a banana leaf.

Among the agricultural people the after-birth was buried in the doorway without any ceremony. Among the cow-people the woman retired to bed as soon as the after-birth came away, and four small boys or girls whose parents were alive and well were sent to look for and bring to the house leaves of the trees *nyawera*, *kirikiti* and *mulokola muhiri*. A hole was dug in the doorway and these were put in and the placenta laid on them; it was covered with more leaves, and the hole was filled up with earth which was beaten hard. This was said to ensure that the child would grow up strong like the children who performed the ceremony, and that its parents would live, like theirs, to look after it. If a child was still-born the placenta was thrown away.

After the birth, the mother lay on her usual bed, a platform of earth beaten hard with, if possible, a cow-skin to lie on and bark-cloths to cover her. During the next four days care had to be taken that the fire in the hut was kept burning brightly, and no one might take any of it away from the hut, for, if they did, the cord would not drop from the child but remain sticking out during its life. Leaves of the sacred trees *kirikiti* and *mayingo* were put on the fire, which made it sacred and gave it power to purge away evil from the child. If the child was a boy, the father brought one of the logs used for filling up the gateway of the kraal by night and placed it on the fire; he gave the thong (*mboha*), which he used for tying the legs of restive cows during milking, to his mother to use as a waist-belt for his wife. If the child was a girl, ordinary fire-wood was used for the fire and the belt for the mother was of bark-cloth.

For the next eight days the mother had to remain in seclusion. She was not allowed to leave the house by the main door, so a second door was made at the back and a court built round it to ensure privacy for the mother and the mid-wife. The midwife boiled a kind of grass (*nstemwe*) and used the juice to wash the lower part of the woman's body each day. She also massaged her daily and tightened her belt. On the eighth day the mother was bathed from head to foot outside the hut in the enclosure, and after that her husband might join her again, and he remained with her all the time she was nursing the child.

Among the agricultural people, if the woman was torn in giving birth, a medicine-man was sent for. He might not enter the house, for no man but the husband was allowed to do that. He made his medicine and passed it through a tube in the wall into the house, where it was put in a hole in the ground, which was lined with plantain leaves to make it hold water, or in a stool with a hollowed seat. The woman sat in this and was washed with the medicine. If the child was a boy, a special log was placed on the fire and kept burning for four days and nights and a knife was stuck in the head of the bed to avert evil influences. The stump of cord, when it fell, was thrown on the mother's bed and left there. For ten days the woman remained in seclusion and apart from her husband, who was careful to have no sexual relations with other women during this period. His mother, who acted as midwife, also looked after his requirements. At the end of the ten days the mother smeared herself all over with clay, which was allowed to dry and then rubbed off, and she washed with water and oiled herself before re-joining her husband.

Among the pastoral people, for a month after the birth of a child, no man but the mother's husband was allowed into the house, and both husband and wife had to be careful to have sexual relations with no one but each other. During the first eight days, the mother refrained from touching the milk-pots and from doing any work, and the midwife managed the household arrangements and handed out the milk-pots. When the woman had re-joined her husband, she took up her usual duties, for after eight days she was supposed to have no more need of the midwife's attentions.

When the umbilical cord fell from the child, the mother kept it until the husband was present. He took a calf and bled it, taking only a little blood. This his wife mixed with milk and added to it the cord chopped very small. The mixture was boiled slowly until it formed a cake. A number

PLATE XXVI

Medicine-men. Agricultural class

PLATE XXVII

Medicine-man about to take an augury

of small children, who were in good health and had both parents alive and well, came with a bunch of the purifying herb *enyamwerha*. A pot of fresh water was placed before each child and each dipped the bunch of herbs in the water and sprinkled the baby, saying, "Grow up strong and good." The children then ate the cake containing the cord and went away. In some cases, however, the cord was not used in this way but was stitched into a leather bag which was worn by the mother in her girdle.

A continuation of this ceremony, performed in some instances, is described in *The Northern Bantu*:

After the meal the children sweep out the hut in which the mother has been secluded; the dust they collect and throw on the kraal dung-heap, and to make quite sure that there is no dust or grass left they sweep the hut out four times. While the children are sweeping out the hut, the mother is undergoing a purificatory ceremony: she washes from head to foot and smears her body with a kind of brown clay which has a sweet smell and is reserved for ceremonial uses. The mother discards all her old clothing, her husband provides her with quite new clothes, she returns to her hut to receive her relatives and friends, who by this time have congregated to see her baby and to congratulate her, and the baby is taken and examined by the women.

If a husband was absent from home when a child was born, he brought a bunch of the herb *muhire* to the house. Putting on his shoes and spreading a mat by the side of the bed on which his wife lay, he took the bunch of herbs, urinated on them, and sprinkled his wife on the inner side of her right thigh to drive away any evil which might have been attracted through his absence or any magic which might have been worked on her.

During the first four months of a child's life it was kept lying upon its back and never allowed to touch the ground with the soles of its feet. It was never carried about unless it was necessary to go on a journey, but it lay on a bark-cloth with another for covering.

A mother always nursed her own child for two or three years except when the man was anxious to have another child soon, when the baby was taken away and artificially fed and the nurse was responsible for it. It was, however, given cow's milk daily in addition to the mother's milk from the day of its birth. This was given to it through the narrow stem end of a bottle-gourd or the end of a cow's horn with a small hole pierced in it. This was called *nkolo*. After the child had finished its meal any milk remaining in the horn was wiped off and smeared upon its navel.

There was no test to prove the legitimacy of a child, for it was impossible to say who was the father, but the husband claimed it.

At the end of four months, among the cow-people, the father took a boy child, and, choosing two cows, brought them before the house and placed him on the back of each in turn. These two animals were thus dedicated to the boy's use and belonged to him. The father then scraped a shallow hole in the floor of the hut, and, putting a bit of bark-cloth in it, he made the child sit in it and gave it the name of one of his ancestors. The ghost of this ancestor became the patron spirit of the child and looked after it, and the child had to act in such a way as to please the ghost.

If the child was a girl, the mother took her at three months old, made her sit in a hole in the floor of the hut, and gave her the name of an ancestor. She then carried the child outside the kraal and told her to look over the plains to the other kraals, for it was from there that her wealth and fortune, that is, her husband, would come.

A child's first teeth were always watched anxiously, for, if they appeared in the upper jaw, it was an ill omen for the parents, and the child was taken away and cared for by some relative until it cast these teeth. If, however, the first teeth appeared in the lower jaw, all was well. Should a father die before his child cut its first teeth, the mother and child left the kraal and lived elsewhere, for they might not be seen by any members of the kraal until the child had cut its teeth, after which they came back.

If the child was a boy, the father, when it cut its first teeth, made a small bow and arrow, leaving a loose end of the string of the bow hanging with a few beads strung on it. The child's head was then shaved for the first time and the mother and the father's sister, or, as some said, the mother's sister, accompanied by some children, carried the child on a round of visits to relatives and friends, who added more beads to those on the string of the bow. On their return home the beads were made into bracelets and anklets for the child to wear.

In some cases, as described in *The Northern Bantu*, when a female child cut its first teeth, the father placed it to sit on the floor and brought an empty gourd such as was used for churning. The child was made to rock this about as if churning and the mother then stowed it away. When the teeth were cast, they were preserved with this gourd.

The mother then made the girl a little belt with a loose end of string, and, accompanied by her husband's sister, she carried her on a round of visits and received presents of beads which were put on the string of her belt and later were made into ornaments for her wrists and ankles.

When a child cast its first tooth, it was made to take the tooth and throw it towards the setting sun, saying, "Grandmother, this is bad, give me a good one."

Among the serfs, the ceremony of naming a child was gone through, but a boy was given no cows and was simply put to sit on the floor. Both boys and girls slept on their parents' bed until quite big, when the boys were given a bed near the fire and the girls slept in a secluded place at the head of the parents' bed.

Among cow-people, if a child was slow in learning to walk, the parents took it to the Mugabe who, taking his stick, tapped it gently, saying, "I drive you from the country." The child would then walk in a few days. If it was slow in learning to talk, a bird, *kanyonza*, which was noted for chattering and was said to be almost able to talk, was caught and the child's tongue made to touch that of the bird, after which the child would speak in a few days.

A girl was often bespoken in marriage at one or two years of age either by a man who wanted her himself or by one who wanted a wife for his son, who might also be only a child.

When the parents consented to the engagement, the man lent them two cows for the child's food. The milk from these, however, was not reserved for her use alone but her father and others might drink of it. As the prospective husband grew up he was expected to make periodical visits to the girl's parents with small presents but he never saw the girl, and he might never take tobacco, for such a gift would cause his prospective wife to be barren.

During the first six or seven years of their lives, boys and girls played together. They were taught to guard the calves which roamed near the kraal and they played together while thus engaged. They had games of warfare, marriage, herding, building and so on, and they, as well as their elders, were fond of wrestling, shooting at a mark with arrows, and spear-throwing. Neither boys nor girls wore any clothing during their early years and their food was milk, of which they were expected to drink large quantities and they were punished if they refused to take what was considered enough. The milk for the children might be set aside and drunk at any time during the day, whereas older people drank it while it was warm or soon after the milking.

At about seven years of age a boy was expected to be useful in the kraal, and about eight he began to go out with the men who took the cattle to pasture. He had to learn to herd the cows, to milk them and to treat their various ailments. This necessitated knowing the different kinds of herbs, their preparation and their use. He had also to learn to protect the cows from wild beasts, especially lions, of which herdsmen, however, seem to have had no fear, merely driving them off with spears or even with their staffs.

A boy underwent no ceremony at puberty, but he was expected to be able to support himself and to obtain a wife without asking for much help. Among the poorer class he was also expected to be able to support his parents in their old age and to take his part in any family feuds and quarrels.

At about the age of eight a girl began to prepare for marriage. She was no longer allowed to play and run about unrestrained, but was kept in the house and made to drink large quantities of milk daily in order to grow fat. Her mother had to teach her to wash milk-pots, to churn and to prepare food, and she would occupy some of her time in making bead-ornaments and weaving the wicker lids for the milk-pots. The rest of her time was spent in sitting about, talking, sleeping, and drinking milk.

When a girl had her first menses, her mother kept the fact secret, if possible, even from her husband. The girl was not allowed to drink milk from the ordinary cows, but the mother, if she could do so, would give her milk from a cow that was past bearing. If a woman during her menses drank milk from a young cow, it would sicken and the milk dry up, and it would probably become barren. A woman who neglected this taboo was said to be stealing her food. The mother concealed the condition of her daughter in order that she might not be taken at once in marriage or be led astray by some other man, for it was a very serious matter for a girl to bear a child before marriage and the mother was responsible for her virtue.

Twins were not welcomed as they were in some of the neighbouring tribes, but they were not treated unkindly. No ceremonies attended their birth except among the members of the Batwa clan whose totem was twins, and they had no more honour given to them than any other child. The procedure in the Batwa clan is described in *The Northern Bantu* as follows:

> The mother and her children are taken to her parents' home and she remains there until the children have cut their first two teeth and the father has performed the ceremony of moving from the old home and building a new kraal. The husband brings his wife and children to their new home and she goes about her duties as before.

Women sometimes became mentally deranged when pregnant, and this was attributed by the women-doctors to some ghost. A medicine-man was summoned to discover by augury what ghost was causing the trouble, and the treatment in such a case differed from that of an ordinary ghost-possessed person. A hut was built at a little distance from the woman's home and she was taken to live there. Her mother-in-law stayed with her and guarded her and tended her with special

care, for it was feared that the ghost would injure the family
in some way should they neglect the mother. The child, when
born, was called the child of the ghost, and particular care
was taken of it lest the ghost should not be satisfied with its
progress and should afflict the family.

When several children of a woman died in infancy, the
next born was often taken away and nursed where the parents
did not see it until it was grown up, though they were kept
informed of its progress. Sometimes the medicine-man was
called in and given a male sheep or goat. He killed the animal
and made the scrotum into a bag, filling it with herbs and
roots, over which he pronounced incantations. This was
fastened up and used as an amulet for the child to wear to
keep it from suffering the fate of its brothers and sisters.
Many amulets of bits of wood and herbs were tied on the
necks, wrists and ankles to keep children from harm.

When a child died at birth, the mother was given special
medicine to make her bear a healthy child the next time.
When a mother died after giving birth, the baby was reared
on cow's milk or by a foster-mother.

If a woman had only girl children she was given medicine
to make her have a son, and, if this failed, her husband might
divorce her; but, even if he married again and had children
by his second wife, he might not arrange the marriages of
the daughters of his first wife without calling her in to take
part in the arrangements and ceremonies. She herself might
by that time be married again, but her husband could not
object to her returning and living as the wife of her former
husband during this time.

If a man and his wife had a quarrel during the time she
was nursing a child and she went away in anger, leaving the
child with its nurse, she might not return to the house until
her husband brought one of the logs for filling up the kraal
gateway and placed it in front of the door. She had to sit
on this and suckle the child before she might step over it
and enter the house.

CHAPTER XI

MARRIAGE

Marriage among the cow-people—clans not entirely exogamous—
preparing a girl for marriage—chastity and punishment for fornication—methods of inducing abortion—polygamy and divorce—adoption
—polyandry—morality after marriage—arranging marriages—the
marriage-fee—washing in the new moon—going for the bride—capturing the bride—first part of the compact—drinking milk—feasting
—the staff of peace—another form of marriage ceremony—tug-of-war
—marriage consummated at the bride's home—going to her new home
—reception by the bridegroom's parents—a young wife remains at
home—rules of consanguinity—agricultural marriage—pre-marriage
chastity and post-marriage freedom—elder sister must be married
first—the marriage-fee—preparing the bride—fetching the bride—
leaving the bride's home—reception at the bridegroom's home—
consummation of the marriage—three months' seclusion—visiting the
bride's parents

T HE marriage customs of the pastoral people of Ankole
differed from those of many of the surrounding tribes in
that they were not entirely exogamous. They had no rule to
prevent members of different sub-divisions of the same great
clan from intermarrying. A man might marry a woman whose
primary totem was the same as his own, provided that her
second or even a third totem differed. Thus the royal clan,
Abahinda, had as totem *nkima,* a monkey with a black face
(*colobus?*), and millet (*bulo*) uncooked and unhusked. They
might not marry into divisions of the clan which retained
only these two totems, but they might marry into such
divisions as the *Abasonga* which had a third totem, *kozi,* a
black cow. The members of the three great clans of the tribe,
the *Abahinda, Abasambo* and *Abagahe,* might intermarry without further enquiry, but within the clans marriage between
members of the sub-divisions was forbidden unless they
differed in at least one totem.

The preparation of a girl for marriage started about the age of eight or nine, as judged from her appearance, for years, being never remembered or counted, formed no guide. From that time she was most carefully watched over by her parents especially the mother, and kept from all contact with men. She had to live a sedentary life, drinking large quantities of milk and eating beef and, at times, millet-porridge. The mother was responsible for the conduct of her daughter, and if she left home for a visit would take the girl with her, unless some trustworthy person could be left in charge of her at home. By the end of a year of this confinement, the girl would lose all desire for any form of activity and even lose the power of walking, so that she could only waddle. The fatter she grew the more beautiful she was considered, and her condition was a pronounced contrast to that of the men, who were athletic and well-developed.

It was a very serious matter for a girl to bear a child before marriage and it seldom happened, for several reasons. Marriages were generally very early and as a rule the girl was married before sexual desires had developed any strength. Then, too, a girl was carefully guarded and seldom left home, so that it was not easy for a man to approach her. The penalty inflicted for such offences, moreover, was so severe as to deter both men and women from their commission.

Of later years more lenient methods have come into use, but at one time a girl of the better class who went wrong was taken to the river Kagera, a stone was tied to her neck, with a bundle of the herbs *etimbwe, busa, ereme* and *bitezo*, and she was cast into the river and drowned. The man, if caught, suffered in the same way. Should the Mugabe or a prince marry a girl and find that she was with child, the girl would be drowned and messengers would be sent to kill with spears her parents and as many of her clan as could be found. A girl who had gone wrong and was being taken away for trial or punishment was never allowed to pass out of the kraal by the main gate but had to go through a gap broken in the kraal-fence at the back. This treatment, besides increasing her shame and furnishing an example to the rest of the community, removed the danger of harm to the cattle.

When more lenient methods were employed, the girl was driven from the kraal to find asylum where she could. If the man consented to marry her, he took her to his own house until the child was born, after which he paid the usual marriage-fee and she became his legal wife. If, however, he refused to take her, she generally wandered to the agricultural people, who might take her in. She might marry one of their men and live an outcast from her tribe, eating the food and doing the work of the despised serfs. In some cases, a poor herdsman, who could not afford to pay a marriage-fee for a wife, would take such a woman, but more often she would simply take refuge among the agricultural people and, after the child was born, would pass from man to man. Unless she married a man of the pastoral tribe she might never return to her own home until the child was grown up. Should it be a girl, its grandparents might then take it and would permit the mother to return.

A girl who had erred and found herself pregnant would often seek her mother's assistance and attempt to bring on abortion. There were several methods of doing this. A bark-cloth was spread over a large frame as if for fumigating it and the girl went under the frame where a spot of hot embers, with a herb *migege* burning on it, was put. The smoke brought on sickness and invariably led to abortion in a short time. Another method might be applied by the girl herself. She inserted into her vagina the juice of the herb *kitezo* or *musong-yesongye*, and repeated this several times in quick succession until it brought about abortion. Another method was to drink the juice of the leaves of a herb *omuwhoko* mixed with water. This brought on violent vomiting and soon produced the desired effect. The mother was the only person in whom the girl confided, and she nursed the girl during the subsequent illness and concealed her true condition. Methods of a magical nature were sometimes adopted by an unmarried girl, who had gone wrong, to prevent conception; she might urinate into a hole in an ant-hill or take the spear of a visitor in the house and, removing the blade, urinate into the socket and replace the blade.

Monogamy was customary, though polygamy was permissible, and the Mugabe and wealthy men often had many wives. In most cases, however, a man would only marry a second wife if his first wife turned out to be sterile. In such a case the man had to decide whether he would divorce his first wife and send her back to her people or whether, if he could afford it, he would keep both wives. Frequently a wife, who found herself to be sterile, encouraged her husband to marry again. If the man divorced his first wife he lost the marriage-fee which he had paid for her, for it was not usual to return it under these conditions. She, however, might remarry, if she wished, or she might remain unmarried with her people. Very often a divorced woman went to live as the wife of some person who could not afford to pay the marriage-fee for a wife; if she bore him a son, he had to pay her relations the marriage-fee to legalise the marriage before his son might inherit his property, for otherwise it would go to his brother or some other member of the clan. In such a case the parents got two marriage-fees for their daughter. If, however, a man could afford to keep two wives they lived in the same kraal, but he built a new house for the second wife. Should the first wife later bear a son, he inherited before any son of the second wife, even if he was younger. If the first wife bore only daughters, the son of the second wife was the heir, but his half-sister had to assist his own sister, if he had any, in performing the purificatory rites of inheritance, when she also took possession of cows or something else from the father's property. A man might even marry a third wife if his second wife was also barren, and in this case the barren wives generally lived together and the wife with children had a house to herself. The first wife retained the duty of looking after the milk-pots for the family and setting apart the milk for the ghosts.

Sometimes a man would not wish to take a second wife and he would adopt a boy, the son of a clan-brother, if possible

PLATE XXVIII

Pastoral (*Muhuma*) girl, twelve years old, being prepared for marriage

PLATE XXIX

Bahuma women and child

a near relative. If the father of the boy consented, the man would take him home and, without any ceremony, the child was accepted as a son and was looked upon as the eldest son and heir of the adoptive father, even if other sons were born to him later. Sometimes a kind of ceremony was gone through at the adoption of such a boy. The barren wife squatted down as though about to bear a child, the boy was placed between her legs, and the husband handed her a thong used to bind the legs of a restive cow when being milked; this she tied round her waist as was done after birth. She told the boy that he was her son and her husband, holding his lower lip, puffed some saliva over the child and took the oath, "You are my own child till death."

In the case of poor herdsmen, a man might have a sufficient number of cows to pay the marriage-fee but not enough to feed his wife afterwards. In that case, he would hire himself out as herdsman to some wealthy cow-owner who would supply him with cows to herd for him. The herdsman would then pay his own cows as the marriage-fee for his bride and become entirely dependent upon his employer for food for himself, his wife and his family. Another course sometimes taken by poor herdsmen was for two or more clan-brothers to pool their cows and share a wife. The eldest went through the marriage ceremony and the children were looked on as his, but all shared the wife and helped to feed and clothe her.

Though before marriage a girl was most strictly guarded and kept from any contact with men, after marriage it was accepted as an essential part of the entertainment of a visitor that he should sleep in the same bed as his host and his wife and have the use of the wife. If the visitor was the husband's father, the husband left the bed and his wife entirely to him and went to sleep with a neighbour who would share his bed and wife with him as long as the father was there. When, however, a man visited a friend whose wife was the visitor's sister, his mother's sister, or his mother's sister's daughter, the visitor slept on another bed. Even unmarried boys were allowed this right as soon as they became of an age for sexual intercourse, and when a boy visited his married brother he had the use of the wife, who might unveil in his presence. A woman never paid visits except to her father or her own near relatives.

It was usual for parents to arrange for the marriage of their children when they were quite small, and an infant girl might be betrothed to a boy one or two years' old. The father of the boy made the arrangements with the girl's parents and, if they were agreeable, he gave them one or two cows for her use. These were not part of the marriage-fee and the milk from them was not reserved for the girl alone, but her father, if he had other cows to feed her, might drink it or give it away. During his childhood and youth the boy had to pay periodical visits to his prospective parents-in-law, taking small presents of beer, butter, or bark-cloths. He might never take tobacco, for such a present would cause his bride to be barren. He never saw the girl on these visits, nor indeed did he meet her until the day of marriage. The girl herself had no voice in the arrangements, though any other members of the clan might protest if they were not pleased[1].

When the girl was old enough to be married, the bride-groom went to visit her parents, taking with him two pots of beer. The father called in the members of the clan to drink the beer and help to settle the amount of the marriage-fee. This varied, according to circumstances, from twenty cows to two in the case of a poor man. The parents of the bride took possession of the cows and they were expected to give something to the maternal grandmother[2].

[1] *Northern Bantu*, p. 119: "Before marriage a girl does not cut her hair, nor is she permitted to wear any ornament on her waist or legs. As her hair grows beads and cowry-shells are worked into it and are a token that she is unmarried."
This custom was evidently more universally observed in earlier days than it is now when some girls wear the straw veil and most have their heads shaved.

[2] *Northern Bantu*, p. 119: "Among the lower classes of pastoral people there are many parents who are unable to betroth their sons in infancy; these grow up to manhood and obtain the necessary means for marriage as best they can. When a young betrothed couple grow up to maturity and

In the past it sometimes happened that a girl who had been betrothed would be desired by some prince. If so, he simply sent for the girl and married her, paying the usual amount to the parents and compensating the man who had hoped to marry her. In later days, princes generally married the daughters of neighbouring rulers who could claim royal blood.

When the marriage-fee had been paid, the man was told to come for his bride at the appearance of the new moon. When the time had come, he fastened a pot of water on the roof of his house where the moon shone upon it, and awaited the final summons. When the call came, he washed with the water, which he said was the moon, and went to fetch the bride. No marriage could take place during the waning of the moon and placing the water was the sign that the new moon was visible. Should there be any hitch in the arrangements, the water was taken into the house and kept there as a sign that the promised time was past.

When the appointed day came, the bridegroom, with some companions, went to the kraal of the bride's father, arranging their arrival to correspond with the return of the cattle from pasture. They squatted down with the men of the kraal and drank beer until about ten o'clock, when they were taken to the house and squatted on the floor near the fire, either next the door or on the inner side of the hut near the bed. The bride, who had fasted all day, was inside the hut in a separate compartment with some companions who wept and wailed. Some of her family then heaped dry grass on the fire until it blazed up and endangered the house, whereupon the bridegroom's party remonstrated, asking if it was their intention to burn them to death. They beat down the fire, promising to add another cow to the marriage-fee, and a little fire was allowed to burn while they sat round drinking beer until about two in the morning.

the youth wishes to marry, he brings his future father-in-law a milch cow and a heifer. This gift confirms the first promise made by the parents on his behalf and gives the girl's parents to understand that he means to hold to the early promise made for him."
In all cases the beer had to be given as part of the marriage settlement.

The bride's relations asked for the man who had come to marry their daughter, and he stood up with one of his friends and declared himself to be the man. The noise of weeping and wailing which had gone on steadily in the bride's chamber increased in volume at this, and the friends closed round the bride to protect her. The bridegroom stepped on his father-in-law's bed and the father-in-law's sister took him by the right wrist and led him to where the bride and her companions were. Her friends strove to prevent him from reaching her and his friends joined in the struggle which then took place. The girls scratched at the faces and arms of the men, causing blood to flow, and the fight sometimes became quite serious. At length the bride's aunt remonstrated with them and separated them, restoring peace and order, and the girls agreed to give up the bride.

The bride's aunt took the left hand of the bridegroom and placed it on the inside of the bride's thigh, saying, "This is your wife." The bridegroom passed a little urine into his hand and rubbed it on the thigh where his left hand had been and this was the first part of the compact between them. This part of the ceremony had to be finished before jackals began to call on the hills or there would be no children from the marriage.

The bridegroom then returned to his companions near the fire, and they continued to drink until about four o'clock when he was conducted to a small hut outside the kraal near the gate. The bride was also brought there and sat in front of the bridegroom. A cow that had one or two calves alive and well was milked and the bridegroom took a mouthful of the milk and puffed it over the bride, who then took a mouthful and puffed it over him. A relative of the bridegroom, a boy whose parents were alive and well, was chosen to drink any milk that was left over. He was called *Mwana wa chora*, and in some cases he afterwards slept with the bride and bridegroom for a few nights to ensure that the bride would bear healthy children.

The rest of that day was spent in feasting and merry-making. The bride's father killed a bull, which was cut up, cooked, and eaten outside the kraal by the men who danced there, while the women sat inside the kraal and played their harps and sang.

In the evening, the bridegroom returned to his bride in her father's house and slept there. When entering, he carried a branch of a tree, *munayafu* or *mulokola*, the kinds which were used for driving cows: this he gave to his father-in-law, who put it in the roof of the house, where it remained until the couple were settled in their own home when it was taken down and burned in the house. It was an emblem of peace and happiness, warding off evil and causing the wife to have children. It might not be taken out of the house or thrown away but had to be burned there, or their happiness would be destroyed.

During the first two or three nights someone always lay with the bride and bridegroom, who slept near the fire. In some cases it was the bride's aunt, in others her young brother, and in others the relative of the bridegroom who had drunk the milk.

In some clans this marriage ceremony differed in certain respects. On the day appointed the bride's father prepared a feast for the bridegroom and his companions and the men of the kraal, and this might last two days. On the second day the young men of the kraal (clan-brothers of the bride) came to the house and asked for their sister in order to give her to her husband, but her father's sister and her girl friends refused to give her up. They tied a rope to her leg and held on to one end, giving the other to the men outside, who pulled and overcame them. The bride was hurried to a place where a party awaited her with a litter, often only a cow-skin, into which she was put and carried away, followed by a party of friends, to the hut where her husband was. There a pot of milk was brought and each puffed milk over the other. When these ceremonies ended, the bride went back to her father's house, where her husband joined her and they slept on the floor by the fire. The bride's father's sister lay with them and the marriage was consummated. On the following day the bride was taken to her new home.

If a boy was married while still too young to complete the marriage, his father took his place with the bride by night and she might not refuse his advances.

The couple might remain two or three days in the bride's home before leaving. The length of their stay depended upon their own desires and the way in which they were treated. When they left, they timed their departure to arrive at the kraal of the bridegroom's father as the cows returned from pasture. The bride and her aunt (her father's sister, who was known as *Isenkazi*) were carried in litters by friends of the bridegroom. The bride's brother also accompanied her. In accordance with the custom of women, the bride was closely veiled when she travelled.

At the gate of the kraal the bride was given a little millet (*bulo*) in each hand as she stepped from the litter, and she scattered this as she walked across the kraal to the hut. As she entered the hut she was handed a gourd such as women used for churning (*ekisabo*), as a sign that she was a mistress in the place and had the right to churn.

In the house the bridegroom's father and mother were seated on the bed and the bride's aunt led her up to them and seated her in the lap first of her father-in-law and then of her mother-in-law. When they had embraced her, she was put to rest on the bed before she was allowed to do anything, because the journey was supposed to have tired her. The young couple lived in the house of the bridegroom's parents until the first child was born, when they moved into their own house. If, however, the man had already a home of his own, he would stay a short time, at most two months, in his father's kraal and then move to his own home.

The girl's father always gave his daughter ornaments and a complete set of milk-pots, churn and butter-pots when she got married, and the bridegroom's father built a house for them. If the bridegroom's father was dead, he built his own house before he got married. The bride's father usually gave his son-in-law a present of some of the cows from the marriage-fee.

In some cases the bride was taken to her home on the day her husband went for her. A feast was made at her father's kraal in the earlier part of the day and she was afterwards taken to her new home. If a girl was very young, she remained with her mother and the husband came and lived there. An extension was made to the parents' house to form a separate room for them, but the husband had to pass through the house to reach it and the bride's mother could enter it at any time.

The children of brothers and sisters were forbidden to marry, but the next generation might intermarry. A man might never marry into the clan of his father, for that was his own clan, and he was also forbidden to marry into the clan of his mother or of any of his grandparents, but he might marry into the clan of his grandfather's mother.

AGRICULTURAL MARRIAGE CEREMONIES

Though the serfs in Ankole were more numerous than the cow-people, they seldom seemed to have large families; possibly the custom by which a woman had sexual relations with large numbers of men had an effect in limiting the number of her children. Most of the agricultural customs were either borrowed from or identical with those of the cow-people, though there were differences.

In the same way as among the cow-people, the chastity of a girl before marriage was the object of the greatest care, and if a girl went wrong she was driven from home and utterly disowned by her parents. If she married after being expelled from home, though they might hear of it, they asked for no marriage-fee. If, however, she had a daughter who was the fruit of the first irregularity, and this daughter was betrothed, the mother's parents might claim a marriage-fee for her.

Once a girl was married, on the other hand, both husband and wife enjoyed the greatest possible sexual freedom. The wife might allow any man she pleased to come to her bed and the husband consorted with any woman he desired. The man claimed the woman he married as his wife and any children she bore were said to be his, but it by no means followed that he was their father.

No younger daughter might be married while there was an elder sister still unmarried, and if any man wished to marry the younger daughter, he had to wait. If the elder sister had some deformity or defect which prevented her being married, she was given the dress of a married woman, and after that the younger sister might be married. The elder sister might then allow any man to come to her bed, but, if she bore a child, the father of it had either to marry her or pay a fine.

When a youth made up his mind that he wished to marry, he asked a friend to go for him to the girl's parents and tell them of his wish. If they consented to the marriage, they sent for the youth, who came, bringing with him a pot of beer. He arranged for another pot to be brought while they were drinking this, and they sat round and discussed the marriage-fee. A few relatives were called in by the parents for this discussion, the chief persons concerned being the father and his brother. The usual amount demanded for a marriage-fee was a cow-calf and a young bull, but, should the youth be unable to procure these, he was asked for fourteen goats, which were divided thus: seven for the father, three for his brother, two for the mother's brother, one for the father's sister, and one for a younger brother of the father. When this matter was settled the tube through which the beer had been drunk by the bride's father at this meeting was put in the roof of the hut as a sign that the marriage agreement had been made.

After the marriage-fee had been paid, the bridegroom had to wait, probably for some weeks, until the bride was made ready for marriage. Sometimes a poor man was given one or even two years to procure the marriage-fee, and during the time of waiting the bride made a large basket of four colours, in which she collected food for her husband. When the fee had been paid, the bride's father told the bridegroom to prepare beer and be ready when the new moon appeared. The father obtained a cow-hide dress, a bark-cloth, amulets, anklets, bracelets and necklets for his daughter. The bride's nails were cut on hands and feet and her hair was all shaved off, except that on the pubes, which was pulled out by her mother, a very painful process which took several days to complete.

When all was ready, the father sent for the bridegroom, who came and kissed the palms of both his hands. The father then brought out a large pot of beer with four tubes and he, his brother, the bridegroom, and the bridegroom's friend, drank beer at the same time from the one pot. After them other friends drank and the pot was refilled and all drank again.

The bridegroom then returned home and made a feast with about twenty or thirty friends, who danced there all night. In the morning two goats were brought; one was taken to the shrine of the bridegroom's grandfather and either killed there or taken back and killed at the door of the hut by having a knife run into its heart so that it bled internally. They ate the flesh of this animal and then the bridegroom's friends started to fetch the bride, taking one goat with them, the bridegroom remaining at home. A small boy whose parents were alive and well had to accompany the party and bear a spear before them.

On their arrival at the bride's father's kraal, the friend who was specially chosen to represent the bridegroom went into the hut where the father and mother awaited him with the bride; they took their daughter on their laps in turn and took leave of her. The father then took her by the hand and presented her to the man who was to take her, who thereupon went out to summon the bearers to carry her. Meanwhile another brother of the bridegroom climbed upon the roof of the hut and stuck a spear through the thatch. The bride touched the spear with her tongue and then the tube through which the betrothal beer had been drunk was substituted for the spear, and water was allow to trickle into the bride's mouth to prevent witchcraft being used against her.

When the bridegroom's representative came back with the bearers, the bride's friends surrounded her and a fierce struggle took place, for they refused to let her go and fought until they were overcome. They scratched and bit and the bride clung to the posts of the hut and refused to enter the litter. When at last she was put in the litter, her brother came and tied a fetish of pig-skin on her ankle as a charm against witchcraft. She was veiled with a cow-skin and took with her a mat (*kirago*). With her went three men and a girl, if possible brothers and a sister, and some girl friends. This struggle is to-day but rough play, representing what was doubtless at one time a real fight to defend a girl from capture.

When the bride arrived, the father and mother-in-law received her sitting on the edge of their bed and she sat in the lap first of one and then of the other. The bride and bridegroom then sat upon the mat she had brought and a little grain (*bulo*) was handed to them. The bridegroom first puffed a little over the bride and she puffed a little over him. A pot with water was put on the fire and, together, the couple sprinkled some millet-flour in the water and, holding on to the same stick, they stirred the porridge and made a little meal of it.

The people who accompanied the bride remained outside and were supplied with beer and food. They all went into the house to greet the bride, and the men afterwards retired outside to dance during the night, while the girls remained and drank beer with the bride.

At about ten o'clock the bride and bridegroom retired to bed, where a young brother of the bridegroom slept on one side and a young sister of the bride on the other, the newly-married couple being between them. The marriage was not consummated until the second night, and should a man find that the girl was not a virgin, he sent as a sign to her parents a hoe-handle with a hole cut in it for the insertion of the iron blade. Should the bridegroom, as was sometimes the case, be too young to consummate the marriage, his father took the bride as his wife until the real husband was old enough to do so.

On the third day some of the bride's relatives came bringing the large basket she had made filled with millet, and also ten to twenty small baskets of food, a bunch of plantains and a pot of plantain-wine. The husband drank first from the pot and then his wife and after her the guests. The girl sister of the bride was given a hoe, and a goat was given to the other guests, who then returned home.

For the next three months the bride remained in seclusion in her own house and took care that the fire did not go out. At the end of this time the husband made a feast, and she came out. The man and wife, accompanied by his brother and her sister, who remained with her until this time, went to visit her parents, who killed a goat and made a feast for them. The tube through which the betrothal beer had been drunk was taken from the roof, and the husband, the wife, and her father and mother drank beer through it. The bride's mother then broke it in pieces and put it in the basket in which she stored her treasures. When the daughter's first child was born, she made a necklet of the bits and put it on the child's neck.

CHAPTER XII

ILLNESS

Causes assigned to illness—gods, ghosts, and magic—methods of working magic—methods used by diviners—treatment of illness caused by a god, by magic, by a family ghost, by a hostile ghost—methods of medicine-men—treatment of child with swelled spleen —bleeding and blistering—small-pox—venereal disease—bubonic plague—coughs and pains in the back

IT was seldom that people assigned any natural cause to illness, but there were times when it was evident that no supernatural cause need be looked for. Old age was regarded as sufficient reason for serious illness, for they thought that the gods called away old people who had fulfilled their allotted time upon earth. They acknowledged, too, that fever might be contracted by eating too freely of beef from a cow that had died of some disease, or by going out in the sun when it was too hot. In most cases, however, illness was attributed to the agency of some god or ghost, or to magic.

Though it was not often that illness could be ascribed to a god, there were occasions when, in consequence of some neglect of his rights and desires or the appropriation for other purposes of cows which had been dedicated to him, a god would attack the guilty person with illness.

A far more common cause of illness was the anger of some ghost, which might be roused by any of a multitude of causes. Some of the cows which had been dedicated to a family or clan ghost might have been sold or exchanged without its sanction; offerings or observances which it considered as its due might have been neglected; it might feel a desire for meat; some of its family might have been ill-used or might have committed some crime against the clan-laws, such as marriage within the forbidden degrees or some immoral action which required punishment; or on the other hand a ghost from a hostile clan might be sent by a member of that clan to attack and harm someone.

Magic was another common cause of illness, for any person who had a grudge against another had not much difficulty in finding means of working magic against him. Sometimes a man would find some method of conveying enchanted beer, over which he had performed magical rites, to his enemy. He would carry the beer to some place where he would not be recognised and there he would hire some unsuspecting person to take it to his enemy. He would give a false name to the bearer, saying that the beer was a present from some other man who was a friend of his intended victim, and the unsuspecting recipient would drink it and fall ill. At once he realised that not only was the beer from an enemy but that magic had been used over it, and he would give up hope of recovery, so that unless the author of the mischief could be discovered and persuaded to raise the spell, the victim would certainly die of fear, though from the enchanted beer alone he might easily recover.

The magic-worker might also blow a spell on to his enemy or insert some magic herb amongst the tobacco in his pipe and get the other to smoke it. If he could obtain a shred of his enemy's garment, a little hair, spittle, grass that had been in his mouth, earth, on which he had stepped, tobacco dust from his pipe, or anything that had been in contact with him, he would take it to a medicine-man who would work magic with it and cause the owner to fall ill. The medicine-men were able to work spells and make medicine to kill a man even at a distance. Sometimes the magician worked against a whole family by secreting some charm in his enemy's house or putting a bone, if possible that of some dead person, over which he pronounced spells, in the thatch of the house or hiding it in the path where the inmates would certainly step over it. The magic would affect all the members of the family but more especially any person against whom it was definitely directed, and nothing would remove the effects until the object was discovered and taken away.

When a man fell ill, it was the duty of his wife to look after him and to inform his relatives of the matter. If it seemed to

be some slight ailment, she would doctor him herself and
resort to blistering or bleeding, or treat him with herbs. If
matters got beyond her skill, the first thing to be done was
to call in a medicine-man or diviner to discover the cause
of the illness. Among the wealthy classes the diviner summoned was always one who did his work with some fowl
or animal or with the insect *ntondo* and two sticks in the
manner already described. A preliminary fee of a cow-skin,
a goat, a sheep, or something of less value was paid to him,
and when he came he was given a fowl which he killed to
examine the intestines. Should he find small specks upon
these, he pronounced the case hopeless and proceeded to
determine the length of time the patient had to live. This he
told by examining the specks on the lungs, inserting a finger
to stretch them and counting the markings. Instead of this
he might give an emetic or draw a little blood from the chest
of the patient and, by an examination of the contents of the
stomach or of the blood, he would determine the cause and
nature of the illness. By these means he also told who should
be summoned to treat the patient, for the diviners themselves
never undertook any treatment.

The poorer classes sent for another kind of diviner who did
not work with animals but with seeds, stones, or sticks. One
would use a pot of water and six, twelve, or fourteen bits of
stick. He first made a noise over the sticks as if spitting on
them and stated his desire to them, saying, "Tell me what
is the cause of the illness; is it the ghost of so-and-so?"
or, "Is it magic worked by so-and-so?" He then cast the
sticks into the pot and from their position he was able to
tell which was the true cause and to decide who could treat
the case, for these diviners, like their superiors, never treated
cases themselves.

Another diviner of this class used a cup of millet (*bulo*) and
six, twelve, or fourteen bits of stone or lumps of mud. He
made a noise as if spitting on the cup of millet and asked the
question to which he wanted an answer. He then threw the
millet from the cup with the bits of stone or mud and watched

their position as they fell on a piece of skin which he had spread for the purpose. This told him the cause of the illness.

When the cause of the illness had thus been settled, the diviner told the patient's friends whom they must call in to carry out the necessary treatment. There were women-doctors (*Omusuzi*) who dealt entirely with women while the men-doctors (*Bafumu*) dealt with both men and women.

If, however, the cause of the illness was found to be the action of some god, the priests of that god were called in and they informed the relatives what offering must be made to propitiate the god, who generally demanded a number of cows. When the god Kagoro attacked a man, the diviner ordered that the priest who represented him should be sent for. This was the same man who was sent for in the case of sickness among the cows in a kraal, and he came with his spears, dancing and pointing them at the house. After dancing round, he entered the house, and holding the man by the knees he smeared him with butter. He then gave him a mixture of the herbs *olugaliramwe, ehoza, honi, omugosora, omuisya* and *ereka*, and pronounced incantations over him. He waited for about a week until the man was well again, and during this time he had to be kept supplied with milk or beer, and beef. When he left he was given a cow and a bark-cloth.

Should the case be ascribed to the working of magic, a fee of a calf-skin was sent to the medicine-man who was asked to treat the case. When he came to the place he usually demanded that a bull or a cow should be killed, and he made a meal of the meat before he started work. In some cases he gave his patient an emetic and a purgative to cleanse him from the spell, and then went on to treat the symptoms with herb-medicines. Should the patient recover, he had to pay the medicine-man a calf, but, if he died, the relatives did not pay anything further. A more elaborate cleansing might, however, be necessary, and in this case, a bull was brought to the medicine-man, who killed it by cutting its throat. He had a bunch of herbs which he dipped in the blood as it flowed from the bull and with this he smeared the sick man's forehead, chest, arms, and legs. The family, who had gathered beside the sick man, the hut with all its contents, the cattle, the kraal, and especially the gate of the kraal and the door and door-posts of the house, were also sprinkled with the blood, and the bunch of herbs was cast on to waste ground, after which the man was expected to recover.

Another method of dealing with magic was to attach it to some animal or fowl. The medicine-man came, and, taking a bunch of herbs, passed them round the house to sweep up evil influences; he then tied the bunch to a fowl, which he buried alive. Should this prove insufficient to remove the magic, a goat or a sheep would be used and treated in the same way. The fee paid to this man might be a calf, a goat, a pot of beer, or a new hoe.

Illness caused by a ghost required more careful treatment. Such a ghost was either that of some person of another clan or of some relative, but never that of a father, for a father's ghost was always good and might never be driven away. The ghost of a man's father might forbid any other man to sleep on the bed with the man's wife and the guest who did so would feel a sense of suffocation or of being strangled and would have to leave the bed. The woman whose husband's father's ghost acted in this way would warn guests and give them some other place in which to sleep, for they might not sleep in her bed as was the usual custom.

Again, the ghost of a man's deceased wife might forbid the husband to marry again; should he disobey, his new wife would fall ill, and, unless she was properly treated, would die. She had to apply to a medicine-man who would find out whether offerings would propitiate the spirit and see that they were properly made. If the man also fell ill, a fowl was killed, dried, and divided into two pieces. The pieces were made up into fetishes and worn by the man and the woman. If, however, the ghost refused to be satisfied, the new wife might not remain in the house of her husband but had to go back to her parents.

PLATE XXX

Medicine-men preparing to exorcise a ghost from a sick man

PLATE XXXI

Medicine-men exorcising a ghost from a sick man

When a ghost had to be forcibly removed from a patient the diviner told the relatives what medicine-man to send for and what preparations to make. A goat of a particular colour, always either black or black and white, was tied to the head of the patient's bed during the night so that the ghost might pass from the patient into it. The medicine-man came in the morning, dancing and singing, and passed a bunch of sticks and herbs all round the house to sweep together all the evil influences into one place. He put the sticks at the head of the bed or outside the door and proceeded to kill the goat, which had been tied to the bed and which was now supposed to contain the ghost. He sprinkled some of the blood on the bed, the patient, and his family. A fowl was brought and passed round the body of the goat so that the ghost passed from the goat into it, and it was buried alive in the gateway through which the cows entered the kraal, thus preventing the ghost from returning. The head of the goat was then cut off; the sticks with which the evil in the house had been swept up and sometimes also some fetishes, which had been hung up round the house, were tied to it and it was buried by the side of the man's bed so that he stepped upon it when getting into or out of the bed. The patient was then treated for the illness with herbs and drugs until he recovered, and if at any future time he dreamed an unpleasant dream, he rose from the bed and spat upon the place where the goat's head was buried which removed any evil influence which was acting upon him. The flesh of the goat was taken by the medicine-man, who was also paid a calf for this work.

Two old medicine-men of Egara went through their healing performance for my information, using a stuffed otter-skin for a patient. It was plain that they were quite convinced that their work was effectual in driving the ghost out. These medicine-men belonged to the agricultural class but attended both pastoral and agricultural people. Some of them wore bark-cloth robes decorated with beads while others wore skins round the loins and over the shoulders, and in all cases they wore special head-dresses. These were either bands of leather with eagle-feathers sticking up from them or tall caps consisting of strips of leather some ten inches deep on which were stitched cowry-shells, beads, feathers and sometimes the claws of birds and beasts. The bag in which the medicine-man carried all his materials for work was the skin of some animal, jackal or wild cat or, more usually, badger or otter. When skinning the animal, an opening was made at the anus, just large enough to remove the bones without damaging the skin. This hole formed the mouth of the bag, which was stuffed with a collection of instruments and drugs. The instruments usually consisted of knives of different sizes for surgical purposes, horns for cupping when bleeding was necessary, blistering irons, and gourd-cups for mixing the drugs. The other contents of the bag were herbs, roots, shells, birds' claws, bits of skin, small gourds containing various mixtures, and anything else the medicine-man might desire for medicinal or magical use. He carried also a rattle made of a bottle-gourd in which seeds or beans were put. The noise of this helped to work upon the feelings of the patient and render him more susceptible to the uncanny influence of the whole performance, and the medicine-man added to the effect by keeping up a kind of growling chant all the time.

When the medicine-man and his assistant arrived at the home of a patient they took their rattles and bags and danced round the outside of the house; then, entering it, they went through a performance of sweeping evil from the walls with brooms of the herbs *muwingula, muzimbazimba* and *mulokola*. Having collected all the evil from the walls, they rubbed down the patient with herb-leaves and put the herbs outside the door.

The patient was then placed on a cow-skin or bark-cloths spread on the floor, where the men could easily get at him and move round him. The chief medicine-man took up a position at his head while the assistant sat at his feet, and they chanted an incantation, accompanying it with the noise of their rattles. The assistant used his rattle during the whole performance, and both kept up a growling chant which was supposed to terrify the ghost.

The chief medicine-man then chose from his bag various drugs and implements which he intended to use and placed them on a skin beside him. He ground to powder some of the herbs, and, making two or three scratches on the patient's chest, he rubbed the powder into them, making the patient writhe with the smarting pain. The medicine-man then bit off a piece from the ends of some of the roots from his bag, returning each root to the bag when he had used it. He chewed these pieces up and, seizing the patient by the head and jaw, opened his mouth and spat the medicine into it. He also put a little powder into the patient's nose, causing him to sneeze, which was a hopeful sign. The ghost by this time was ready to flee, for the bitter medicine the man had swallowed and the smarting of the incisions made its abode uncomfortable. The medicine-man fanned the patient, uttering incantations over him, and then rubbed him down with his hands, pressing the ghost from his head out at his feet and the tips of his fingers. When the ghost sought to escape it was caught in a pot which was placed ready and was either burned or drowned, while the patient was put back to bed and treated with medicines, according to the symptoms, until he recovered. The fee paid to such medicine-men varied from a cow, a goat or a sheep to a hoe or some butter.

When a child suffered from swelled spleen (*akabango*), the parents took it and put it to sleep by the bedside of the Mugabe through the night. The following morning, when he rose, before he spoke to anyone, he put his foot on the child's stomach and pressed gently, then he spat upon it and it was expected to recover in about four days.

After the cause of an illness, were it god, ghost, or magic, had been dealt with, the patient was treated by the medicine-man according to the symptoms. Cupping or bleeding and blistering were often resorted to, sometimes, for what was considered a minor trouble, by the friends of the patient without the aid of the medicine-man. The blood was taken from the temples or the head, and the instruments used were the end of a cow's horn and a small knife. A few scratches were made with the knife, the place was moistened with water, and the broad end of the horn held over it, while the air was sucked out through a small hole in the pointed end of the horn, which was then closed with a plug of fibre inserted by the tongue when the air was exhausted. When a certain amount of blood had been drawn off the cup was removed. Blistering was done with a small round iron about four to six inches long and a quarter of an inch in diameter or smaller, which was inserted in a wooden handle. The iron was heated until hot enough to raise a blister and was then applied to the skin quickly in several places. Sometimes two or three irons would be fastened together to make more blisters. Blistering was practised for headache and cold in the head, when the blisters were made on the head; for cold in the chest, when they were made on the chest; and for rheumatism, when they were made wherever required.

When a man was found to be suffering from small-pox, he was isolated and someone who had had the disease was chosen to look after him. For the first three days he was given little to eat and lived on milk and hot water. He was encouraged to sleep as much as possible. On the fourth day the pustules were pricked with a thorn and as a rule the pus was left to dry on them, care being taken that it did not get into the eyes, but some people mopped it up with a sponge made of some herb or of plantain-fibre. On the sixth day, the patient was bathed with warm fresh water, and on the seventh he was smeared with white clay, which absorbed the pus and cleaned off the peeling skin. This was continued until he was well and he was also encouraged to take as much nourishment as he could.

In cases of venereal disease (*enjoka*), roots of the herb *kagendazada* were pounded and the juice put in the sun for twelve hours and then drunk, which caused the blood and pus to come away. A man in feeble health who was childless was given juice obtained by pounding the roots of *saru* and *gugu*, and also of *mziramfu*, mixed with milk. These were said to strengthen him so that he soon became a father.

Peasants suffered from bubonic plague, but it was almost entirely confined to them. When one or more of the inmates of a house died, special medicine-men went and either cleansed the hut or destroyed it entirely, as they considered best for the purification of the locality. Should a cow-man contract the disease, he was smeared over from head to foot with cow-dung and recovered.

A herb, *omusongyesongye*, was given to women when attacked by a kind of fit which made them fall down and struggle. The juice of the herb was extracted and poured into the patient's nose.

Sometimes, when a man suffered from a cough due to a cold or some chest complaint, a cow or bull was brought and a vein in its neck opened. The patient put his mouth to the place and drank the blood as it gushed out. When a man suffered from pain in his back, blood was drawn from a cow, mixed with milk, and given to him to drink.

CHAPTER XIII

DEATH AND INHERiTANCE

Disposal of property before death—preparing a dead body—the grave —milk for the dead—the burial—the mourning—purifying the mourners—coming of the heir—purificatory ceremony—end of the mourning—the widows—the ghost—death of women—death ceremonies among agricultural people—burial—purification—widows— inheritance—right of the eldest son of the first wife—appointing an heir—division of property—levirate custom—inheritance by children —heir of a dead woman—right of a slave's son—inheritance among peasants

DEATH

WHEN a man was seriously ill and was not expected to recover, he was pressed to announce the name of the son whom he chose as his heir, for it was not necessarily the eldest son who inherited, though he usually did so, and a man might name as his heir anyone he chose. Even then it was possible for the clan-members to override his wishes and appoint someone else to inherit, and, if he did not make his desires known, the Mugabe might claim the property and take possession of it, handing it over to whomsoever he would. The relatives, therefore, were much disturbed if the sick man refused to speak, and they sent for some responsible member of the clan who would do what he could to induce the sick man to declare his wishes. Should he still persist in his silence, they feared that someone among them had done something wrong for which the sick man intended to punish him, and this was considered to be so serious that relatives whose consciences reproached them have been known to die of fright. Should he, however, wish to dispose of his property himself, he would state the number of cattle which each child was to receive and give instructions as to the treatment of his widows. The relatives also asked him whether there was anyone against whom he had a grudge, and, if he named anyone, that person was told and would bring a cow or some other gift to make his peace before the dying man became a dangerous ghost.

When a chief fell ill and his recovery was despaired of, an old cow was selected to supply him with milk until his death. When the man died, his relatives gathered from all parts and the widows, with some of the relatives or some chosen men, prepared the body. It was washed, the legs bent up into the squatting posture adopted by cow-men when resting, the eyes were closed, the right arm was placed under the head and the left arm on the chest. In some cases weeping and wailing went on all this time, but usually there was silence during the preparation of the body for the grave. All the members of the clan were expected to be present at the washing of the body as a leave-taking.

Meanwhile some male relatives or some of the dead man s slaves dug the grave in the dung-heap in the kraal; except when dung was scarce and the dung-heap not big enough, it was not dug below the surface of the earth. Burial in the earth was considered to be objectionable and was always avoided, unless it was forced upon them by dire necessity. The grave was lined with grass and a mat put in for the body to lie upon, and all had to be ready by afternoon when the cows returned from pasture. In exceptional cases, should a chief die during the night, he might be buried in the early morning before the cows left the kraal, but, should he die during the day, his body had to wait for burial until the cows returned in the evening. This was the procedure adopted whenever possible.

When the cows came home, the old cow which had been chosen to give milk to the dead man during his illness was milked and the milk poured into the mouth of the dead man, whose face was then covered over. This cow was not milked again but was kept until the day when the heir came to take possession, when it was killed and the meat divided among the mourners. In the case of a wealthy man a sprig of *esoghi*, some of the herb *nyawera*, some wool from a white sheep and the milk of a white cow were brought and put on his stomach to persuade the ghost to remain quiet.

The body was laid in the grave on its right side looking up the hill towards the gate of the kraal, never down the hill, and, when the grave was filled, a cow was killed and eaten beside it, and the mourning began and went on until the heir came. During the interment silence was observed by all; no sound of sorrow might be heard. All the full-grown bulls of the dead man's herd had strings tied round their scrotums to prevent them from mating with the cows, and they were killed as required during the period of mourning. None of them was killed until all the members of the family were assembled, which was usually by the second day after the death. When the grave was filled in the mourners washed their hands, shaved their heads, cut their nails, and gave themselves up to weeping and wailing for the period of mourning, during which they ate meat but might not drink milk until after their purification when mourning ceased. Any relatives who had urgent duties which prevented them from taking part in the mourning left for their homes after the funeral.

Among poorer pastoral people two bulls were brought immediately after the funeral. These were killed and the blood sprinkled over the house and goods of the dead man and over the people. The mourners washed and shaved their heads, feasted on the meat and drank beer all that night, leaving the milk for the children. Next morning the man chosen to inherit was brought and the mourning ended. Four days was, however, the usual time among the more wealthy people, and, if all things were not ready by that time, the mourning might go on longer, ending always after an even number of days. The heir would endeavour to have everything ready by the fourth day, for, the longer the mourning went on, the more meat was eaten and the more beer drunk. Delays might be caused by the absence of some important relative or by the fact that some of the herds were at a distance from the kraal. It was not necessary that all the cattle should be present, but some hair from each animal in the herd had to be brought before the purificatory ceremony could be performed.

During the time of mourning, the mourners slept on the ground near the fire and not on beds, the kraal was not swept out and the main fire was put out and not re-lighted. Even the calves had no fresh grass put in their huts. Any cattle which the heir did not want were used for food, sold, or given away.

On the night before the heir was to come, the mourners had their heads shaved again and a bunch of the herb *mwetengo* was rubbed over them to remove any evil resulting from the death. The herb was then cast out on waste land where no one was likely to pass and be contaminated by it. This was called *kuliasirira* or purification.

Early on the next morning, the heir came, bringing with him a sister to perform the purificatory ceremony. This sister might be married or single, and if the heir had no sister, the clan-members appointed for the purpose a woman of the clan, who was his "potential sister," that is, a woman of the same clan and generation, who could take the place of his sister as a "potential mother" might take the place of his mother, should she be dead. The mother of the heir had also to be present, and, if she was dead, a "potential mother" was appointed to take her place.

The heir and his sister, both wearing new clothes, took places outside the gate of the kraal, and the people and cattle were gathered round them. All the pots and other goods of the dead man were brought from the house and anything that was not in perfect condition was broken and placed upon the grave, while the good pots and other possessions were brought out to be purified. A little of every kind of food which a cow-man might eat was also brought to be cleansed.

When all was ready, a healthy boy whose parents were alive and well was sent to bring a pot of water from a well. This was mixed with white clay and a bunch of the herbs *nyawera* and *mugosola* was prepared. The sister of the heir took the bunch of herbs, dipped them into the water, and touched her brother on his forehead and knees; she then sprinkled the people, the vessels, the food, and, lastly, the cattle. As she finished, she dropped her bunch of herbs before any cow or cows which she desired, and these became her own and were separated from the rest of the herd. To prevent her from taking the best of the cows, the herdsmen usually brought these up close to the heir and kept them there during the ceremony; these were called "the herd of the shoes," and she might not take any of them. Should this sister not be married, the cows were left as hers in the charge of her brother, for no ordinary woman might possess property. Should she be married but have no son, she also left them with her brother, for, if she took them away, they became her husband's and might be inherited by a stranger if she remained without children. If she had a son, however, she took them away, for they would be inherited by him.

Another account of this purificatory ceremony stated that the heir sat upon his stool and the sister took a seat beside him, while any children of the family were gathered near them. The headman of the clan dipped a bunch of *nyawera* and *mugosola* into the mixture of white clay and water and touched the foreheads and knees of the heir, his sister and the children. The sister then rose and proceeded to purify the people, the goods and the cattle. The bunch of herbs was thrown away, and, if any one came upon it in the path or in the grass, they would walk round it and not step over it, lest the evil of death should come upon them. This purificatory ceremony (*kuliasirira*) marked the end of the mourning.

The heir put on the dead man's shoes and sat on his stool, and the cows were all milked. The headman of the clan milked a new pot full to the brim and presented it to the heir, who drank as much as he could at one draught. His sister then drank some and the children finished it. In the case of important chiefs this part of the ceremony was repeated on the following day.

The first duty of the heir, when the purificatory ceremonies had been completed, was to see that the fire in the kraal was re-lit and everything cleaned up and put straight. Then feasting began, bulls were killed for meat and the people drank beer and made merry.

As soon as the heir had time to build a new kraal, the old one was either broken down and the house destroyed, or they were left to fall down. The heir was given a new stool and shoes and took up his abode in the new kraal. He was responsible for any debts incurred by the dead man, but there was no set time for presenting claims, which, if they could be substantiated, had to be paid at any future time.

The widows of a dead man, especially if they were too old to marry again, would commit suicide by poisoning or by hanging themselves. Wives, as they grew old, often carried poison about with them so that it was ready for use, but no one as a rule attempted to prevent their taking it, as this was looked upon as a laudable action. Younger widows, however, might be taken to wife by the heir, or they might return to their own homes without repayment of the marriage-fee. Such a widow might marry again, in which case the man paid no marriage-fee for her unless she bore him a son, when the marriage-fee had to be paid before the boy was considered to be a legitimate child or could inherit.

When the heir had left the old kraal, the grave was no longer cared for and no attention was paid to the bones of the dead, though that part of the country which contained the dead was taboo to the family. The ghost accompanied the family, for a special place was dedicated to it in the new house and offerings were made to it there. Cows were dedicated to the ghost and the milk was placed in a special wooden pot and put in the place sacred to the ghost near the owner's bed. A shrine was also built for the ghost near the kraal-gate, where offerings were made when the medicine-man announced that such were necessary. The medicine-man often declared that the ghosts of other relatives required offerings, and then shrines had to be built for them also, for no ghost would share a shrine with another. Thus even forty shrines might be found at times before the entrance of one kraal.

When a woman fell ill, she was nursed by her mother or her sister who came to her for the purpose. When she died, she was washed and her legs were bent up as in the case of a man, but it was her left arm that was placed under her head. Her grave was dug in the dung-heap and she lay on her left side as if facing her husband's body. Her husband did not at once leave the kraal though he did not enter the house again, and before long he would arrange to have a new kraal built and leave the old one to fall down.

When a woman died while with child, the child was removed and buried in a separate grave. No blame was laid on the husband, and he might marry again.

If a mother died after the birth of a child, her sister or a clan-sister might come as her heir, marry the man, and look after the children. A motherless infant might either be fed on cow's milk or brought up by a foster-mother.

Death Ceremonies among the Agricultural People

The body of a dead man was prepared for burial in the same way as among the cow-people, but the body was not washed and the burial could take place at any time. The grave was dug in the earth near the house, and the man was laid in it on his right side. The widow had to go to sleep in some other house, for the door-posts were taken down and laid on the bed and the centre ring of the roof and the main central post of the house were taken down and laid on the grave. The bow of the dead man was broken and laid on the grave with the wooden shaft of his spear, the handle of his hoe, and his shield, and his widow added a bangle from her arm. A male goat took the place of the bull of the pastoral ceremony; its scrotum was tied and it was kept until the heir came, when it was killed and eaten.

Four days were given to mourning, and during this time the children of the family might eat no salt, nor might they eat with children whose parents were alive.

After four days the heir came and three baskets filled with food were placed before him. His sister then proceeded to purify the heir, the family, the pots and other goods, and the animals, with water mixed with white clay. When she had finished, she laid her bunch of herbs at the feet of a goat which became her property.

Any childless widow who did not wish to become wife to the heir might return to her family, who had then to refund the marriage-fee which had been paid for her. If a widow had children, she continued to live with them and care for them while the heir took the place of their father.

INHERITANCE

It was usual, though not an invariable rule, for the eldest son of a man's first wife to succeed to his office and property. A man could, however, if he so desired, nominate any other son to be his heir, and it was also possible for the clan-members to appoint someone whom they considered more suitable and to reject the heir nominated by the deceased owner of the property. It sometimes happened that the first wife had only daughters, and the man married a second wife and had a son by her who became heir to his property. If, however, the first wife later bore a son, this child would take precedence and inherit, though he was younger than the son of the second wife. In like manner, if a man married his slave as his first wife and she gave birth to a son, he would inherit even though the father later married a free-woman and by her had a son. When the members of the clan refused to allow the eldest son to inherit, it would be because of some mental or physica disability or because of some known evil habit.

If a man died without an heir, the head of the clan might appoint a clan-brother to take possession of the property. To show that he had thus inherited property otherwise than from his own father, he was thereafter known as the "little father" of himself. It was a rule never to mention the name of a dead man, and a child who inherited property from his father was called "the father of himself"; thus, if N died leaving a son L who inherited, L was never called the son of N but "the father of L," which made it clear to everyone that he possessed property inherited from a dead father. In cases where there was no heir, the Mugabe might take possession of the property and give it to whom he would.

A man usually left instructions for some of his property to be divided among the other members of his family in addition to his heir, who would take charge of younger members. Some might even be left to widows who had small sons, but, as women were not supposed to possess property, it would become the property of the children as soon as they were old enough to manage it. A childless widow became the wife of the heir or of some relative of the dead man, and therefore any property she received remained in the clan, becoming the property of her new husband, who was a man of the same clan as the former owner.

Younger children of the family often remained with the heir, though the grandparents were their rightful guardians. The cattle which younger children inherited remained with the heir until the children were of an age to take charge of them.

Should a man die childless, his brother was, in some cases, expected to take the widow to wife, and the first son she bore was looked upon as the son of the dead man and inherited his property. This, however, required the special sanction of the Mugabe, and as a rule an heir of the same clan was appointed who took the childless widow to wife, and her children shared the property with any other children he might have.

Young children sometimes inherited property and performed the purificatory rites with a real or clan sister. In such a case the mother looked after the property until the child was old enough to do so. If a man died leaving his wife with child, the family waited until the birth before deciding on the disposal of the property, for, if the child was a boy, he would inherit and the mother would manage affairs until he grew up; if, however, the child was a girl, the heir was appointed by the clan and the widow became his wife.

As a woman did not possess property, she had no heir,

but, if a wife died leaving children, her sister might come and take charge of them. She was then known as the heir of the dead woman, and generally married the husband.

A man might marry a slave-woman, and any son she bore to him might inherit his property. When a male slave was given a wife by his master, any children born to them were slaves.

Among the agricultural people, the heir took about ten out of every thirty animals, all the implements, the house, which he repaired and used, and any personal property. The chief wife took five goats, and the rest were divided amongst the family. A peasant usually had four or five wives and these went to the heir.

CHAPTER XIV

WARFARE AND HUNTING

Cattle the only cause of war—raids by the Baganda—raids on the Baganda—preparing to meet invasion—the safety of the Mugabe—preparing an expedition—auguries—work of spies—magic-working—the leader—assembling the army—commissariat—entering the enemy's country—methods of fighting—the women—treatment of the dead and prisoners—home-coming—the wounded—hunting among pastoral people—the Mugabe at a hunt—hunting among peasants—dividing the kill

WARFARE

THE Banyankole were not a warlike people and suffered much from attacks of neighbours who knew their peaceful disposition. Their principal enemies were the Baganda, though other dwellers on their borders, such as the Bakitara, would also seize any opportunity to raid their country and carry off cattle. When cattle were thus stolen from them, the Banyankole would rise and make an attempt to get them back and now and then, tempted by the sight of ill-protected herds near their own borders, they would rise of their own accord and raid a neighbouring country, carrying off the cattle, but nothing unconnected with cattle was able to rouse them to war. The cow-men scorned and despised all who cultivated the land or lived on a vegetable diet, but they would do and bear anything for the sake of their cows, to which they became very much attached.

As their principal aggressors were the Baganda, cattle grazing on that side of Ankole had to be very carefully guarded, but it often happened that Baganda raiders would succeed in carrying off herds to their own country. The difficulty then was to raise a body of men quickly enough to get the cows back before they were driven too far into Buganda. The Banyankole had the advantage of knowing the cows, who would obey their voices, and of being able to move about by night, for they had little fear of wild animals. They would therefore gather as many men as they could get and follow the raiders by night, for they knew that they were no match for the warlike Baganda in open warfare. In the dark they would make a sudden rush upon the raiders and some of them would gather together and drive off the cows while others attacked the men and kept them from following up the cows. By this means they were frequently able to recover the greater part of their lost cattle without much loss of life.

A pastoral chief on the borders of Buganda might make a sudden raid into Baganda territory to carry off, at the risk of his life, some of their herds. These he would hurry into the heart of his own country before their guardians had time to raise the alarm and get help. After such a successful raid, the chief would carry his tale to the Mugabe, taking to him some of the spoil and making scornful remarks about the other chiefs, who would be roused, by jealousy of the rewards and praise given to him, to emulate his feat.

While the chief was receiving honour and commendation, however, arrangements had to be made to meet an almost certain invasion of the Baganda. The Mugabe consulted diviners and medicine-men, who, by their charms, discovered where the Baganda army was and whether they were coming to attack. Further information was got by sending spies into Buganda to find out what they could about the doings of the people. When these scouts or the people on the borders found that an army was on its way into the country, the news was sent by a runner to the Mugabe. He called out as he went, to warn the people on the way, and, as soon as he reached the Mugabe, messengers were sent out to carry the news all through the country.

Meanwhile steps were being taken for the safety of the Mugabe and of the cattle. The herds, especially those of the Mugabe, were driven into the far parts of the country, while a new kraal was built and the Mugabe's women and his property were taken to it. The Mugabe himself remained in the old kraal until the enemy came near, when he also retired to the new place. If the enemy came on so rapidly that there was not time for the Mugabe to flee, he remained where he was and took part in the fight, but as a rule he was kept in a place of safety. When he left the old kraal, a guard was put in charge. This man had to watch until he was sure that there was no hope of turning the enemy back, when he had to set fire to the royal kraal. The Mugabe might never return to a kraal in which the enemy had been, for it would be bewitched, and the fact of their entering a kraal in which he had resided might also do him harm, so that all such danger was averted by burning the kraal. These invasions never lasted longer than a day or two and the greatest difficulty was to prevent the enemy from capturing and carrying off women and cattle.

Sometimes a chief would inform the Mugabe that there were many cattle in a certain district which was easily accessible, that they were inadequately guarded, and that an attack in force would easily capture them. When an expedition on a large scale was planned, it took some time, often about a year, to make all the preparations.

The Mugabe first consulted diviners and medicine-men to find out whether the expedition was advisable and whether it would be successful. About fifty cows and two hundred fowls were collected and brought for the purpose of taking auguries. A cow was milked and the Mugabe squirted a little of the milk into the mouths of twenty cows, whispering into the ear of each what he wanted. These cows were separated from the fifty and kept apart, and next morning early one of them was killed by having the arteries in its throat opened. This was done by cutting down them, not across in the ordinary way, and the medicine-man watched to see how the blood flowed. The lungs and intestines were then examined, special attention being paid to the way in which the dung was cleared from the stomach. If there was any stoppage it meant that the Mugabe would meet with evil. The skin had to be flayed carefully from the animal, and the meat was cut so that no bones were broken, and eaten on the spot.

The fowls were treated in the same way. The Mugabe spat into the throat of one at night and the next morning it was killed and the flow of blood, the lungs and intestines examined. When the augury from a fowl was good, its head was taken and made into a fetish for the Mugabe to wear.

Sometimes the Mugabe gave the diviner a white bull from which to take the augury. If the augury was good it was accepted and preparations went forward, but, if it was bad, another was taken before they acted upon it.

While the preparations at home were going on, spies were sent out into the enemy country under the pretence of trading. These men wandered about the country and brought back information as to the strength of the enemy, the size of their herds, their methods of herding, and the protection of the animals by night. Some of the spies carried with them magic which would prevent the people from knowing that any expedition was being planned and from making any preparations. These men travelled into the country as if on their way to buy goods. They visited the people and often stayed some time in different kraals, where they gathered things with which to make magic, and deposited the magic objects they had with them. They carried as a rule nothing but a bag for tobacco and a pipe, but under the tobacco in the bag were concealed all sorts of objects, things they had picked up in the kraals, on the roads, or in the grass, and also medicines prepared and brought from their own country. They buried things in the roads and stuck them in the roofs of houses, and by such means the people were enfeebled, the cows were bewitched so that they came away quickly, and all things were made easy for the attackers. Sometimes these men took a bull on which they used magic. In the evening they turned it loose among some cows and it accompanied them back to their kraal and bewitched them, making them desire to wander. They believed that the magic made the bull able to wander invisible during the day so that it reached fresh kraals each evening and bewitched many cows.

At home the Mugabe, in consultation with the diviner,

appointed a leader for the army. He was given a special royal fetish, *Luwoma*, and a drum and fifes, and while the final preparations were being made he lived at home with his wife. Meanwhile a special kraal was built for the Mugabe near the frontier from which the raid was to be made. Here he took up his abode with a special woman to look after him and cows to feed him. Here also came the royal medicine-man with his fetishes and the royal spear. Messengers came from the army daily with news and the medicine-man took auguries and sent messengers to the leader with blessing and advice.

When the time came to gather his army together, the leader camped at the place from which he meant to start the expedition, and the various chiefs with their followers came to him there. The Mugabe sent messengers round the country to call the people by a special cry, for no drums were used. Herdsmen and serfs both answered the call and came to join the army without any auguries or blessing from the medicine-men. No women, however, went to war, those of the cow-men being too fat to travel and the serfs being forbidden to bring theirs.

The leader had his hut in the centre of the camping-place and others camped round about, leaving a clear space round the hut where his special fetish was placed; no person might pass in front of his hut but had to go round behind it.

The Mugabe usually gave a number of cows for the food of the army and these were killed and the meat dried to carry with them. The leader and chiefs carried beer, honey and millet, as well as dried meat, but the rest of the army expected to be supplied by the people as they passed along. For arms the men carried one or two leaf-shaped spears, a small shield with a boss, and a bow with arrows in a wooden quiver.

When the army was ready to start, a fetish of herbs was placed in the road so that they might step over it as they passed. This was said to give the men courage and to make their arms strong and sure so that they might kill men and secure many cattle. The Mugabe wore a fetish and carried a fetish stick to which a number of roots and herbs of special powers were tied.

While the army was away, the Mugabe and the royal medicine-man remained in the new kraal and messengers went constantly between them and the army bringing information as to the doings of the forces. The royal medicine-man took auguries daily to keep the Mugabe informed of the progress of the expedition, and he sent his blessing by messengers to the leader.

When the army reached the enemy's country, it was divided into small parties so that it would not attract attention, and the men travelled by night, resting during the day. When they came to the pre-arranged place, a few chosen warriors went forward by night to attack and carry off the cattle. When they had succeeded in getting the cows away, the rest of the army rose and attacked those who tried to follow up the stolen cattle. These were driven by day and night until they crossed the border and reached a place of safety.

If the retreating invaders found that the enemy's forces were coming very near them, they killed a cow and left it half cooked near fires, to look as though they had been disturbed in the midst of a meal. The warriors would certainly stop to eat the meat thus provided and this gave the others more time to make good their escape with the cattle.

When possible they avoided an actual fight, but if they were forced into it, they attacked in large numbers, shooting arrows and casting stones from slings. When the fight came to close quarters, they attacked with their spears, which were never thrown but reserved for hand-to-hand fighting. Whenever possible archers would conceal themselves in the grass or bush and attack unseen while the spear-men would seek to cut off and attack isolated members or small groups of the enemy. Strategy was more admired than bravery in the field and a leader was more praised for avoiding a pitched battle than for any show of bravery.

While the expedition was going on, the women who had husbands or sons in the army went out to a *kirikiti* tree with their milk-pots. These were placed before the tree and they called upon the god to keep their relatives safe and prosper the expedition, smearing the tree, as they prayed, with butter. The tree was watched and if any insect climbed the trunk they thought that a battle was going on and redoubled their intercessions and prayers for victory. In the afternoon they drank the milk as a solemn meal in the presence of the god. Women whose husbands were out with the army had to keep all men away from their beds and be strictly chaste.

When the news came that the men were returning, bead head-dresses were put upon the milk-pots, and thanks and praise were offered to the god, who had brought them back in safety and given them success. In addition to as much milk as could be kept, beer and the best of food were prepared for their arrival, when they feasted on the meat and beer and later drank milk.

The bodies of warriors who were killed in the field or died of wounds were put out of the camp and covered with grass, leaves and branches to keep wild animals from carrying them off. The dead of the enemy were never mutilated and prisoners were brought to the Mugabe and kept as slaves, one or at times both their ears being cut off to show that they were slaves taken in war.

When the army came near home, messengers were sent to the Mugabe who sent cattle to be given to them and a medicine-man to purify the warriors and the spoil, after which the greater part of the army departed and went straight to their own homes. The leader with the chiefs and his special followers went to the Mugabe to report the doings of the expedition and to divide the spoil. The Mugabe sent his herdsmen to pick out cows for the royal herds, after which the leader might choose what he wanted, and presents were given to any chiefs or men who had specially distinguished themselves. Any which then remained were divided among the other chiefs and the army. The Mugabe might also grant special cattle or even chieftainships to men who had shown great bravery, but any who were accused of cowardice were not punished, though they knew that they might never hope for promotion.

The warrior who had killed a man was treated like a murderer or a hunter who had killed a lion, leopard, antelope, or hyaena (because these animals belonged to the gods); he was not allowed to sleep or eat with others until he had been purified, for the ghost of the man was upon him.

The wounded were carried home with the army and if a man's wounds were not serious, he was looked after by his wife in his own kraal and the wife had to be strictly chaste until he recovered. A sick man might be fed on milk warmed by adding hot water, though milk might never be boiled. More seriously wounded men were also brought home, but they were looked after by surgeons and nursed by some old woman who was a widow or by a woman who had had no sexual connexion with men for some time.

The surgeon took leaves of *ekitobotobo* or *ntengo* and laid them on stones heated in the kraal fire. When the sap flowed from the hot leaves they were applied to the wound until it appeared clean and healthy. If a wound was very unhealthy, the surgeon heated a spear and thrust it inside to burn away the bad place and stop bleeding. To stop excessive bleeding in a limb, a pad of fibre was placed over the wound and a bandage bound tightly round. A barbed arrow or spear which was left in a wounded limb was forced through and no attempt made to draw it back. A special surgeon (*abagyengi*) was called in to treat bone fractures. In the case of a broken limb he applied some herbs, bound the limb to splints, and kept it thus until the fracture had healed. In the case of a skull fracture, the surgeon removed any splinters of bone, bound herbs over the wound and left it to heal. From time to time he put on fresh herbs, using kinds which he had found by experience to have healing properties, though he knew nothing of their antiseptic action.

When the wounds had healed, the old woman took the man to some waste land near, where she washed him from head to foot with fresh water and purified him with the herbs *mwetengo* and *omubuza* and then with *nyawera*. She then put new clothes upon him, taking the old as her perquisite. After this purification the man returned to his wife and family.

HUNTING

Among the cow-men hunting was only a form of sport and was not followed for the sake of food, for it was not permitted to eat the meat of the animals killed, though their skins were used for rugs and sometimes for clothing. Some people declared that the cow-men might eat certain kinds of antelope, but if the animal saw the hunter approaching before it was killed, he might not partake of the meat. The only professional hunters kept by the Mugabe were a few elephant hunters of the peasant class. As, however, the people did not value ivory for its own sake and never worked it, it was only used for sale to adjacent tribes, and the hunters were few.

The Mugabe had large numbers of dogs for hunting and these were kept for him by his peasants, though he kept a favoured few in his own kraal. These were distinguished by wearing special collars, made from the skins of animals, to which bells were attached. The dogs were used in the hunts to drive the game.

When the Mugabe desired to go to hunt, messengers were sent round the night before to warn the people, hundreds of whom went out as beaters with the dogs. The Mugabe set out in the morning about nine or ten o'clock and took up a good position with a number of assistants. The beaters drove the game past him and he might shoot them with arrows or throw spears at them, or even spear them down if they passed near him. The guards who were with him quickly brought down any animal which he had wounded and he himself at times became excited and ran after a wounded animal. The present Mugabe has become too fat to think of hunting and even moving about is difficult to him, but the rulers of old were active and took part in such sport.

The meat of the animals killed was given to the peasants who accompanied the hunt and to the dogs, and the skins went to the royal skin-dressers to be prepared for use.

Hunting was, however, a different thing among the peasants, for it was their chief means of securing meat. They kept dogs which were used for putting up small game and these sometimes also caught gazelle or other animals, being rewarded with the entrails.

A peasant might hunt alone or with one or two companions but sometimes a man, generally one of the medicine-men, would prepare a bigger hunt. In this case he blew his horn at night and the next morning early those who cared to hunt assembled at his hut. The leader placed a fetish in the path and all jumped over it, thus removing any evil that might be hanging over them and giving them strength and skill for the chase. Nets were often used in these organised hunts and the animals driven into them.

If the leader of the hunt killed an animal, he took a shoulder, the back, the legs and the skin, while the second man took a shoulder. If the man who called the hunt had not killed the animal, he took a shoulder by virtue of his office, and the man who had killed the animal divided up the rest of the meat as he wished. They never ate the flesh of pigs, but used the skin and gave the flesh to the dogs.

When a man was out hunting, his wife refrained from sexual intercourse with other men and she had to be careful not to kill anything; even vermin, if caught, must be thrown away and not killed. She might let no man pass behind her back but warned him to keep in front of her. Should she neglect any of these precautions, her husband's chances of obtaining game in the hunt would be ruined.

CHAPTER XV

FOLK-LORE

The Hawk and the Hen—the Rabbit and the Leopard

THE HAWK AND THE HEN

A HEN went to some cow-men to buy meat. She brought it away with her and immediately met a hawk also going to get food. When she saw him coming she tucked her leg under her wing. The hawk asked her, "Where did you get your meat?" The hen replied, "From the cow-men." The hawk asked, "What did you pay for it?" and she answered, "I bought it with my leg; those who go to buy take legs." So the hawk cut off its leg and then could not walk, and in anger declared that hawks would always hunt hens and chickens and kill them. Since then when a hen sees a hawk coming she always hides her leg under her wing.

THE RABBIT AND THE LEOPARD

A rabbit and a leopard lived together and the leopard borrowed a cow from the rabbit. Afterwards the rabbit wanted the cow. The leopard wished the rabbit to die, so that he might keep the cow, so he said, "To-morrow bring nine portions of cooked millet. We will cross the lake and when I throw one portion in you will also throw in a portion to pacify the lake spirit." The leopard took nine stones and nine portions of food. They reached the lake and as they began to cross the leopard dropped in a stone. The rabbit threw in a portion of food and they went on until the nine portions were finished. The leopard when he landed took out a portion of millet and ate it. The rabbit asked, "Where did you get that from?" and the leopard replied, "Is there nothing at the bottom of an old man's bag?" They went on and the leopard said, "If you get any wine, come back here to get a reed for a tube to drink it through." The little rabbit said, "I must go and relieve myself," and went back, picking a reed, which he carried. They went on a little and the leopard saw a tree and said, "If they give you anything to eat, come and break a piece of wood to help you eat it." The rabbit broke a piece off and carried it. When they reached their destination, the people gave them some wine and the leopard said to the rabbit, "Go and fetch a reed from where I showed you." The rabbit went just outside and came back with the reed. The leopard refused the wine in anger because he had been so quick, for he had meant to drink all the wine while the rabbit was away. The people brought food, and the leopard told the rabbit to go and bring a stick to serve out the food. He went again just outside and returned with the stick. The leopard refused the food as he did the wine, and then he was hungry and went at night and killed a goat. He returned and found the rabbit asleep and rubbed blood on his mouth, knowing that the owners of the goat would come next day and question them as to the goat. When they came, as he expected, he said, "I did not steal it, but see on whom the blood is to be found; catch him and kill him." They came to the rabbit, who was asleep and did not know what was happening, found the blood, and killed him. The leopard then went away satisfied.

Some time afterwards, the younger brother of the rabbit learned all that had happened and he wanted to have revenge on the leopard for killing his brother. He went to the witch-doctor to get advice. The witch-doctor said to him, "Take shells and when you reach the place where you will stay the night, put them on your eyes; and take nine portions of cooked millet and nine stones. When you cross the lake with the leopard and he says, 'Throw in food,' throw in a stone." The young rabbit went and made friends with the leopard and suggested a visit to the island. They crossed the lake and the rabbit threw in a stone whenever the leopard suggested millet should be dropped in to appease the water spirit. On the road the leopard broke off a reed and the rabbit did so also. The leopard was very troubled and told the rabbit, "If they give us wine come here to fetch a reed to make a drinking tube"; and again when they reached the tree, he said, "Come here if food is given to us and get a stick to make a spoon"; but the leopard was unable to trick the rabbit. As before, the leopard was angry and ate no food, but when they went to bed, the rabbit fixed the shells into his eyes to make them look as though he were awake. The leopard slipped away and killed a goat and came to rub the blood on the rabbit, but seeing the white shells he thought he was awake and stole away to wait until he should go to sleep. In the morning the owners of the goat came to enquire for it, and the rabbit said, "You see us. I did not do it. Kill the thief." They found the leopard with blood on him and killed him, and thus the first rabbit was avenged.

RELATIONSHIPS

Son, omwana wangye (used by the father).
Father, tata (used by a son).
Mother, mawe.
Elder brother, mukulu wangye (m.s.).
Elder sister, mukulu wangye (w.s.).
Sister, munyanyaze (m.s.).
Father's brother, tata nto.
Father's brother's wife, muka tata nto.
Father's brother's child, murumuna wange (if younger than speaker); mukulu wange.
Father's sister, tata nkazi.
Father's sister's husband, iba tata nkazi.
Father's sister's child, mwojo wa tata nkazi.
Mother's brother, marimi.
Mother's brother's wife, muka marimi. ·
Mother's brother's child, mwana wa marimi.
Mother's sister, mawe nto.
Mother's sister's husband, iba mawe nto.
Mother's sister's child, mwojo wa mawe nto.
Sister's son's wife, mukamwana wangye (m.s.).
Sister's son's child, mwana wangye (m.s.).
Sister's daughter's husband, mulamu wangye (m.s.).
Sister's daughter's child, mwana wangye (m.s.).
Father's father, tata nkulu.
Father's mother, mawe nkulu.
Mother's father, tata nkulu.
Mother's mother, mawe nkulu.
Younger brother, muganda nto.
Wife, muka.
Daughter, muhala.
Son's son, mwana wa mwana wange.
Son's daughter, mwana (muhala) wa muhala wange.
Daughter's son, mwana (muhala) wa muhala wange.
Daughter's daughter, mwana (muhala) wa muhala wange.
Husband, ibanyi.
Wife's father, tatazara.
Wife's mother, mazara.
Husband's father, tatazara.
Husband's mother, mazara.
Wife's brother, mulamu wangye.
Wife's sister, mulamu wangye.
Husband's brother, mulamu wangye.
Husband's sister, mulamukazi wangye.
Wife's sister's husband, mushawzire wangye.
Husband's brother's wife, muka ibanyi.
Son's wife's parents, baishezara mwana wangye.

INDEX

UGANDA PROTECTORATE

Boundary of Protectorate — — —
Railways ━━━━━━━━ Main Roads ....

Scale: Miles

0   20   40   60   80   100 120

THE BAGESU

PLATE I

Commissioner's camping ground

Commissioner's camp

Scenery on Mount Elgon

THE BAGESU

AND OTHER TRIBES OF THE UGANDA PROTECTORATE

THE THIRD PART OF THE REPORT
OF THE MACKIE ETHNOLOGICAL
EXPEDITION TO CENTRAL
AFRICA

BY

JOHN ROSCOE, M.A.

Hon. Canon of Norwich and Rector of Ovington, Norfolk
Formerly of the Church Missionary Society

CAMBRIDGE
AT THE UNIVERSITY PRESS
1924

Reprinted by permission of Cambridge University Press
ⓒ Cambridge University Press

S.B.N.-GB: 576.59255.2
Republished in 1968 by
Gregg Press Limited
1 Westmead
Farnborough Hants
England
Printed in Germany

PREFACE

IN sending forth this, the third and last volume of the report of the Mackie Ethnological Expedition, my feelings are mainly those of dissatisfaction at the incompleteness of the work, but there is some consolation in the thought that there may be here something new both for the scientist and for the ordinary reader, and that some light may be shed on matters which hitherto lay in the twilight of uncertainty and doubt.

It is for those who undertook the responsibility of arranging and directing this expedition to judge in how far it has fulfilled their expectations. The writer, who had the great privilege of undertaking the actual investigation, can only wish that it could have been carried further and that discoveries of greater value to science had been made.

Though information concerning many hitherto little known customs has been obtained, the origin of these pastoral people of the Lake Region still remains a mystery. We may hope that in due time it will be possible to piece together items of knowledge thus gathered from different sources and to make from them a complete story. The student of these matters can no longer doubt that these pastoral people entered the Lake Region as immigrants from the north east and that they were associated with the people who in remote ages made Egypt so interesting. There remains still to be accomplished the more difficult, and, I venture to think, the more interesting, task of procuring information from the tribes along the frontier of Abyssinia. Such an investigation will supply much that is missing and might possibly give some reliable indications of the dates at which migrations took place. To those tribes we must look for the solution of what is still overshadowed by mystery, and the necessary investigation is rendered very difficult by the suspicions of these people and their desire to remain free from the intrusion of the white man.

In this third volume I have brought together scraps of information gathered mainly while travelling from place to place. With the exception of the notes on the Bagesu, Basabei, and Bakyiga, the information was collected in places where the expedition halted to spend the night and to obtain fresh porters for the baggage. Any experienced traveller will readily understand how impossible it is to be sure that information obtained from the casual informant is reliable. He may be useful and his information valuable, but it is also quite possible that if you knew the man better or could hear what his companions and clan-fellows think of him, you would place no trust in him. Information thus obtained must therefore be imparted with a reservation: it is the best procurable under the circumstances.

The notes have been arranged in a geographical order. Taking Mount Elgon as the starting point, we move westward to Lake Albert, then in a south westerly direction round the Uganda Protectorate boundary to the Kigezi country bordering upon the new Belgian state, Ruanda. The tribes are dealt with separately, some, where conditions were most favourable, being more fully considered than others. The languages of these tribes differ considerably and these at times made it difficult to investigate such delicate subjects as the secrets of their social life, for enquiries often aroused suspicion as to the motives of the investigator.

There are points of divergence from, and in some instances of open contradiction of former statements given in the "Northern Bantu"; these I have thought it well to leave without any attempt at explanation, for the present notes were jotted down at odd times and in places where it was impossible to compare them with my former notes and to enquire into the causes of differences. Indeed no opportunity occurred of reading or copying these rough pencilled notes until after I had left the country. These brief accounts, however, may be of use to future workers who undertake the task of a more detailed and careful examination of such people as, for example, the Basoga.

The Lake dwellers, or Bakene, whom I sought carefully, I found to have deserted their papyrus island homes both along the rivers and in the lakes, and settled on the mainland, so that their former mode of life has ceased and a new order begun. This was due to the settled state of the country brought about by the British Government. As the lake life which I desired to investigate was gone, I made no examination of the people but turned aside to other fields.

The Expedition was carried out after the Armistice during the years 1919–20. Owing to the restricted shipping and the number of applicants for passages it was only possible to reach Africa in 1919 by travelling in a cargo steamer *viâ* the Cape of Good Hope to Mombasa. I am deeply indebted to the Directors of the Clan Line, whose kindness and courtesy made it possible for me to reach Mombasa sooner than I should otherwise have done.

To that Company I tender my grateful thanks, and to the officers of the ships in which I travelled.

The actual work of the Expedition began with the journey from Kampala to Ankole, and from there the route followed was by roads less used and more circuitous than those the natives ordinarily follow. My mode of travel was on foot or riding an ordinary bicycle while the goods were carried on the heads of native porters. The route taken was the reverse of the order in which I have arranged the ethnological information in the text.

The journey home was by the Nile from Lake Albert to Khartoum and Cairo. When travelling by the Nile steamer it was impossible to make any notes of the tribes encountered worth recording: the brief stops, to take in wood for the engines, did not give time to make more than a few enquiries from the people.

Readers who desire more detailed information as to the route of the Expedition, the scenery of the country traversed, and incidents of travel, may be referred to my book *The Soul of Central Africa* (Cassells, London, 1922), where I have touched on these topics more fully than seemed necessary in the present report.

I am indebted to Sir James G. Frazer for again reading over my proofs and making valuable suggestions; to Miss Cook, of Murtle, Aberdeenshire, a former student at Newnham College, Cambridge, who kindly undertook the work formerly done by my late friend the Rev. W. A. Cox, and read the manuscripts, giving valuable suggestions; and to Miss Bisset, my faithful and indefatigable co-worker, who has done so much for me in the preparation of this report.

To Sir Peter Mackie, the generous donor who made the expedition possible, I would not only renew my thanks for what he has done, but also express the hope that he will feel satisfied with the results. May others be stimulated by his example to assist this great cause. To the Royal Society I would again tender grateful thanks for help, advice, and sympathy.

I should like to urge most emphatically the importance of an investigation of the tribes from Lake Rudolf to the Nile along the borders of Abyssinia, and also of the Pygmies in the Semliki valley or in the Dark Forest near the river, before their habits of life are lost. It is a duty we owe to science and to posterity to secure while possible an account of the social life and customs which are rapidly vanishing. A right understanding of these people is not only of value to science, to education, and to the spread of Christianity, but facilitates the sound and peaceable government of the country.

J. ROSCOE

OVINGTON RECTORY,
July, 1923

CONTENTS

THE BAGESU

CHAPTER I. THE PEOPLE

CHAPTER II. RELIGION

CHAPTER III. OCCUPATIONS OF THE BAGESU

CHAPTER IV. BIRTH, INITIATION, AND MARRIAGE

CHAPTER V. SICKNESS, DEATH, AND INHERITANCE

CHAPTER VI. LANGUAGE

CHAPTER VII. THE BAKYIGA CLAN, A SECTION OF THE BAGESU OF MOUNT ELGON

THE BASABEI

THE BATESO

BUSOGA

CHAPTER XVI. RELIGION

CHAPTER XVII. OCCUPATIONS OF THE PEOPLE

CHAPTER XVIII. BIRTH, MARRIAGE, ILLNESS, AND DEATH

THE BAKONJO

CHAPTER XIX. THE PEOPLE

CHAPTER XX. BIRTH, MARRIAGE, ILLNESS, AND DEATH

THE BAMBWA

CHAPTER XXI. THE PEOPLE AND THEIR OCCUPATIONS

THE BATUSE OR BALYANWANDA
OF RUANDA

LIST OF PLATES

THE BAGESU

CHAPTER I

THE PEOPLE

Origin—flight to the mountain—caves of refuge—houses—villages—
clans—clan exogamy—enmity between clans—harvest festivities—
marriage—uncleanliness of the people—clothing—hair—ornaments—
food—government—taxation—slaves—fire

MOUNT ELGON consists of a large range, or rather group, of mountain peaks, some of them rising to great heights, and it covers an area of many square miles. On the higher peaks snow lies for long periods but is not perpetual, and water is plentiful, for many streams flow from the heights. In some parts the rocky sides of the mountain rise precipitously for some hundreds of feet and streams fall over these precipices into rock basins below. In these rock walls are many caves, some of them large enough to shelter two hundred cows and several families of people. In the gorges watered by the streams there grow luxuriant forests both of fine trees and of bamboo, the latter being used for building and also cut up to form water vessels and for other purposes.

The mountain is so extensive that, although small villages are numerous, they are often separated by as much as ten to fifteen miles, and the cultivated land which surrounds each village seems but a speck on the vast slope of wild mountain.

The Bagesu tribe on Mount Elgon is one of the most primitive of the negro tribes of Africa, and was driven from the plains to the east of Mount Elgon by the attacks of the Masai and Nandi. To escape the ravages of these warlike tribes, the Bagesu fled to the mountain, only to find that on the lower slopes they were subject to periodical raids by the Abyssinians and those tribes who inhabited the borders of Abyssinia. They therefore made their way to the less easily

accessible heights and seldom left the high valleys and plateaux
of the southern and western sides. Their foes, though deterred
by the cold and by the ease with which missiles could be
hurled on them from above as they climbed the steep paths,
did at times attempt raids on the Bagesu villages; and on
such occasions the inhabitants, with their flocks and herds,
found places of refuge in the large natural caves with which
certain parts of the mountain were honeycombed. Most of
these caves were reached by steep and narrow paths, easily de-
fended against attack, and some of them were kept provisioned
and ready for occupation in case of sudden need. As long as
raiders remained in the district the cattle were kept in the
caves during the day and taken out to graze during the night.
Though several of the caves were examined, no sign of
permanent habitation was found, the floors being smooth
rock without any deposits.

Bagesu houses were built in groups forming villages which
varied in size from ten, the common number, to forty houses
in the case of a large settlement. No attempt was ever made
to build stockades to protect these villages, for the long and
arduous climb which was necessary to reach them from the
plain not only deterred foes from frequent attacks, but gave
the people time to escape into places of safety after the raiders
were sighted.

The tribe was not a large one, but numbered possibly some
two thousand. It was divided into a number of clans, two
or three of which had gathered round Mbale, where the
Government Station is situated, while the others were scattered
about the slopes of the mountain. The names of some of these
clans were:

1. Bankoko	7. Bafumbo	12. Basiguya
2. Bakonde	8. Bahalasi	13. Balucheke
3. Bakyiga	9. Balago	14. Bavutu
4. Babuya	10. Balugenya	15. Basuguya
5. Bahugu	11. Baginyanya	16. Basihu
6. Bayobo		

The large clans were sub-divided, each small division claim-
ing to be the head or principal division of the clan and there-

PLATE II

Entrance to cave

View of caves

Caves on Mount Elgon

fore masters of the part of the country in which they dwelt. The following are the names of some of the sub-divisions of the two most important clans, the Bankoko and Bakonde, though in neither case is the list exhaustive:

Bankoko

1. Bamboi	10. Bambubi	17. Babezi
2. Basamaga	11. Bakigoti	18. Bachelwe
3. Bamwonyi	12. Bamukuma	19. Banababe
4. Bamdudu	13. Bamudoda	20. Banafuna
5. Basakya	14. Balebe (who claim	21. Batunda
6. Bamugeni	a totem *ifumbo*)	22. Barujeka
7. Babirabi	15. Bamasika	23. Bamwali
8. Bakigori	16. Banakamyu	24. Bagaza
9. Bakumwa		

Bakonde

1. Balweta	4. Bawongolo	6. Bamiyaga
2. Bamwangu	5. Balwaso	7. Bamuluya
3. Bakikale		

It is probable that these clans were not totemic, for not only did they refuse to acknowledge the existence of totems, but they seemed most surprised when questioned on the subject. It is, however, quite possible that they were totemic and that some special conception of the meaning and use of totems led to this complete reticence on the subject. Clans and divisions were clearly marked and clan exogamy was enforced, while there was at the same time constant enmity between the clans, and, to a lesser degree, between the sub-divisions of the same clan. It was indeed unsafe for any man, even if armed, to wander alone into the territory of another division. Women who were found unprotected would not be attacked, but if they were unmarried they ran the risk of being captured and given in marriage to some member of their captor's clan.

At one period of the year, however, this hostility ceased and the people went about from village to village in safety. This armistice took place immediately after harvest, when beer had been brewed. At this time no man might carry any weapons; spears and knives were carefully stowed away, and the people went about armed only with long bamboo staffs, inside which they carried beer tubes sometimes as much as four feet long, with a cane work filter in one end. As long as the beer lasted, people went from village to village drinking, dancing, and singing by day and by night. The beer was brought into open spaces in great pots, round which men and women sat in separate groups, each group having one pot in the centre into which all put their tubes. These gatherings became regular saturnalia, for men and women lived together regardless of marriage relationships. This was especially remarkable because at other times the women of the tribe were strictly chaste and the men guarded their own wives with jealous care. Though a visitor in a man's house slept near the same fire, the code of morality forbade his having any familiarity with the women of his host If a man had several wives living in different houses, he might put a visitor into one of these houses to sleep, but he first removed the wife, who had to sleep elsewhere.

It was at this time of festivity, too, that young men and women who were ready for marriage, that is, men who had been initiated and women who had completed the keloids on forehead and body, chose their mates. The two might simply go to live together, and after they had become husband and wife, the man learned from his wife's relatives what they expected as a marriage fee. and matters were settled while the young couple continued to live together.

This feasting and merry-making was the one great event of the year. After it was over the clans returned to their usual hostile attitude towards each other, and even the marriage relationships which had been formed had no influence, for a man would kill his wife's brothers or his sister's husband as readily as anyone else. The women, however, were free to return to their old homes on special occasions, such as funeral ceremonies, and it was no unusual thing to find a wife attending the mourning ceremonies of her father or brother who had been killed by her husband.

These people were uncleanly both in their persons and in

PLATE III

Young man of Bagesu tribe with load of building material

Old man of the Bagesu tribe

PLATE IV

Girl of the Bagesu tribe, showing keloids

their houses, where they made no attempt at sanitation. The floors were sometimes swept out and occasionally smeared with cow-dung to make them smooth, for they were both bed and sitting-place. Pots were rarely washed; all that they considered necessary was to scrape them out with the finger after a meal, though sometimes a stick would be used to scrape out the remains of one meal before cooking the next. The people sometimes washed their feet on a muddy day, but they never troubled to wash their bodies, though they might bathe if a stream or pool tempted them when the sun was hot. When they could procure any oil or fat they would rub it over their bodies, but otherwise they paid no heed to the filth which accumulated. Carrying water to their houses for the purpose of washing was never even thought of.

The clothing of the people was never intended either for warmth or covering. Before initiation a boy went naked, but when his initiation was complete, he was entitled to wear the dress of a full-grown man, which consisted of a skin, usually a goat-skin. Two of the legs were joined with string about a foot long. The skin was put under the right arm and the string passed over the head on to the left shoulder, so that the left side was completely exposed, though the skin covered the right side and reached halfway down the thighs. If a man refused to undergo the ceremony of initiation, he was not allowed to wear this skin, to marry, or to sit in the council of the men.

Until marriage girls also went naked or wore a sort of apron measuring some six inches by three, sometimes made of coarsely woven fibre and sometimes consisting merely of strings to which were tied the stem ends of bottle gourds. After marriage a woman wore a girdle from which, at the back, hung a fringe of banana fibre twisted into strings like cord. The ends of these strings were tied together and bound with fibre for about an inch of their length, a piece of work which only the owner of the belt might do. This end was brought between the legs from the back to the front, passed under the belt in front and allowed to hang down. When a woman became a widow, she burned this girdle and went naked unless she married again, when she made herself another. This is still the dress worn by the married women except in the vicinity of European settlements.

Both men and women shaved all the hair off their heads, faces, and bodies at frequent intervals, often monthly.

The ornaments of unmarried girls were as a rule only bracelets, but married women wore anklets as well. The workmanship of these was crude, in fact they were of the most primitive and unfinished type to be found in this part of Africa, for there were no able artisans among the people. The bracelets and anklets were merely iron or, if possible, brass rods, about as thick as a slate pencil; these were bent round the limb and no attempt was made to join the ends or to decorate them. Though younger members of the tribe are now refusing to pierce the lips or ears, many people still wear lip ornaments, usually of wood, which is the undress ornament, while a few wear the full-dress lip ornament, a bit of white stone, some two inches long, half an inch thick at the end inserted in the lip, and tapering towards the end which protrudes. When the ornament is not in place, a button of wood is inserted to keep the hole from closing and to prevent the saliva from trickling out on to the chin. As a rule men did not wear this ornament, though there were a few exceptions, but both men and women pierced both the lobes and the helix of the ears, though they seldom enlarged the holes more than enough to insert straws. The most common ear ornaments were small iron, brass, or copper wire rings, which had a few glass beads threaded on them and were passed through these holes.

If a woman possessed any money, in the form of cowry-shells or, later, of the Uganda cents, she usually threaded it and wore it round her waist, while men carried theirs, along with other things, such as their tobacco and pipes, fetishes, and so forth, in bags slung on the left shoulder. These bags were made of goat or even wild cat skins, flayed off whole from the animal, leaving stumps of the legs. Sometimes the skin of the head was left on, but often it was cut off and the neck stitched up.

The most common food was the plantain, but the people also grew and used large quantities of millet of two or three kinds, a kind of pea known as *pokya*, and beans and maize. Sweet potatoes were grown by a few and also marrows and small tomatoes, though these were not generally used.

The people kept a few cows, but they cooked the milk into cakes and rarely drank it fresh.

Food was eaten straight from the pot, and a man with his wife and family sat round one pot, helping themselves with their hands. A visitor never ate with the family, but was given a share some distance away. A man was expected to supply food for his parents in their old age, and he generally built a house for them near his own so that he could easily attend to their needs.

There was no tribal government, but each clan had its own head who settled serious matters within the clan and also dealt with disputes arising between members of different clans. Each village had also its head-man, who settled ordinary cases of dispute, but any difficult matters had to be submitted to the head or father of the clan. Cases of murder, the kidnapping of women and all matters in which another clan was concerned had to be brought before him.

There was no regular tribute given either to the head of the clan or to the head-man of the village, but both expected to receive gifts of beer about harvest time from the men under them.

The Bagesu sometimes bought slaves, but these were treated as members of the family. Girls were married into the tribe and boys were adopted and allowed to inherit property.

The members of this tribe did not consider fire as in any way sacred. If it could not be obtained in any other way they would make it with fire-sticks, but they preferred, when possible, to carry it with them, in the form of a smouldering torch of wood or tow, or to obtain it from some other member of the clan.

CHAPTER II

RELIGION

The creator—offerings—rock and water spirits—god of plague—god of smallpox—sacred skulls and stones—rain-making—punishment of rain-maker—rain-making ceremonies

THE religious ideas of the Bagesu were vague and unformed, and though there was a belief in a creator, known as *Weri Kubumba,* he was not often troubled with requests of any kind. It was to him that offerings were made during the ceremonies of initiation, and his priest conveyed his blessing to the boys who were undergoing the rites. He might, also, be appealed to at times in cases of serious illness.

If there was a year in which the cows did not bear well, the herdsmen took them to a specially prepared shrine; one barren cow was offered to the god by the priest, who then drank beer that had been blessed and puffed it over the other cows. The dedicated cow was killed and a feast made for all the cow-owners, after which the herds were taken back to their places.

Certain rocks or large boulders were believed to be the homes of different spirits, who at times demanded particular attention and offerings. Very often the chief or head-man of a village near one of these rocks acted as priest or medium for the spirit and would inform the people when the spirit desired a shrine to be built and offerings to be made. The following paragraphs from the *Northern Bantu* give further particulars regarding these rock-spirits:

When a spirit appears to an elder, he announces the fact to his village and orders a shrine to be built at the base of some rock and offerings to be made. The wealthier people take goats, others take fowls, and the children carry plantains or sweet potatoes. The animals are offered and killed, the blood is caught in a vessel and left in the shrine for the spirit, and the meat and food are cooked and eaten by the people on the spot. After one of these visions the elder of the village takes two fowls to the rock and dedicates them to the spirit. One fowl he kills and eats on the spot, the other he takes home to breed, the eggs being saved and hatched, and the chickens reared and cared for until there are enough to exchange for a female goat. The goat is then kept, together with any young it has, until the elder is able to exchange them for a cow, when this and any calves it has are kept for the spirit by the elder, who may use the milk, and the animals continue to breed and form a herd of cows.

Mothers frequently betake themselves to a rock-spirit when a child falls sick, or when it does not make the progress it should. An offering is made at the base of some rock and she calls to the spirit to have pity on her child and make it well and strong. A man or a woman who is in delicate health will also go to a rock, make an offering and ask the spirit to make him well.

Waterfall-spirits. Each waterfall is supposed to have a spirit, and these spirits are thought to be of the greatest help to mothers to make their children thrive. A mother will take her water-pot and climb the steep side of the mountain, get between the rock and the falling water, fill a pot with it and carry it home. 'It is a dangerous and a difficult task, calling for a cool head and strong nerves. The water is used to sprinkle over the head of the child and is said to give it health and to make it thrive.

Gibini was the god of plague, and to him offerings were made when plague attacked anyone. The people offered meat and vegetable food beside trees which were planted before the house, and then, saying "We leave you yours and we eat ours," they took some of the meat and ran away into the forest, where they ate it and deceived the god by returning by a different way.

Enundu, taking his name from the disease, was the god of smallpox, to whom a goat was offered whenever the disease appeared.

The only part of a dead man which was not destroyed was his skull, which was kept in the house or set upon a stone outside. A large stone was always placed near the door for the residence of the ghost, and this was called *Mboge*. Frequent if not daily offerings of food and beer were made beside this stone and prayers were offered to the ghost which was supposed to possess it.

RAIN-MAKING

The rain-maker was one of the most important and influential men of the tribe. His ability to procure the kind of weather that was wanted was considered beyond dispute and when rain did not come after he had gone through his incantations, no one dreamt of considering him incapable, they said he had not exerted himself and must be induced to use all his power. When the weather continued dry and the people wanted rain, they visited the rain-maker, taking with them a number of fowls of either sex and any colour, and also some food, as gifts to him. He might, however, refuse to act without something more, and might demand a goat or a cow, which he had seen somewhere and coveted. This would then have to be brought before he would begin his work.

When he considered that the gifts were sufficient, he arranged in his house his fetishes, which he kept covered until they were needed, and told them that he wanted rain. He offered a fowl to rejoice the heart of the god and usually smeared some of the blood on the fetishes. Then, going to a well, he brought to the house a pot of water into which he put certain herbs. Up to this point the work was done in his house, but now he brought out the fetishes and sprinkled them with the medicated water from the pot. He also sprinkled the water upwards towards heaven and round him on every side, calling upon the spirit to give rain.

Should this attempt fail, the people brought further presents and the man tried again, but should the rain still refuse to come, the people began to threaten him, and after warning him once or twice, they beat him, carried off all his goods, and burned his house. When such extreme measures had been taken and still no rain fell, they came to the conclusion that they had been too severe in their treatment and they would return all his goods, adding presents, and beg him to bring rain.

When rain had continued too long and dry weather was wanted, the medicine-man went out to a spot where he had planted some sacred trees. There he called to his fetishes and waved his sacred stick to drive away the clouds. If this was unsuccessful, he scraped up some sand soaked with rain which had fallen from the roof of his house, and wrapped it in a bundle of grass. This he took into his house and put over the fire, so that as it dried it would dry up the rain. If his methods failed, the people treated him in the same way as when he would not bring rain, but he could usually terrify them by the threat that he would retaliate by drying up the rain when it was wanted or sending it when it was not wanted.

More elaborate rain-making ceremonies are described in the *Northern Bantu* as follows:

The usual procedure of a rain-maker is to take two fowls which some suppliant has brought. One fowl he kills by hitting it on the head with a sacred stick; he then cuts it open from the under-side of the beak to the tail, removes the entrails and examines them for marks, these markings being the signs which enable him to tell when the rain may be expected. Some markings cause him to re-place the entrails in the fowl and expose it to the heat of the sun; after a time he shakes the fowl about, and, if the entrails make a noise, he announces that there will be a strong wind which will destroy the crops. The second fowl is killed after the manner of the first and is intended to confirm the inferences drawn from it. Should the rain still delay, the people threaten the man and, unless it comes then, they carry out their threats and punish him, because they are convinced he has the ability to help them and is not using his influence. In most instances, after making an attack upon the rain-maker, the people restore his property, thinking that otherwise the god will be angry with them for their doings, and they make special offerings to the man for the damage they have done.

The rain-maker may consent to take the extreme measure of climbing the mountain and paying a visit to the deity on the top, a step which he asserts is fraught with danger to him and may cost him his life. A black ox and a quantity of beer are brought and taken up the mountain by several village elders, who accompany the rain-maker to a plateau near the top. Here the ox is killed and eaten by the company, with the exception of one leg, at a sacred meal at which the blood is offered to the god. The leg is carried up the mountain to a priest who lives near a sacred pool in which is said to be a large snake which is the god. This pool is the spring which supplies many of the waterfalls upon the mountain. The priest takes the meat and hears the request of the rain-maker. The priest and rain-maker then make a trough of clay near the pool and pour the beer into it. The priest stands near the trough and puts a long beer-tube into the spring in order to suck a little water through it. The snake resents this, for it guards the spring against any person drawing water and is said to capture any man who rashly attempts to do so. When, therefore, the priest attempts to draw water, the snake darts forth and winds its deadly coils round him, but the odour of the beer saves him, for the reptile smells it, hastily uncoils itself, drinks the beer and is soon helplessly drunk. As soon as the men see it is helpless, they break its fangs and proceed rapidly to fill a number of water-pots from the sacred spring, arranging them round the pool. The water thus drawn and set on the top of the mountain will without fail bring rain, which will continue to fall daily until the priest takes steps to stop it by emptying the pots again. The rain-maker descends the mountain with the elders who have waited for him on the upper plateau and in a short time rain begins to pour down.

The rain-maker now waits, knowing that the people will soon come with offerings and requests to have the rain stopped. When the people have had enough rain and see that their crops will be spoiled for want of sunshine, they go in a body to the rain-maker to beg for sunshine. The rain-maker has now to make a second visit to the serpent-god with an offering of beer, and has to go with the priest through a similar performance to that above described in order to make the god drunk, after which he empties the pots and turns them bottom upwards to ensure sunshine. Thus the harvest is assured. the seasons are readjusted and the year proceeds in its proper course.

CHAPTER III

OCCUPATIONS OF THE BAGESU

Possession of land—cultivation of millet—sowing the seed—harvest—granaries—the firstfruits—plantains—other crops—beer from millet and plantains—harvest festival—tobacco—cows, goats, sheep, and fowls—building houses—interior of a house—ghost-stones—potters—smiths—hunting—fishing—warfare

AGRICULTURE

WHEN the Bagesu settled on Elgon, the different clans took possession of land on the upper slopes of the ridges and this land was meted out to sub-divisions and within these sub-divisions to the families. These plots of land might never pass out of the sub-division which had taken possession of them, but they might be given by the head-man to different members. When a man was given a new plot and cultivated it, it became his own and he could pass it on to his family. As families grew and increased it became necessary to take in more land, and the fields gradually extended down the slopes. When the arrival of the British guaranteed their safety from raids, the descent became much more rapid, and the lower valleys and slopes and then the plains were brought under cultivation. The old fields, however, still remained the property of the different clans and members of other clans might not encroach.

The main crop, and now practically the only crop which is grown on the higher slopes, was the small millet, *bulo*. This was as a rule planted only once a year, though at times a catch crop might be raised. They seldom sowed in the same land for more than a few years, for they preferred to let it rest and break up new land or re-plant land that had been resting. The men did the first rough work of cutting down the shrubs and coarse grass and preparing the place for digging, but the women turned up the soil with wooden hoes or digging sticks, for until within recent years iron hoes were unknown. In the *Northern Bantu*, I have noted the fact that women did the rough digging, leaving the work to be finished by the men. This arrangement is to be found among some of the clans on the south-east slopes of the mountain, and is opposed to the practice of most tribes. In later years, the people bought hoes from smiths of other nations and used them until they were worn out, when the local smiths made them into spears or knives. There were originally no smiths in the tribe, and those who appeared in later days made only knives, arrow-heads, and spears. The earth was turned over with hoes or digging sticks to a depth of some eight or ten inches, and the grain was sown upon this land without further preparation.

Sometimes before a woman sowed, she took some of her seed to be blessed by a medicine-man and mixed this with the remainder; as a rule, however, she paid no attention to such precautions, but simply set out in the early morning with the basket of seed and a few hot embers or a smouldering torch to make a fire. When she reached her field she first lit her fire, to which she would retire for rest and to light her pipe. During the sowing the fire had to be guarded lest anyone should take any of it, for this would rob the grain of its vitality. The woman sometimes put a few seeds in her pipe and blew the smoke over the field to make the seed grow. A pot of beer was sometimes poured out on a new field before the sowing took place to secure the favour of the earth spirit. With her hoe or stick the woman raised a little earth to a depth of two or three inches, dropped in a few seeds, and pushed back the earth with her foot; then taking a short pace she repeated the performance. Sometimes the husband assisted his wife with the sowing, and then she made the holes for the seed while he followed, dropping two or three grains in each hole and pushing a little earth over them with his foot.

When the crop had grown to a height of about three inches, the husband weeded it and thinned it out, leaving the plants some twelve inches apart, and as it grew he helped to protect it from wild animals, especially pigs. In some places it was necessary to guard the crops by night, and for this purpose the men built huts in the fields and kept fires burning brightly. The presence of a man with a fire was generally enough to keep animals at a distance. The crop usually grew to a height of some eighteen inches, and when the grain was in the ear, children were employed from early morning until dusk in driving off birds.

When the grain was ripe, husband and wife had to work together to reap the harvest, but before any of the new corn was used for food, some of it was gathered and sent, with a little of the last year's corn and a fowl, to a medicine-man, who offered them to a special deity before anyone in the village might partake of the new corn. Such an offering freed the village from taboo and enabled its members to begin eating the new crop. The heads of grain were cut off short and either spread to dry on ground prepared in the field or tied up in bundles and carried to the hard ground before the hut door, where they were covered at night with plantain leaves. When dry, the grain was stored in the ear, the granaries being large wicker baskets with movable covers, four to five feet high and three feet in diameter, raised from the ground on tree stumps or large stones. The baskets were smeared on the inside and sometimes on the outside with dung, to protect the grain from the weather and from insects and to keep it from leaking through the wicker-work. From these stores the grain was taken out, threshed with short sticks, and winnowed when required.

The first of the crop had to be eaten by the man and his wife together; if he was not at home, the wife used the grain, but put aside a piece of the first porridge cooked for him to eat on his return.

Plantains of several kinds, some used for food and some for beer, were grown, but the trees seldom bore well because of the cold on the high slopes of the mountain. Now, however, that the people have come further down towards the plains, the upper slopes are left for millet and plantains are grown in the valleys. The women did the digging when cultivating plantains, and the men pruned the trees. The plantain as food was generally eaten boiled, as they cooked potatoes, and it was found very useful when their supply of grain ran short, for the trees bore all the year round.

Sweet potatoes were in general use and semsem was grown but was not used as a food. It was ground, mixed with water and boiled, when possible a little salt was added, and it was eaten with other food as a relish. Maize, beans, marrows, and small tomatoes were also grown as luxuries.

Each wife had her own field and kept her own store of food, and a husband visited his wives in turn and ate with them. When he wanted beer they all contributed a share, and when guests came, the men were given one house and the women another, the two parties drinking separately.

Brewing

After the harvest had been reaped brewing commenced, and the people used for this all the grain they could spare. This was prepared by being threshed, sifted, mixed with a little water, and left for about five days until it sprouted, when it was dried in the sun, baked, and ground to a coarse flour. To this flour water was added and this was left standing for two days, when boiling water was poured on it and it was drunk while hot.

When beer was made from plantains, the fruit was hung over the fire and thus artificially ripened, after which it was pulped in large wooden troughs. The juice was drained off into pots and a little malt, that is, millet prepared as described above, was added. After having stood for two days, this was ready for use. This beer was not very intoxicating, but after the men had sat for hours drinking it through long tubes, they were completely under its influence.

Harvest Festival

When the beer was ready, the members from all the clans gathered at the villages for the beer drinking, of which something has already been said. Men and women went together to the different villages, but the women had their own pots and drank as freely as the men, though they were not expected to wander so far in search of the beer as the men did. Both parties sat round their pots at different distances according to the length of their tubes, and talked and drank until they were too helpless to go on longer, when they were carried away to sleep off the effects of the drink. Sometimes a man and his wife would take turns in drinking. The man would drink until he could stand no more, when his wife would put him to bed and care for him until he recovered. She would then take her turn at the drinking and he would care for her. When the beer at one village was exhausted the company went on to another where the drinking was resumed.

Dancing was also indulged in at these festivals, drums and bells being the only instruments used. Under the influence of the beer and the excitement of dancing, all restraint was thrown off and free love was indulged in, though there were a few men who even then jealously guarded their wives. If there was a moon, and the new moon was invariably awaited

before the festivities began, the dancing and drinking would
go on far into the night.

TOBACCO

Tobacco has been in use for so long that no one can tell
how it was introduced. The women grew it on the dust-heaps
near the houses, where they could guard it. Both the ashes
of the fire and the sweepings of the house, in which the animals
were kept by night, were thrown upon this heap, so that the
ground was rich and the plants flourished luxuriantly. When
the leaves were fully grown the women plucked and pounded
them, being careful not to lose the juice, and made them into
cakes, which were dried in the sun until they were a rich dark
colour, when they were considered ready for use and were
stored in the house.

Both men and women smoked tobacco, but women never
chewed it, whereas men at times did so. Of recent years
Indian hemp has been grown and is smoked by many of the
people, much to their detriment.

DOMESTIC ANIMALS

The Bagesu kept only a few cows, three or four being the
largest number possessed by any man, because the chief
object was to gather a sufficient number and with them to
purchase another wife. The cows were kept in the houses by
night and were herded by either men or women, there being
no restrictions to prevent the wife or daughter from looking
after the cattle, and even children frequently herded the
cows with the goats. Several children would combine to do
the work, leaving the animals to roam about on the hill-
sides whilst they played their games. These cows were small,
and hardy enough to endure the cold of the mountains and
also the heat of the day in the more sheltered spots. Like
most African cows they gave little milk, two to three pints
being all that could safely be taken without depriving the calf
of its necessary nourishment. The milk was never drunk fresh
but was boiled, sometimes with salt, until all the moisture

was gone, leaving a cake which was eaten. Butter was chiefly used for smearing on the body, though it was sometimes added to food.

While in the huts the cows were tied by the neck, but a bull was always left free. When a cow calved, the milk for the first three or four days was cooked and the cake eaten by small children.

Each householder had his goats and a few sheep, the latter being always poor miserable-looking creatures, with but little flesh. Goats were the more prized, not only because they multiplied more rapidly, but also because they grew bigger and were always in better condition. Both goats and sheep were tied to pegs in the floor round the side of the hut by night, sheep and female goats by the neck and male goats by the leg. These animals, however, were never kept in great numbers, for the tribe was pre-eminently agricultural, and animals were used mainly as currency, for obtaining wives or for the payment of debts.

Fowls were also kept, and a small cage was built for them on one side of the house to keep them from wild cats by night. They were never fed, but had to hunt for their own food, with the natural result that they were seldom in good condition for the table.

BUILDING

When a man made up his mind that he would leave his old home and build a new house, he first consulted various auguries to see if the ghosts approved of his intention, and if the move would be to his advantage. He arranged the site of the house with the head-man of the village in which he intended to settle, and took up his abode with friends or relatives near the place. He had to observe only two taboos of importance during the time of building: if during the building a child was born in the house where he was staying, he did not go to work for four days, and if a dog had puppies, he stayed at home two days.

The man then cut his trees and carried them to the appointed site. He had to prepare a number of stout stakes some five feet long for the outer walls, a central post and four others to support the roof, a quantity of slender saplings or bamboos to make the roof, and grass for thatching.

When all the materials had been collected, he called to-gether his friends to help him in levelling the ground, for the site was usually on the side of a hill. A circle was then marked out and a shallow trench dug, in which the stakes for the outer wall were planted a few inches deep, making a wall about four or five feet high. These were laced together with creeper rope in two places, about half-way up and again near the top. The posts for carrying the roof were put in, a long one in the centre which decided the pitch of the roof, and four others round it. At times the owner would do the work up to this point himself, but in any case he now called in his friends to help in the finishing of the house, and he brewed a quantity of beer, which was the only payment given to those who as-sisted him in the work.

The saplings or bamboos were arranged radiating from the central post to the outer wall, upon which they rested, looking like the ribs of a great umbrella, and the spaces between them were filled with smaller bamboos, or with elephant grass, laced together with bark rope, and on this frame-work was laid a grass thatch. The ends of the roof-poles were cut so that all projected to an even length over the wall. The grass used as thatch was a coarse kind which grew about a foot and a half long. The root ends were laid uppermost and each layer was placed a few inches higher than the one before, thus making a good thick layer of thatch, and on the pinnacle was a tuft so arranged as to make the point of the roof water-tight.

The wife and her friends then plastered mud over the walls, filling up all the crevices and smoothing the mud with their hands. When the walls were smooth, they smeared them with cow-dung, sometimes mixed with mud. The women also made the floor smooth by beating the earth with the palms of the hands or with the flat side of hoes.

The fire-place was in the centre of the hut near the central post, against which a flat stone was placed to keep it from being burned. The fire was usually brought from another house though, if there was difficulty in procuring it, they made it with fire-sticks, for there was no ritual for the use of fire. There was no chimney or outlet for the smoke except the doorway, but the conical roof drew it up and it filtered through the thatch. No window was ever considered necessary, for the door afforded all the light and air the inhabitants required.

In most of the houses there was no furniture, and the majority of the people slept on the floor near the fire without covering of any kind. In a few cases among the more enlightened people beds might be found. Four posts with forked tops were planted in the ground and in the forks were fixed side- and foot- and head-pieces. Very rough cross-pieces were laid over these and the whole was covered with a cow-skin.

To one side of the doorway one or two large stones were at times placed, and on them might be put the skull of some member of the family who had died. Before these stones beer was poured out for the ghost and other offerings were made. A small shrine for some family ghost might also be found near, and sometimes reeds or trees were planted in front of the house and a few shells were hung on them; these were for the residence of some ghost which had been troubling the family.

POTTERS

Both men and women were potters, but their work was very primitive and the vessels very irregular in shape. Their clay, which they called *lidiri*, was procured from the river beds; and they were careful always to bake their pots between new and full moon and not while it was waning. Any woman with child had to keep away from the pots while they were being made, and no women except the makers might approach during the baking; but their taboos were few and not of much importance.

SMITHS

There were very few smiths and no smelters; indeed iron-stone was not known, and the smiths bought their metal ready for use. They made only spears and knives and rough ornaments. Spades and hoes the people bought ready made from Kitara and Busoga.

HUNTING

Various wild animals, mostly small antelope, were hunted for the sake of their meat, but others, such as lions or leopards, were only hunted when they became troublesome and attacked people. Lions were not common, though a stray beast might wander into the mountain for a few days, but leopards were plentiful, and when one was killed the meat was eaten and the skin used as a rug or sold. Though a few people understood and used nets, practically all hunting was done with the spear.

Herds of elephants occasionally appeared in the district, when a hunting party would be formed and an attempt made to kill one. At one time their only value lay in their meat, but in later years the ivory was sold to traders. When men went out to hunt elephants, the chief hunters concealed themselves in the branches of trees with spears, which were made with heavy shafts and attached by a rope to the tree. Other men acted as beaters and drove the animals under the trees where the hunters could kill them with their spears. The man who first speared an elephant claimed the tusks, which he sold; but there was no specific method of dividing the meat, and the men simply fought for what they could get.

Should a man be killed when out hunting, they brought the body home, in order, they said, that they might mourn. The real reason, however, was that the mourners might hold their feast on the flesh and that the proper ceremonies to release the ghost for its journey to the other world might be carried out.

Large herbivorous rats were a favourite food, and various methods were adopted to catch these animals. Some men might beat the grass, while others remained by the runs and caught or struck the rats with sticks as they ran along. They sometimes also used snares, which consisted of a string with a noose attached to a bent stick in such a way that the rat in passing through the noose released the stick and was caught and strangled.

FISHING

Fish was a favourite food, and men living near streams followed various methods of fishing. They sometimes caught them by hand, but the most common method was to dam a stream and divert its water into pools into which they waded, catching the fish in wicker baskets. Fish were cooked and eaten fresh, or dried over wood fires and boiled when needed.

WARFARE

Clans had frequent disputes, and petty wars of clan against clan were common, while lonely pedestrians would be attacked and even killed by fellow-tribesmen of different clans. War on a larger scale was often caused by an attack by some daring spirits of one clan on the cattle of another while they were out at pasture. As soon as the theft had been committed, the war-horns were sounded and drums were beaten and men from all parts came to join in the fight. The attackers retreated to a hill and the opposing force gathered on another facing them. As soon as a large enough army had come together they advanced until they could shoot their arrows and throw their spears. The arrows were the more effective weapon, for they were always treated with a virulent poison and even a scratch was certain to cause death. The men too were very skilful in their use and very accurate in aim.

As the excitement grew men would rush out from the main bodies and meet each other in hand-to-hand combats. The fall of one of these warriors had an immediate effect on the army to which he belonged and might even put them to flight. When one party fled the others would follow them up into their territory, plundering and burning their houses as they passed along. Any men who were overtaken or who were found wounded were killed, a hand was cut off and tied to a stick and the victor carried it aloft in triumph; women and children were captured and carried off.

When a man who had killed one of the enemy reached home, he had to be purified before he might enter his house. His relatives brought him a goat which he killed, smearing the contents of the stomach upon himself, his wife, the children, and the door-posts. Until he was thus purified he had to eat apart from his companions, taking his food from a bowl with a stick, but after this cleansing he returned to his ordinary life and rejoined his wife in the house.

Wounded men were if possible brought home by their companions and were treated with care. They said that the *Mulindi*, that is, the relatives who ate the dead, came and carried away the bodies of the slain, for should the body be left to decay, the ghost would attack children with various diseases. The relatives of a dead man would keep up a feud against the clan who had killed him and would watch for years for an opportunity of killing some member of it in order to satisfy the ghost; for nothing short of death could compensate for death.

The Bankoko from the south of the mountain would never unite with men of clans from the north against any enemy, for they were deadly foes and only met in amity during the harvest festivals, when the members might even intermarry.

CHAPTER IV

BIRTH, INITIATION, AND MARRIAGE

Taboos during pregnancy—birth—naming children—period of seclusion —death of children—weaning children—making a child sit up—the first teeth—birth of twins—bringing-out of twins—death of twins— training children—extracting teeth—adoption—initiation—cicatrization by girls—initiation of boys—preparation—initiation festival— taking the oath—circumcision—feast after healing—marriage— fornication—clan exogamy and polygamy—arranging marriages—bringing the bride—marriage before initiation—taboos concerning parents-in-law—divorce and adultery

WHEN a woman conceived, her husband's father was informed and he sent a cow in return for the good news. This was killed, and the husband, the wife, and the members of the clan feasted on the meat. A woman during pregnancy observed no restrictions or food taboos, and she might arrange her diet to suit herself. Her husband had to refrain from climbing any trees or high rocks or on to house roofs, and when walking down a hill he had to go carefully, for should he slip and fall, his wife might have a miscarriage.

When the time of birth approached, several friends of the woman came to be with her, but one person, as a rule the husband's mother or aunt, was chosen to act as midwife. The expectant woman stood by a post in the house, and one of the assistants held her under the arms and raised her up and down in order to shake the child down and help on the birth. The midwife stood in front of the patient to receive the child; when it was born she tied the cord a few inches from it and cut it with a strip of reed from the roof. The baby was handed to one of the assistants, who washed its head, face, and mouth, and started respiration. The midwife then waited for the afterbirth, which in most cases was carefully buried outside near the house, in a place where the refuse from the house was afterwards thrown. In some clans, however, the afterbirth was simply thrown out and left for dogs or wild animals to devour.

A little beer was poured out at the post where the child was born, and two trees, named *mbaga* and *mwima*, were planted in front of the house near the door for the residence of the good spirit who came to be the guardian of the child.

The child was named as soon as possible after its birth, by the father if it was a boy and by the mother if it was a girl. In either case, it was called after some deceased ancestor of the father's clan whose ghost was then expected to look after it. If the child did not thrive, the parents consulted a medicine-man, who took an augury, and would sometimes advise them to change the child's name, for the ghost whose name it bore was causing the trouble and another ghost had to be called upon to befriend it.

For fifteen days after the birth, the mother remained in

seclusion in the house, and when this period was over she was taken out and washed all over and the hair on both head and body was shaved off. While she was undergoing this purification, the house was swept out and cleaned.

Children often died at birth or in infancy, and the bodies were thrown out into the bush as with adults. It is most probable that these bodies were eaten as were those of adults after death, but it is difficult to obtain proof.

Women were said to have as many as ten children, but as a rule only about half of them lived. A woman whose children died in infancy had usually a large number, for she returned to her husband and probably became pregnant again very soon, whereas if she were nursing a child she kept away from him for two to three years. A child was generally not weaned until the mother had become pregnant again; there was no ceremony at weaning—the child was simply kept by a relative in some place where it did not see its mother.

When a child was three months old, the mother took it to her mother, who put it to sit on the floor. A goat was killed and a feast took place with much beer-drinking. It was usual for the children of the village to take part in this feast.

Little importance was attached to the order in which the first teeth were cut, though if the lower teeth came first it was considered satisfactory.

TWINS

When the midwife saw that there were twins, she might not remove the children from the spot where they were born before she had obtained the sanction of the medicine-man. He was therefore speedily summoned and was given a fowl which he offered to the gods. After the sacrifice he closed the house against visitors, the husband remaining in one half of it, while the wife and children were in the other.

The cord of each child was cut as in the case of other children and the placenta carried to some place near the house and buried where the sweepings from the hut might be thrown upon the spot. In the early morning, in the evening, and at intervals during the day, two small drums, one for each child, were beaten.

On the third day, the heads of the twins were shaved and their nails pared and then for seven months the father collected fowls, goats and promises of food for the ceremony of bringing the twins out for inspection. The father's parents killed a goat while the mother's parents brought fowls, and large quantities of beer were brewed. The members of the two clans gathered and danced in two parties, the father leading his relatives and the mother hers. They drank beer and blew it over the members of the other party as they danced, the idea, as in other tribes, being to divert from themselves any evil which might be attached to the twins and cast it on the other clan.

There was greatest rejoicing when the twins were one of each sex; for should they both be of one sex, the parent who was not represented knew that the wrath of the gods was for some reason directed against him, and he and his clan had to make many offerings to pacify them.

Should one of the children die before this bringing-out ceremony, a small hut was built over the spot where the placenta was buried and the body was placed in it. One of the drums was removed and only one was beaten daily.

Until they were fully grown, children who were twins wore special anklets, but after puberty and marriage they ceased to be thus distinguished from ordinary people.

Boys and girls were taught to be useful at as early an age as possible. Boys had to go and learn to herd and care for the goats and sheep, and girls had to dig in the fields, carry firewood and water, and learn to cook. At the age of about eight or ten years, both girls and boys had the two lower incisors extracted. This was not a compulsory operation, but anyone who refused to have it done was looked upon as a coward and called "animal" and "monkey."

People seldom adopted children and when they did there was no ceremony. Adoption was rarely permanent and the child would be sent back to its own home after a time.

INITIATION

About the age of ten or twelve years girls of the Bagesu began to make on the body and forehead the markings which were the sign of clan membership. The wounds were made with an iron needle with a point at one end and a ring at the other, which was put round the finger, the needle being curved so that it lay round the back of the hand. The girl carried this about with her and made the wounds on her body herself, though those on the forehead had to be made by someone else. She pinched up a little skin, ran the needle through it, and then made an incision down to the needle at right angles to it. She rubbed wood ashes into the wound and left it to heal; as the wounds often festered and were very painful, it took some time to complete the markings. When healed the keloids stood out in hard lumps like warts, those on the forehead being as large as peas. Some were made oval in shape and others round, and they were arranged in lines, spaced in different ways according to the fashion of the clan to which the girl belonged. Four lines of keloids were usually made running from the breasts downwards, and two lines on the forehead running down the temples. A woman who had not these keloids would not be accepted in marriage and was not allowed to join the grown women as one of them, for she was still looked upon as a child.

Boys had to go through an elaborate ceremony of initiation and a form of circumcision before they were considered fit for marriage or to take part in the councils of the men of the clan. No force was employed to induce the boys to undergo this ceremony, but until they had been operated upon, they were regarded as children and might not wear clothing or join the men either in the councils or in beer-drinking. Parents and friends were therefore anxious for the boys to be initiated as early as possible. No account was kept of a child's age, but as soon as a boy showed signs of reaching puberty, he was told that he should prepare himself to attend the next initiation ceremonies.

These ceremonies took place as a rule every second or third year in each district, and the people chose a year when the harvest was plentiful so that they might brew large quantities of beer and make great preparations. If the harvest yield was a poor one, the ceremony was postponed until another year.

The boys who decided to undergo the ceremony met daily for some two to four months before the day appointed for the event, and they went from village to village dancing and receiving presents from the people. These presents always consisted of animals or fowls and they were collected together at the village in which the ceremony was to take place, because hundreds of people gathered there for the event and all had to be fed and entertained. The boys were led by a man who knew the songs they were expected to sing and undertook to train them. He took them from place to place to dance, and as he sang he instructed them in various clan matters which were of a public character and not of great importance, for the more careful teaching of the clan secrets was undertaken in private by old men appointed by the clan. There was no tune in the songs; words were simply drawled out in a sort of rhythm to which the boys stamped their feet as they moved round in a circle. Whenever they could get them they wore thigh bells, which were three or four iron bells like cow-bells, strung round the right thigh so that they rattled as the wearer stamped to the rhythm. The boys' faces and bodies were painted with red ochre and well oiled, and they carried reeds or thin bamboos which they held aloft as they stamped about and sang.

The time set for the ceremony was two or three days after the appearance of the new moon, when the boys from the different villages met at an arranged place. In the early morning of the appointed day, a priest with one or more followers, one of whom was the chief in whose village the ceremony was taking place, went to the mountain shrine of the creator, *Weri*, which was under the shade of a large tree and near a spring of water. They took with them a fowl, usually white, and two eggs; the fowl was offered to the god

PLATE V

Bagesu initiation dance

Bagesu initiation dance. Thigh bells

PLATE VI

Instructing the youths upon taking the oath

Giving the youths roots to chew
to strengthen them

and was then killed and left at the foot of the sacred tree, while the eggs were broken in the path for a snake who was supposed to be in the tree[1].

The boys, of whom there might be a dozen or more, were then brought by the priest and the chief to the forest. If there were among them any sons of chiefs or wealthy men, one or more bulls might be available for the feast, but failing sons of wealthy men, there would be only goats. One animal was taken with them to the forest and offered to the god, after which it was killed and the contents of the stomach, mixed with water, were smeared over the bodies of the boys. A plentiful supply of cooked vegetable food and beer had also been brought, and the meat of the animal which had been offered to the god was cooked and eaten with this as a sacred meal, while the priest pronounced the god's blessing on each boy.

When the meal was over and they had drunk freely of the beer, the boys went back to the village, going the whole way at a rapid trot, for they were not allowed to walk. If a second bull had been given by one of the fathers, it was killed near the place where the ceremony was to take place, and the meat was taken to the house of the head-man of the village, where the priest cut it into small pieces and, climbing to the top of the house, threw it among the assembled people in the name of the boy whose father had given it. There was a great scramble for the pieces of meat, for they were believed to confer a special blessing if taken home and eaten. The breast was hung round the boy's neck for a time before being removed and eaten.

By this time it would be noon, and dancing went on vigorously, the excitement increasing rapidly. The boys pranced up and down a space about two hundred yards long, brandishing their heavy clubs or sticks in the air. From time to time one of them rushed into the surrounding crowd, striking about

---

[1] In many parts of Africa a green tree snake with an orange tint underneath it near the head, frequents trees by springs to feed upon small birds as they come to the water. This snake is invariably sacred.

in a furious manner. He was said to be under the influence of some spirit and to be driving off an evil ghost; he was usually completely regardless as to where his blows fell and struck at anyone who was not quick enough to get out of his way, so that serious wounds and often deaths were caused at this time. From the appearance of the eyes of the boys I saw undergoing these ceremonies, I concluded that the state of possession was feigned; though they were at a high pitch of excitement, most of them clearly knew what they were doing. The spectators who surrounded the youths and followed them about shared in the excitement, and women often became hysterical and shook all over, dancing, as the people said, under the influence of the spirit.

Early in the afternoon, the boys were summoned by the chief and rushed away to the mountain where the priest awaited them at the shrine. Each boy was again blessed and his face and body was smeared with white clay. This visit took about an hour and by that time the boys, with the beer and the dancing, were in such a state of excitement that someone was needed to guide and help them as they returned to their own villages. This journey had again to be performed at a run; the priest and his assistants followed them, and they were operated upon at their own villages.

When the boys arrived they stood in a line and a log was placed behind them, which they might later use as a seat if necessary. Plantain leaves, sometimes one for each boy, sometimes one between two or three, were laid on the ground in front of them. Each leaf was arranged like a dish and in it was put an egg, covered with a thin piece of gourd, and a little water; a bunch of sacred herbs was placed beside each. A group of excited admirers stood round the youths, singing to them and keeping up their courage and the excitement. The boys stood erect and now and then jumped into the air with both feet together, keeping their legs straight and their arms stretched above their heads.

An elderly man came forward and described to the boys their duty to the clan, admonishing them to be faithful.

PLATE VII

Performing the operation

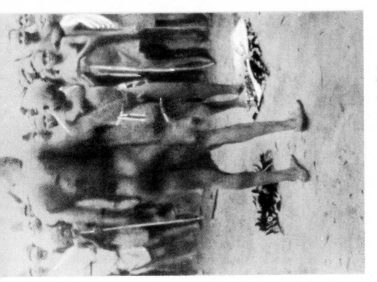

Taking the oath

Bagesu Initiation Ceremony

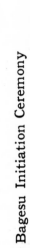

When they had agreed, by an exclamation of "Eh!" to follow the customs and rules of the clan, he took the bunch of herbs, dipped it in the water, and sprinkled each with a sharp swish on the face and chest. One of the youths next jumped forward with his feet together until he reached the plantain, then, making three jumps in the air, still keeping his legs straight, he came down the third time on the leaf and the egg. It was not necessary to break the egg, and in some places one egg did for three or four boys.

When all had thus sealed their vows, a man came with a packet of sacred powder, some of which he placed on a knife-blade and poured upon the boys' heads to give blessing and courage. The mother of a boy also often came forward at this time with a root for her son to chew, which was supposed to check excessive bleeding.

When the boys were all ready, a medicine-man, who had been concealed in one of the huts, came out with a large knife, which looked anything but aseptic. Approaching the first boy he pulled the foreskin forward as far as it would stretch and cut it off, throwing it at the boy's feet. He did not stop to examine his work but passed on to the next boy until he had finished the row, when he went away. The boys paid no attention to what was being done but stood with their arms stretched up and each jumped in the air as soon as the man had passed on to the next one. Another medicine-man followed with an assistant, who held the penis out at full length while the medicine-man pinched up and cut off every bit of skin except a strip along the passage underneath. This took some minutes for he was quite deliberate and cast each bit of skin on the ground at the boy's feet as he cut it off. When he had finished the boy had to keep his arms raised and jump into the air coming down upon his own skin and blood and shouting a special cry. Meanwhile old people examined the member to see that the work was properly done. When the next boy's operation was over, the first might sit down on the log behind him; no dressing was applied, but they waited until all were finished, when they were led away to a special house, where they remained until they were healed. When they had left the place, the foreskin and blood of each were scraped up and buried.

The parents usually stood behind their sons during the operation to encourage them, and to chastise them if they showed signs of fear. The father would whip a nervous boy and, taking blood from one who had already been operated upon, would smear it on his mouth to give him courage, for a boy who showed fear was afterwards treated with scorn. Fainting, however, was not regarded as weak or cowardly, and a boy was caught by the people behind and put to sit on the log; a pregnant woman was brought and dropped millet seeds upon his face and neck to restore him. Boys as a rule healed quickly, and though now and then one would die from excessive bleeding, it was not common.

The morning after the operation two or three elderly women visited the boys and examined them to see that the work had been properly done. Should they find any skin still remaining they cut it off at once.

From one to two months was allowed for healing, and then they were taken to a river where they were washed and shaved and smeared with white clay. Each boy was given a new skin, which was the dress of a full-grown man, and his father presented him with a spear, bow, and arrows. The medicine-man made an offering of a fowl to the god and the boys presented the medicine-man with rings and bracelets. A cow was then killed and a feast made.

These ceremonies usually took place during June, July, and August, and the boys took part in the dancing and festivities of the harvest season when they were healed. The boys of one clan might be healed in time to take part in the dancing at the initiation ceremonies of another clan. These boys were distinguished by the white clay with which they were smeared and by the new skin robe which they wore.

When the boys were healed, they were allowed to join the men in their councils and to put their tubes with the men into the beer-pots. They were also looked upon as ready for marriage and took advantage of the harvest festivities to find themselves wives.

PLATE VIII

After the operation

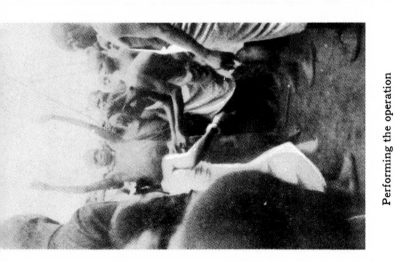

Performing the operation

Bagesu Initiation Ceremony

MARRIAGE

Though boys and girls remained at home and slept together on the floor until they were married, they refrained from sexual relations, for such connection between members of the same clan was an unforgivable offence and death was the certain punishment for the injury. Girls, however, went, always in companies, to the young men of other clans to gratify their passions, and a girl was not blamed for having relations with men so long as she did not bear a child. Even if she did, however, there was no punishment, but the man was expected to pay the marriage fee and marry her. Should he refuse, the child was born at the girl's home, and, unless its father paid a goat to redeem it, it remained with her.

Clan exogamy was strictly enforced and blood relationships were carefully considered in all cases. The tribe was polygamous, but often lack of means prevented men from having more than one wife. No wife objected to her husband's marrying another woman, but each expected to be supplied with a house and field of her own. A man usually refrained from marrying two sisters, and even avoided marrying two women from the same clan because they were regarded as sisters.

Marriages were usually arranged during the harvest season, for at other times it was not safe for members of different clans to enter each other's territory. Fathers sometimes arranged marriages for their sons, but during the festivities boys and girls met and as a rule settled their own affairs with regard to marriage. They might, in fact, as I have already remarked, go at once to live together, and in that case the man had to arrange matters concerning the marriage fee while they lived as a married couple. When a couple had agreed that they wished to marry, the boy might ask his father or a friend to go to the girl's parents and make enquiries about the marriage fee. As it was not safe for a man to travel alone, the messenger had to take three or four companions with him. On his arrival he made an offer to which the girl's parents might agree at once, or there might be some bargaining before the matter was settled. The usual sum was three or four cows, but as many as ten might be asked for and goats might be demanded in addition.

The girl's parents then required some time for preparations, for they had to brew a pot of beer for the girl to take with her. The girl went about her usual occupations, but she was instructed in the duties of a wife; she was fed on the best food her parents could obtain that she might grow fat, and she was daily washed and her body rubbed with oil to make her skin smooth and soft.

When the bridegroom sent the cows, he had also to present a spear and a hoe, and in return the father despatched his daughter with a pot of beer, saying, "Go and rejoice the man's heart." She was accompanied by a number of girl friends who took their hoes with them and remained three days, digging the field for the bride. Men did not as a rule venture to accompany a bride, for only women were safe to travel among other clans once the harvest season was past. The bridegroom supplied the party with food and gave them presents of fowls, spades, or cowry-shells. In some cases, the bridegroom's mother cooked for these guests and invited them to have their meal with her; they, however, were not expected to comply with this invitation but had to take the food and eat it in private when there were no other women present.

At the end of three days the bride and her companions were sent back to her parents with a gift of a sheep. There they feasted and danced before dispersing to their own homes. When the new moon appeared, the bride returned to her husband, sometimes taking with her a pot of beer and a goat, and accompanied by one relative, who stayed for a night.

There was no marriage ceremony and no period of seclusion, because the woman went to work in her field the day after she arrived in her new home. The husband had built his house and prepared his land before he asked her to come to him.

A woman would sometimes agree to marry a man who had not been initiated, and her relatives would consent, on the understanding that he would undergo the operation of cir-

cumcision on the next opportunity. If when the time came
he refused, his wife would leave him and return to her parents,
for no woman cared to live with a man who was too timid to
undergo the trial. She also realised that his refusal placed her
and her children along with him outside his clan, which meant
that she could not count on the help of clan-fellows in time of
trouble.

From the time of his marriage the parents of a bridegroom
never entered his house and never saw his wife nor spoke to
her. If the wife was ill, her mother-in-law would arrange to
meet her at some place outside her house, and she would
attend to her in child-birth, but these were the only occasions
of meeting. The husband might see and speak to his father-in-
law, but he might not meet his mother-in-law and had to
leave the path if she were on it.

If a man found that a wife was barren he might divorce her,
but he often kept the barren wife to cook for him and married
another, by whom he would have children. There was little
jealousy between men on account of women. If a woman
committed adultery, she usually deserted her husband and
went to the man, and the husband demanded from him the
amount of the marriage fee he had paid to her parents and
married another wife, though if the wife who had deserted
him returned, he would accept her. Sometimes, however, a
man who discovered that his wife was unfaithful would vent
his wrath both upon her and upon the man who had wronged
him, and would spear him whenever opportunity offered. A
man who found his brother with his wife might fine him or
seize his goods.

While menstruating, a woman avoided touching her
husband's weapons and, if possible, did not cook his food,
though she would do so if he had no other wife.

Bagesu women were not so docile as wives in other tribes,
and unless a husband asserted himself vigorously, there was
constant bickering. A wife would not hesitate to attack her
husband with her hands, a stick, or a knife, and a man of a
quiet disposition was often completely ruled by his wife.

CHAPTER V

SICKNESS, DEATH, AND INHERITANCE

Causes of illness—bleeding and blistering—illness due to the god *Weri*
—illness due to ghosts—illness due to magic—bubonic plague—small-
pox—other methods of treatment—eating the dead—widows—suicide
—manslaughter—murder—inheritance

SICKNESS

FEW people attained to any great age, for the hardships of
existence were such that both men and women generally suc-
cumbed before sixty. The fact, however, that a few people
lived longer might have been taken as proof that illness and
death were, as was generally believed, due to the influence of
some superhuman power. Illness was therefore always ascribed
either to ghosts or to magic exerted by some ill-disposed
person.

When a man fell ill of some minor complaint, his wife might
treat him. For headache, for swellings on the limbs (such as
abscesses), or for pains in the chest, bleeding by cupping was
often resorted to, and it was essential that this should be done
by a relative and not by a person belonging to a different clan.
The cup used was some three inches from the pointed end of
a cow's horn, with a hole made in the side near the point. A
few scratches were made on the flesh, the spot was wetted,
and the broad end of the horn placed firmly over it. The air
was sucked out and a plug of fibre, previously put into the
mouth, was inserted in the hole with the tip of the tongue.
When the right amount of blood had been drawn off, the plug
was withdrawn, the horn taken off, and the place sponged.
At other times it was considered advisable to blister a patient,
and for this purpose a stick, of the same kind as that used for
the fire-sticks, which had been thrust into the fire or made
burning hot by friction, was applied to the place where the
pain was felt.

If the illness increased, the wife summoned the man's

relatives. If they thought it necessary they called in a medicine-man and gave him a goat that he might by an augury find out the cause of the illness and how to deal with it.

Should the augury indicate that the illness was due to the god *Weri*, a goat and two long branches of a tree were brought to the house in which the sick man lay. The branches were planted outside near the door to form a resort or shrine for the god, and the goat was offered to him beside them. If the goat urinated while the preparations for the offering were being made, it was a sign that the god accepted it, whereupon it was taken away with beating of drums to the forest, where it was killed and eaten. If, however, the god did not thus signify his acceptance, the goat was taken back to the herd and another brought and tied near the trees for a short time to see whether the god accepted it, in which case it was taken to the forest and sacrificed.

When a ghost was causing illness, a bull was brought and killed near the man's house, and the medicine-man examined the entrails. The body was presented to the ghost, which was told to come and eat it; after which the medicine-man and his followers carried the meat to a distance where they ate it, for the members of the sick man's family might not touch it lest they should contract the illness.

When a woman was ill, the husband called in a medicine-man who demanded a fowl or a goat for the augury. If he decided that the illness was caused by a ghost which had taken possession of the woman, he killed an animal, cooked some of the meat, and with it tempted the ghost to leave the patient. If this did not succeed he proceeded to more vigorous methods, and tried to frighten the ghost by threats or to smoke it out by burning herbs, wool, or feathers. He invariably planted before the door of the house two trees or reeds in which the ghost could take up its residence when it had left the patient. Offerings of beer and food for the ghost were placed beneath these trees from time to time.

People who claimed to be magic-workers believed firmly in

their own powers, and the general belief in and fear of magic
was so great that the suggestion of its presence was enough to
throw a man into such a condition of nervousness that he was
quite likely to die of fear.

When a medicine-man found by augury that magic was the
cause of illness, he proceeded to discover the guilty person,
and advised the relatives to call together the members of the
clan and the culprit that they might come to an agreement.
A cow was killed and the people ate a sacred meal, adjuring
the magic-worker to remove his spell. When he had been
persuaded to do so, possibly by the payment of an animal or
by the settlement of some dispute, the illness could be treated
with ordinary remedies.

Should a man die under the influence of magic, his relatives
held the magic-worker responsible for the death, and would
kill him in revenge.

If a man fell ill of bubonic plague, the medicine-man
ordered the relatives to make an offering of an animal, a fowl,
and some vegetable food to the god of plague. The animal was
killed and the medicine-man wore the skin during the ceremony. The relatives offered some of the food to the god
beside trees which had been planted by the door, saying,
"We leave you this and we eat the rest"; they carried away
the rest of the food to the forest, where they ate it, and
returned to the house by a different path.

When smallpox (*enundu*) broke out in a house, a goat was
sacrificed and the villagers built a fence round the hut to stop
the disease from spreading. The inmates of the house were
left to look after each other, and if one died, the body was
carried to waste land and eaten there by relatives who had
already had the disease and who were deputed to perform the
mourning ceremonies.

When a medicine-man succeeded in curing a patient, he was
given an extra present.

The following notes with regard to illness are quoted from
the *Northern Bantu* and were collected among some other
clans of the tribe:

The chief cause of sickness is said to be magic, and to discover its source the relatives of the sick person seek a medicine-man and from him obtain a verdict by divination. He may discover some object hidden in the thatch or buried near the house which he pronounces to have been the cause. It has, he informs the relatives, been hidden there by some ill-disposed person and the magical spell has to be broken and the object in question destroyed before the sickness will yield to treatment. When once the spell of magic has been broken, the medicine-man finds no difficulty in dealing with the sickness. At times counter-magic has to be used to heal a sick person, because a ghost has seized him. In such cases the medicine-man is supplied with a fowl which he divides into four parts, placing them in four shallow holes made on a plot of waste land. Having thus divided the fowl he goes through a form of incantation in which he commands the ghost to leave the sick person and trouble him no more. He then removes the meat from three of the holes; one piece is taken, cooked, and given to the sick man, a second is taken to the deity of the clan, a third piece the medicine-man himself takes, cooks and eats, while the fourth piece is left in the hole on the waste land for the ghost.

Transferring sickness. At other times, it may be, the illness has to be transferred to some other person by means of herbs. The medicine-man chooses his bunch of herbs from an uninhabited part of the country, ties them neatly into a bunch, brushes them over the patient and then carries them to a distant path where, by night, he buries them, covering the spot in such a manner as not to attract attention. The first unsuspecting person who passes contracts the disease and the patient recovers.

Ghostly possession. A medicine-man sometimes attributes sickness to ghostly possession, which he says must be cured by propitiating the ghost. He will probably tell the attendants of the sick person that it is the ghost of some relative who has been offended in some way and has therefore sent sickness. Should the person be a rich man, a hut is built as a shrine in honour of the ghost, with a long pole protruding through the centre of the thatch at the apex. The patient gives the medicine-man a goat or an ox to offer to the ghost; the animal is killed near the shrine, the blood is caught in a vessel and put into the shrine with a portion of the meat. The people assemble in numbers to take part in this ceremony. The medicine-man climbs the hut after making the offering of blood, spikes a large piece of meat on the pole and proceeds to cut it into small pieces, which he throws among the crowd, who eagerly scramble for them and eat them. The sickness is supposed to be so widely scattered by this ceremony that it is rendered harmless, and the patient quickly regains his usual health. Any meat that is left the medicine-man takes away with him for his own use.

When a case of sickness proves fatal, the relatives again appeal to the medicine-man to discover who has caused the death that they may seek the accused person in order to put him to death. When discovered he is tried, but sometimes he may succeed in escaping death by paying a heavy fine.

DEATH

There can be little doubt that the custom of disposing of the dead by eating the bodies during the days observed for mourning was common to all the Bagesu clans. For various reasons, the custom was kept secret, and even members of the tribe were not permitted to look on during the ceremony, which was performed by night. Yet the custom was known to all, and each family was aware of what was going on, though they never sought to watch their neighbours' doings.

When a man died, the body was kept in the house until the evening, when the relatives who had been summoned gathered for the mourning. In some exceptional instances it took one or two days to bring the relatives together, but as a rule all was ready by the evening of the day of death, and at sunset the body was carried to the nearest waste ground and deposited there. At the same time men of the clan hid themselves in different places round about and, as darkness deepened, they blew upon gourd horns, making a noise like the cry of jackals. The villagers said that the jackals were coming to eat the dead, and young people were warned not to go outside. When darkness had set in and it was felt to be safe to work without intrusion from inquisitive onlookers, a number of elderly women relatives of the dead man went to the place where the body lay and cut it up, carrying back the pieces they wanted to the house of mourning and leaving the remains to be devoured by wild animals.

For the next three, or sometimes four days, the relatives mourned in the house in which the death had taken place, where they cooked and ate the flesh of the dead, destroying the bones by fire and leaving nothing. There was no purification or shaving when this mourning was ended; sometimes an ox was killed for a feast when the heir was announced, but as a rule the people simply returned to their ordinary life without any ceremony. The widows burned their grass girdles and

either went naked or wore the small aprons used by unmarried girls.

The reason they gave for not burying their dead was that,
if they allowed the body to decay, the ghost would be detained in the vicinity of the place of death and would, in
revenge, cause illness to the children of the family.

SUICIDE

When a man committed suicide in his house, the house was
broken down and burned. If, however, he hanged himself on
a tree, even if it was near his house, the body was cast into
the grass, the tree was cut down and its roots dug up and
burned near the place, but the people went on living in the
house. The reason given for the destruction and burning was
that the place would influence others to commit the same
deed, for the house or tree was considered to convey infection.

If a wife hanged herself in her house, the husband was
accused of being the cause. He was despoiled of all his possessions and his house was broken down.

MANSLAUGHTER

It required much skill and ingenuity for a man to prove
that the killing of another was accidental. He might, however, succeed in doing so to the satisfaction of the elders of
the clan, and, if both men belonged to the same clan, he was
fined, while the relatives of the dead man gave him a pot of
beer to show that they were reconciled. The smallest fine imposed for manslaughter was the amount necessary to procure
a wife. This was given to the father of the dead man, who was
expected to have another son to take the place of the dead.

In some clans the guilty man had to appease the ghost by
killing a goat, smearing the contents of its stomach on his
chest and throwing the remainder upon the roof of the dead
man's house.

If a man thus accidentally killed belonged to another clan,
the perpetrator of the deed would be protected by his clan
until the case could be tried. If he could prove that it was an

accident, he was fined five cows and probably several goats, sheep, and fowls, while the injured party brought beer as a sign of their acceptance of the terms. Representatives of the two parties met to make an agreement, and an animal, a goat, or sometimes a dog, was brought between them. This animal was cut in two parts, between the fore and hind legs, with one stroke from a heavy knife. The meat was sent to the man who had committed the deed, and in return he sent a live animal, which was killed and eaten on the spot.

MURDER

When one man murdered another who was his clan brother and probably an inhabitant of the same village, all his goods were taken from him, but his life might be spared.

Murders often resulted from quarrels between men of the same clan but of different villages, for they had irritable dispositions and were quick to attack. The murderer would then flee to some other tribe or clan where he would be safe from pursuit, though he ran the risk of being killed as an intruder before he found a place of refuge. The injured party then lay in wait until they found some member of his family, when they avenged the murder by killing him.

When a man killed someone from another clan, he had to be purified before he could return to his ordinary life. Until this had been done, he had to eat his food with two sticks and never allow any food he put in his mouth to touch his hands. He took two goats, one male for himself, and one female for his wife. The male goat was killed at a distance from the house, and the man was smeared with the contents of its stomach, while the other goat was killed near the house and the contents of its stomach smeared on his wife, the children, and the door-posts, and thrown on the house. The family then feasted on the meat.

INHERITANCE

The heir to a man's property was usually his eldest son, but the members of his clan might nominate some other member in his place, simply putting the dead man's son aside, saying, "We are here; you cannot inherit now, nor can you go to your father's widows."

If the eldest son inherited, he generally provided for younger brothers as they grew up, and he kept his sisters until marriage, when he took the marriage fees which were paid for them to help him to get wives for himself and his brothers.

Should there be no child or none old enough to inherit, a brother of the dead man took the property. He looked after the children, gave the sons some of the father's property as they grew up, and arranged the daughters' marriages.

If a son inherited, his mother lived either with or near him. Other widows were generally taken to wife by the heir, but they were at liberty to return to their own homes if their relatives would refund the original marriage fee paid for them. A widow who thus refused the heir was free to re-marry; and her new husband paid the marriage fee to her relatives or, if the original marriage fee had not been returned, to the heir.

Women might never inherit or possess property, though a mother might at times keep the property of her husband for a son who was still a junior.

CHAPTER VI

LANGUAGE

Seasons—salutations—relationships—counting

THE divisions of the year among such primitive peoples were arbitrary and variable, depending on the length of the rains. There were two chief divisions, those of the great rains and the smaller rains, and these varied in length from four to six months. During the dry weather between the rains practically no work was done but when, after some weeks of sun and hot dry winds, clouds began to appear, it was known to be time to prepare any new ground for sowing. Later on ground which had been already cleared was dug and made ready. About eight weeks after harvest the sound of thunder would be heard and the people said "the year has begun." The digging of the fields was then hurriedly finished and after the first shower of rain the seed was sown. During the heavy rains beans and the principal crops were sown, for this season lasted some five to six months. The season of the smaller rains was shorter, lasting sometimes only some four months, so that certain quick-growing crops were sown.

NAMES OF THE SEASONS

Mwaka, munane, sambya=the great rains; time for sowing millet and beans.
Luwhira=the dry season.
Kimiyu, buhi=sunshine.
Mwesi=a month.
Mwaka=the year.

SALUTATIONS

Watulire?=How are you? The greeting upon meeting. Answer, *Natulire nili mlahi*=I am quite well.
Nzia wefwe=I am going. Used on leaving. Answer, *Nozia mwuliko*= Go with peace.

RELATIONSHIPS

Father, baba.
Mother, mai.
Brother, yaiya omulebe wase.
Sister, mai wase.
Husband, musiza wase.
Wife, makasi wase.
Son, mwana wase.
Daughter, mukana wase muwala wange.
Father's father, guga wase.
Father's mother, kuku wase.
Mother's father, kuku wase.
Mother's mother, kuku wase.
Father's brother, baba omugyaka.
Father's sister, sengawe or sengawase.
Mother's brother, mama.
Mother's sister, mama.
Father's brother's wife, mai.
Father's sister's husband, mai.
Mother's brother's wife, muko mai or mai.
Mother's sister's husband, baba akwali mai.
Father's brother's son, yaiya.
Father's brother's daughter, mugogo wase.

Father's sister's son, musala wasenge.
Father's sister's daughter, mugogo wasengawe.
Mother's sister's son, masala wase wa mama.
Mother's sister's daughter, mugogo wase wa mama.
Son's son, muzukulu wase.
Son's daughter, muzukulu wase.
Daughter's son, muzukulu wase.
Daughter's daughter, muzukulu wase.
Brother's son, mwana.
Brother's daughter, mwana.
Sister's son, mwiwa mwana.
Sister's daughter, mwiwa mwana.
Wife's father, baba wase.
Wife's mother, muko (mukyienta).
Wife's brother, musani wase.
Wife's sister, musani wase.
Wife's sister's husband, wasagwa wase.
Husband's father, baba muko wase.
Husband's mother, mayi.
Husband's brother, mulamu wase.
Husband's sister, mulamu wase.
Husband's brother's wife, wangoye wase.
Son's wife, muko.
Daughter's husband, mwana.
Elder brother, muganda.
Younger brother, muganda muto.
Elder sister, muganda mugogo wange.
Younger sister, muganda mugogo wange muto.
Father's elder brother, baba.
Father's younger brother, baba muto.

COUNTING

1. *ndwera*, index-finger stretched out.
2. *zibira*, two fingers stretched out.
3. *ziolatu*, index bent in and others extended.
4. *zine*, four fingers extended.
5. *zitano*, closed fist.
6. *zisesaba*, three fingers on each hand extended.
7. *zitano zibira*, three fingers of one and four of the other extended.
8. *zitano ne ziolatu*, four fingers of each hand extended.
9. *zitano ne zine*, four fingers extended and laid on the closed fist.
10. *zikumi*, both closed fists.

They have no higher number than 10 but they go on to multiply it in various roundabout ways.

Vocabulary

All, byosi
arm, mukono
arrow, luhembo

Back, mabega
beast, nsolo
believe, wekiriza
bird, kanyonyi
bitter, mbi (?)
black, kimala
blood, mafugi
blue, nabufu
boat, lenkolo (for beer)
body, mubiri
bone, ugumba
born (to be), kuzala
bow, buhingo
breath, gumuka
bright, kasamirira
burn, wokire

Carry, wetwika
chief, mwami
child, mwana
cloud, enfule
club, mpimbo
come, ija
command, nku
cut, sala

Dance, kukina
dark, mahalire
day, gumumu
die, wafa
do, kola
dream, alotira amulotu
drink, kunyue

Ear, kutu, matu
earth, ridoha
eat, kulya
enemy, zoneboneko
eye, monye

False, bulimba

fear, tire
few, bijeke
fight, kulwana
fire, muliro
fish, zingane
food, madote
foolish, musiru
foot, kitandagire
forest, misala
friend, busare

Ghost, misambwe
go, kuzi
god, mweri
good, kirabi

Hair, ezune
hand, chaba
hard, kihandalafu
hate, lobire
head, mutwe
hear, wawulira
heart, moyo
heavy, kizito
high, ndahi
house, enzu

I, nje

Kill, mwitire
know, nahulihe

Large, kigala
leg, kigere
lie, nogone
lightning, fulatu lutulikire
live, mulamu
liver, amani
long, kihavu
loud, lugale
love, gana
low, nyimpi

Man, musindi
many, kingi

marry, kuwabintu
moon, mwesi
mountain, lusozi lumya
mouth, mumuwa

Near, ligosi
new, kisyaka
night, kiro
no, sinalubiri, ah ah
nose, muru

Old, akade

Past, kanyuma
priest, mufumu

Quick, kuzi

Rain, enfula
red, mbisima
river, gamezi
run, dima

See, tunula kusirira
shadow, kisigo
shield, ngabo
short, kijeki
shoulder, libega
sing, imba
sit, kalasi
skin, kikoba
sky, lugulu
sleep, kugane
slow, mpola
small, kijake
smell, funye
soft, kidembu
sorcerer, mufumu
soul, mwoyo
speak, alamu
spear, ifumu

stand, imamo
star, namwemi
stone, ibare
strike, kuba
sun, gumumu
sweet, kireme

Take, hire
taste, komba
tell, gumuganıkira
that, ekyo
they, abo
thing, kintu
think, walumire
this, kino
thou, wewe
thunder, nagulu, enfula
tongue, lulimi
tooth, gameno
touch, sawo
tree, kisala
true, bulahi

Ugly, mbi

Walk, kuze
war, kusolana
water, mezi
white, mwanga
who, nana
whole, kyosi
wind, mbeho
wise, ndahi, bulahi
wish, ngama
woman, mukame
word, luma

Yellow, nabufu
yes, eh nihawe wena
you, mwe (plur.)
young, mujake

CHAPTER VII

THE BAKYIGA CLAN, A SECTION OF THE BAGESU OF MOUNT ELGON

Origin of the clan—sub-divisions—religion and customs—marriage—inheritance—relationships

ON the northern slopes of Mount Elgon there lived a clan called the Bakyiga who, though regarded as a section of the Bagesu tribe, held little communication with the other clans. They had a tradition that at one time they lived in Kavirondo and were forced up the mountain slopes by constant raids of tribes from the north and east. They said too that the clan separated and one branch wandered off to the west and were not heard of again. The forefathers of the tribe who first settled on Mount Elgon were Mutula, Ukuyo, Kiyemba, and Benkoko and the present head of the clan is Maguma.

The main clan had several sub-divisions between which there was always enmity, so that it was not even safe for a man to go alone among the members of another sub-division of his own clan. The names of the sub-divisions were:

1. Bukyunya	4. Zuzeni	7. Mufuma
2. Kimatya	5. Kufula	8. Kiribo
3. Kibe	6. Nakayode wa Kimatya	9. Fukula

The Fukula branch were not agriculturalists like the rest of the clan, but were hunters and kept cattle which they herded in the plains.

In clothing and in most of the customs and ceremonies they followed the clans of the Bagesu. Their god was *Weri* who could work both good and evil, but ghosts were the responsible agents and to them offerings were made when demanded by the medicine-men. Their huts were of the same type as those of the Bagesu and they followed the same customs during the building.

Slavery was unknown and prisoners taken during war were received into the families of the captors and treated as members of them, the only difference being that a captive might never inherit property even if there was no son to take possession. In exceptional cases a man might sell a child to a tribesman in order to pay a debt, but such a child was taken into the family and not treated as a slave.

The treatment of sickness and death and their burial ceremonies were identical with those practised in the other Bagesu clans, but they continued to mourn for one month after a death. A murderer if caught was killed, but if he escaped, his division of the clan was plundered and some member of it was killed in his stead.

MARRIAGE

The clan followed the rules of exogamy but permitted marriage between members of different sub-divisions. Originally the marriage price demanded from a man was one cow but this has increased until now they ask for six cows.

Men before marriage underwent the initiation rites common to the whole Bagesu tribe and the women made cicatrizations on their bodies so that the keloids were well formed before the time of marriage came. Originally marriage was always by capture, but this led to such fierce fighting that the clan gave up the practice and settled marriages by negotiation.

After marriage the bride remained in seclusion ten days. Should the bridegroom have no house of his own, he placed the bride with some friend and after the time of seclusion she went out to dig in her own plot of land while her husband built a hut.

Polygamy was common and a man might have as many as four wives, each of whom had to have her own house in his village and her own plot of land. Each wife kept the grain she grew in her own granary but she might not sell any without her husband's permission. Neglect of this rule often led husbands to beat their wives but wives would stand up for themselves and fight their husbands to get their own way. The wives of one man were usually on friendly terms and one wife would look after the children of another if necessary.

They had a custom that if a child died and the mother was suffering from swollen breasts, a dog might be put to suck from her.

INHERITANCE

The eldest son was the legal heir of a man's property but should a man die without a son, his brother inherited. Women were never allowed to possess property, but if a man died leaving a son who was still a child, the boy's mother looked after the property until he was old enough to manage it himself.

RELATIONSHIPS

Father, lulawefe.
Mother, mawe.
Brother, yayawefe.
Sister, mugogowefe.
Husband, omusezawefe.
Wife, makazozi.
Son, mwana.
Daughter, omukamwana.
Father's father, muzukulu.
Father's mother, muzukulu.
Mother's father, kugawefe.
Mother's mother, guguwefe.
Father's brother, salawefe.
Father's sister, sengewefe.
Mother's brother, mawase.
Mother's sister, kyananyino.
Father's brother's wife, mamafe.
Father's sister's husband, mukwewase.
Mother's brother's wife, mukaziwase.
Mother's sister's husband, lalawefe.
Father's brother's son, yayawefe.
Father's brother's daughter, mugogowefe.
Father's sister's son, muhimwana.
Father's sister's daughter, muhimwana.
Mother's brother's son, kyanyanino.

Mother's brother's daughter, kyanyanino.
Mother's sister's son, yayawase.
Mother's sister's daughter, yayawase.
Son's son, muzukulu.
Daughter's daughter, muzukulu.
Daughter's son, muzukulu.
Son's daughter, muzukulu.
Brother's son, mwanawase.
Brother's daughter, mwanawase.
Sister's son, yayawase.
Sister's daughter, yayawase.
Wife's father, tatawase.
Wife's mother, mawase.
Wife's brother, mukowase.
Wife's sister, mulamuwase.
Wife's sister's husband, mukwawase.
Husband's father, bapawase.
Husband's mother, mai.
Husband's brother, mulamuwase.
Husband's sister, maiwase.
Husband's brother's wife, wangoye.
Son's wife, mukanawase.
Daughter's husband, mwanawase.
Elder brother, mukulu.
Younger brother, muduwa.
Elder sister, mai mugibola.
Younger sister, mai muduwa.

PLATE IX

Woman carrying milk in gourds at Sabei

PLATE X

Waterfall at Sipi, Mount Elgon

THE BASABEI

CHAPTER VIII

GENERAL

The Basabei, a semi-pastoral tribe—origin of the tribe—clans—
government—chiefs of the clans—head-men of the villages—murder—
clothing and ornaments—scarifications—food—carrying loads—fires

ON the north and north-eastern slopes of Mount Elgon
there is to be found a semi-pastoral tribe, divided into
two sections, the Basabei and the Bambei. Though not so fine
either in feature or physique as the pastoral people of Ankole,
they resembled the Negro-Hamitic tribes of the Lake Region
in appearance, but differed from them entirely in their mode
of life. They might have come from the same stock, but in
that case they must have entered the country during another,
possibly a later, migration. Much in their general behaviour,
however, seemed to connect them with the pastoral groups of
the north-east, the Masai, the Nandi, the Wahumba of the
Usagara Hills, and the Wakikuyu, rather than with those of
the south-west. They practised initiation ceremonies which
included circumcision, while the Baganda and Banyankole
avoided all mutilations and the Bakitara confined themselves
to the extraction of certain of their teeth. Both men and
women of the Basabei had to undergo initiation ceremonies
before they were recognised as full members of the clan; until
these rites were performed they might not enter into the
councils of the adults, nor might they marry. Their use of
milk and their methods of building also differed from those
of the Baganda, Bakitara, and Banyankole.

The people said that they first lived in Sengweri, on the
plains to the east of the mountain, and were forced by the
constant raids of the Masai upon their cattle to betake them-

selves to the hills. It seems possible that they were the most north-westerly representatives of the same race as the Masai; they might indeed have been a branch which, having cut itself adrift from one of the larger tribes, was forced to move up the mountain for safety. The Suk, Turkana, and Karamojo tribes might also belong to the Galla, but as I was unable to reach them I cannot judge with any certainty. The remains of the Galla have been swept further north and absorbed by the Abyssinians and the border tribes of that country.

The mountain homes not being favourable for the breeding of large herds of cattle, the people took to agricultural pursuits; and, as generations passed, milk fell into a secondary place in their diet and vegetables became the staple food. Their huts were similar in style to those of the Wagogo and other belligerent tribes of East Africa, that is, they had flat roofs which were made of mud, not of thatch, and which therefore protected the huts against incendiarism by night-raiders who might try by such means to drive out the occupants in order to attack and slay them in the open. The milk vessels too, like those of the Masai, were chiefly gourds, while the clothing, the ornaments, and even the method by which the women carried loads, were like those of the Masai and Nandi. Both men and women were tall with finely cut features and no spare flesh; their voices were high-pitched and their conversation sounded short and abrupt.

The Basabei said that at first their tribe was composed of three clans:

1. *Gibisisi*, who avoided dogs (*embwa*);
2. *Goboro*, who avoided a kind of mushroom (*butiko*);
3. *Kyemwehe*, who avoided all kinds of vegetables.

The founders of these clans were said to have come into the country with a cow and a calf and a bride called Yaboro.

The tribe has now two main divisions, Basabei and Bambei, and the clans are numerous, though the tribe is numerically small, not amounting to more than several hundreds. Each clan has its own totem, which was, however, known only to a few of the principal members, who could not be induced to divulge it. The clans were all exogamous, and, with the exception of a few dwellers near rivers, none of them would eat fish.

BASABEI CLANS. PATERNAL DESCENT

Kaboroha	Kamelogot	Kabukya
Mandani	Kabusuriti	Kasongeni
Kamehi	Kabukyabikweni	Kabukyebai
Kasuleri	Kamaseki	Tobani
Kabukeriwo	Kabukweti	Abuheri
Kabukyemori	Kabogi	Atamuto
Kabekyebukutwa	Kabukyemehi	Kyakyebasu
Kabisi	Kabugyorwa	Abukyesiri
Abusyosya	Kabuyesukwa	Kabukyelemeti
Kabukyemiro	Kabungora	Kabunga
Abikibingoye	Kabukyemeseki	Kabungarha
Akwasanhi	Kabusabugi (totem, monkey)	
Kamundi	Kaburob	·Kaputen
Kamuhoyi	Kaburini	Kabilelo
Kapekumuro	Kabukerege	Kabukerotiki
Kabukyeburoni	Kabukyetoromu	Kabukyemeri
Kabukyemeyo	Kabukyemu	Kabukyebukyui
Kabukyebuteri	Kabukyereteregeyi	Kamaruyu
Kamyeronyi	Kabutigori	Kabutomamu
Kamitwa	Kabusogahi	Kabyemeti
Kamarange	Kamalemet	Kabukyemes
Kabuyes	Kabisigoha	Kametwa
Kabusuwi	Kabufubiti	Kamatwi
Kabukorot	Kabuhyerobi (rhinocerus or donkey)	

CLANS OF THE BAMBEI. PATERNAL DESCENT

Bagweri (chief)	Bometi	Kabusesi
Kabikwakoi	Kamoko	Kaputuyi
Kapujogeni	Kabukekya	Kamunatiri
Kabunaronge	Kabusamasama	Kabusirikwa
Kamenwa	Kapuchawiloti	Kaputoki
Kabeti	Kabuchai	Kabukerani
Kamujaki	Kabusomini	Kabukyekosomi
Kama	Kabuseroti	Kabuchesongoli
Kabunyai	Kasumbata	Kabukamai
Kabukyemuroi	Kabuchoiki	Kamere
Kabukyerobı	Kabukweki	Kabubyekyoko
Kabukyasaga	Kabukuti	Kabukyebereni
Kabis	Kabit	Kaboro
Kabukyabasa	Kabukarimenkat	Karema
Kamulyingama	Kamunangori	Kamuranyemi

Kalimet	Kabukyekwek	Kabukyorokwa
Kabwari	Kabuna	Kamagina
Kabukendui	Kamilil	Kaputo
Kamuriyoni	Kabukyaleli	

Government

The members of each clan lived on their own particular part of the mountain, and had their own head-man who was responsible for all affairs concerning the clan and its relations with other clans. He claimed no rights as ruler over the clan, for he was its Father, and not its king. His power was greatest in connection with the land, and it was to him that all disputes concerning the boundaries of cultivated plots or of clan land were brought. These, however, were not frequent, for unclaimed land was so plentiful that quarrels on this account were few. There was seldom a case of theft to be tried, for theft among themselves was, so far as I could discover, practically unknown. They took any opportunity of stealing, or, as they called it, "snatching away" animals belonging to any other tribe, but this was regarded as an act deserving of praise and not of punishment. The Father of the clan demanded no payment of taxes or rents, but he expected to receive a pot of beer each year after the harvest was over.

The villages varied in size, some containing as many as forty houses and others as few as four. They were situated on the sides of the mountain wherever an even place gave room for their houses and fields, places with an area of about one square mile being generally chosen. Countless cascades fell down the mountain sides and ran over such level places as clear streams, which supplied the people with water. The trees on the banks of these streams were often of gigantic size; and vegetation of all kinds, from the tropical growths of the lower slopes to the plants and flowers of temperate zones on the cooler heights, flourished luxuriantly.

In each village there was one man who was looked upon as the head, often because of the site he occupied. To him the members of the village brought their difficulties and disputes, and all ordinary cases he settled himself. If, however, anyone refused to accept his decision or if a case concerned any person outside his own village, he would appeal to the Father of the clan. A man who refused to accept the decision of the head of the village and was judged in the wrong by the Father of the clan, was flogged, or, if he was an old man, was fined a cow, which was killed and eaten by members of the clan.

Murder

When two members of the same clan quarrelled and fought and one killed the other, no compensation was claimed by the parents of the dead man but, if he was married, the parents of his wife claimed a cow and a sheep.

Should a murderer and his victim be of different clans, the clan of the murdered man would demand compensation. The murderer brought to an appointed place ten cows, two bulls, and two sheep, and members of both clans met there. One bull and one sheep were killed for the men and the same for the women, and the clans ate a meal together and were smeared with the contents of the stomachs and some of the blood of the animals. The spear, shield, and knife of the murdered man were brought and given to his brother, who also took the skin of one bull and one sheep, while the brother of the murdered man's wife took the rest. The fine was intentionally heavy in order that it might act as a deterrent and the man was often financially crippled for years before he could pay it off.

For one man to curse another in the name of the rainbow was a serious offence, and the man thus cursed was justified in spearing the other to death. He was, however, tried for the murder and might be fined as much as five cows.

Clothing

In spite of the fact that many of these people lived at great heights on the mountains, where the cold was often extreme, they wore practically nothing in the way of clothing; and though they took shelter in the warmth of their huts when the sun went down, they never allowed cold to interfere with their ordinary out-of-door tasks. Boys when small might go naked, or they might wear a skin slung from one shoulder and long enough to reach the hips, which was also the only dress of a full-grown man. The skin was that of a goat or calf; two corners were fastened together and the robe put over the head and under the left arm so that the fastened corners were on the right shoulder and the robe was open down the right side.

A girl before she was of an age for marriage wore only a small apron four inches by six. This was often merely a fringe of grass twisted into strings, but sometimes seeds or the ends of bottle gourds were pierced and threaded on the strings. After a girl had reached marriageable age and had been initiated, she wore a robe over her shoulders and one round her waist hanging to her knees. The shoulder robe was usually a cow-skin; two corners were fastened together and it was slipped over her head, hanging over her shoulders to her waist with the opening in front, so that she could have her arms free or wrap the robe round her as she wished. The other robe was generally made of two or three goat-skins sewed together and hung from the waist to the knees.

The ornaments worn by women were iron bracelets and anklets, and on the latter were generally strung numbers of iron rings like large washers. They did not pierce their lips, but wooden discs were inserted in the lobes of the ears and bits of straw stuck through the helix.

Men also wore bracelets, often ivory rings, above the elbow and above the biceps, while round their necks they wore iron rings. The lobes of their ears were pierced for large discs and small rings were put through holes pierced in the cartilage of the helix.

Women made keloids on the sides of the body, running in lines from above the ribs down to the stomach; but they had no other markings. The men only made these keloids on the body when they had killed some enemy in battle, for they were regarded as a mark of courage. Boys sometimes made keloids on their shoulders.

Food

Milk, which was at one time regarded as an essential article of diet, gradually became less used, until it was looked upon by adults more as a luxury than a necessity, though mothers still declared it essential for the children. It was drunk fresh and whenever possible was mixed with blood, either of cows or of wild animals killed in the hunt.

The chief food of the people was millet, which was ground between stones and made into a thick porridge. Sweet potatoes were boiled and eaten whole, as were also plantains, though the latter might be baked in the embers of the fire. Maize when young was roasted in the cob, but when it had been left to ripen fully it was first boiled and then roasted. Various kinds of dwarf beans were grown; these were seldom used fresh but were removed from the husks, dried, and stored until required, when they were soaked for some hours and boiled until soft. Numbers of wild plants were also used as vegetables.

They ate all kinds of animals except lions, leopards, dogs, and hyaenas. The blood of the animals killed was caught in vessels, cooked, and eaten.

Salt they obtained from various trees, which were burned and the ashes washed with water. The water was then filtered off and evaporated over slow fires.

The people had two meals daily, one in the morning and one in the evening. In fine weather they ate their meals outside, but, if it was wet, in the hut. The husband, wife, and family ate out of one pot, sitting in a circle round it.

Fires

The only fuel used for fires, both for warming the houses and for cooking, was wood, which was plentiful on the mountain. The women went out to gather it and bring it home. Men sometimes performed such tasks as building huts and digging in the fields, but most of the manual labour was carried on by the women. Men when carrying loads put them on their heads, but women preferred to bear them on their backs. They made up great bundles of fire-wood, binding them with thongs of cow-skin of which a loop formed a sling for carrying the load. The woman sat on the ground with her back to her load and passed the thong over her head, placing it round her forehead. Then, rising, she walked in a stooping attitude with the weight of the load resting on her back and supported by the strap. All kinds of loads, even food and water-pots, were carried in this way by the women.

The fires in the huts were practically never allowed to die out, but if one did so and there was no other fire near from which some might be brought, fire-sticks were used, and every house kept these in readiness for emergency. The sticks were called *tembererwa*, the hard wood stick which was used to bore into the other being known as the male, while the soft stick was the female. The point of the hard stick was bored into the soft wood by twirling it rapidly between the hands until the dust from the soft wood was ignited, when the flame was blown into tow which readily took fire. So far as could be learned, fire had no sacredness and there were no taboos connected with it.

CHAPTER IX

RELIGION

The creator—ghosts—names of children—offerings to ghosts—
magic—rain-making

THE Creator was *Oiki*, and prayers and offerings were made to him, especially in cases of illness. He had many shrines in the country, and when anyone was ill, a few old people, men or women according to the sex of the patient, went to a shrine with a pot of beer or, if they could not get that, a pot of milk instead. They stirred the beer, saying, "This is for you, spare so-and-so, let him get well." In addition to the beer a goat or a fowl might be offered and killed at the shrine, and cows were often presented to the god and kept alive. An animal

PLATE XI

Men and women of Sabei carrying loads

which belonged to the god might not be killed and eaten
except by a gathering of the whole clan, and another animal
had always to be dedicated in its place.

The most important supernatural beings were, however,
the ghosts, that is, the spirits of the dead. These ghosts had
a special place of abode, but the people had no idea of its
whereabouts. The ghosts spent most of their time in the
vicinity of their old haunts, exerting their influence for good
or ill upon the living. Dreams were regarded as conversations
with the ghosts, who took this means of warning and advising
their living relatives. Illness might be caused by a ghost who
desired a gift of a sheep, a goat, or a cow.

The name given to a child in its infancy was that of some
departed member of the clan, and it was given at the instiga-
tion of the ghost, which remained with the child and took
charge of it. Though the ghost used its influence generally for
good it might also punish the child for any failure in clan
duties or observances. It would resist any attempt on the
part of another ghost to influence the child, telling the other
to wait for another child to be born and take charge of it.
A child was always given a new name at initiation, and in
this case the name was that of the father if he was dead, or
of some member of the clan recently deceased. This was the
name afterwards used, and the name given at birth was
merely retained for identification purposes.

When a man brewed beer, he always poured a little out for
the ghosts of his father and grandfather, for if this attention
was neglected, they would be offended and bring illness into
the family. People also offered cows to the ghosts of their
ancestors, and kept them alive. There was a recent case where
a man, pressed by hunger, sold first one and then the other
of two cows which he had given to the ghost of his father.
The ghost came to him and, seizing him by the throat until
it nearly choked him, demanded why he had parted with the
cows without first obtaining its permission. The man promised
to supply the ghost with others and, being released on this
understanding, obtained two new cows as soon as possible.

A person who was accused of using magic was tested by the poison ordeal. He was given certain drugs to drink, and if he became intoxicated under their influence, he was judged guilty and was killed by being struck with a club on the neck so that it was broken. Old people were often accused of being the cause of a death, and if on being tried they were judged guilty, they were killed by having the neck broken with a blow from a club.

Rain-making

The rain-maker, though well known and feared, did not practise his art in public. When rain was wanted, the people took a goat and several pots of beer and went to the rain-maker's village in the evening. When they arrived, they presented their offering and made their request. They remained in the village for a night, during which the rain-maker made his incantations in secret; and in the morning he told them that they might expect rain after a certain number of days.

The people went away, but, should the rain not come at the promised time, they appealed to him again and he gave them pots of beer which he had blessed and told them to go to a certain place and pour the beer into a particular river. The beer had always to be thrown into a calm pool and not into a part where the stream flowed rapidly.

CHAPTER X

OCCUPATIONS OF THE PEOPLE

The cattle—breeding—milk-vessels—use of milk—sheep and goats— agriculture—brewing—tobacco—building—flat-roofed and bee-hive huts—pottery—iron-work—hunting small game, buffalo, and elephants —fishing—warfare—scarifications of a warrior—dancing

The Cattle

THE cows bred by these mountain people were of a small type and inferior to those of the plains; but they were possibly more hardy and better adapted to the colder climate and rougher conditions, requiring less care and attention. During the rainy season they were pastured on the hills and brought back to the villages by night; but when the grass on the hills was dried up by the sun, it was burned off and the cows were taken down to the lower plains, where the grass had been burnt off earlier in the year and was growing again. They were not brought back from the plains to the villages by night, but were gathered together into small zarebas or, during heavy rains, into caves, which are numerous on this side of the mountain. The herdsmen also did not return home but remained with the cattle to herd and guard them, while the women came daily from the villages with large gourds to carry home milk for their families.

As in Kitara, one fully-grown bull was considered sufficient to serve a herd of one hundred cows, and two young bulls were also kept in the herd. Care was always taken that a bull did not serve its own calf, and a heifer was usually sent away from the herd in which it was born, to one in some other place to mitigate the risk of in-breeding. A cow might have as many as ten calves before it was considered too old to bear.

The men took the cows out to pasture, but the women cleaned the kraal and milked the cows when they returned at night. The milk-vessels were gourds, those in common use varying in size from small gourds which held about a pint to large vessels holding a quart, while some large bottle-gourds held as much as two gallons. Leather straps were attached for carrying the gourds, and after use the vessels were washed out with water and grit of pounded stone, and hung up to dry. When dry, they were fumigated with burning reeds or elephant grass, after which some of the ash was dropped into them, stirred round with a stick and shaken out, any that remained inside being allowed to mix with the milk.

Milk was usually drunk fresh, though clotted milk was also largely used. Little milk was kept for butter, for the people did not eat it and only used it in small quantities for rubbing on their bodies. The dung from the cows was used for smearing the floors of the houses to give them a smooth surface, but it was never used for fuel.

When a cow calved, a boy, or, should there be no boy in the family, a girl was chosen to drink the milk until the calf was able to go out and eat grass, which would be when it was about two weeks old. During this time the boy might not drink milk from other cows, and had also to abstain from all animal and vegetable food. When the calf began to eat grass, the father of the family alone drank the milk from the milking of that day, after which it became common and anyone might drink it.

It was customary for parents to prepare for the initiation of sons or daughters by setting aside milk for them some years before the event. This was usually taken from a cow which had just had a calf, so that the milk was discoloured with blood, or a cow might be bled and the blood mixed with milk, which was then put in a large pot and placed in a cave or hung in a tree. It might be kept four or five years, and it set firm like a large cake, which was eaten by the boy or girl when the initiation ceremony took place.

Sheep and goats were kept in fairly large numbers. They were herded during the day by children, both boys and girls, who gathered together from their various homes and played while they watched the herds. In the early evening they returned to the village, and the kids and lambs, which had been shut up in huts during the day, were turned out and allowed to feed before all the animals were taken in for the night.

Fowls were kept in the houses by most wives, and a few dogs were kept for hunting purposes.

AGRICULTURE

When new land was being brought under cultivation, the men did the clearing; but they never used the hoe, and the preparation of the ground for sowing was left to the women. When her husband had cut down the trees, scrub, and grass, the woman burned them on the ground, which was the only fertilising the soil ever got. When land was worn out and

PLATE XII

Sabei granaries

yielded poor crops it was left to lie fallow for two or three years, and the owner either broke up new ground or returned to a field which had been out of use for some time. There was no method known of fertilising such land, nature being left to restore it when it ceased to yield good crops.

They followed a certain rotation of crops, for millet was seldom grown on the same ground for two successive seasons. Other grains or potatoes were planted in the place where millet had been grown in the previous year.

While the millet was ripening, children were sent to keep off the birds; and when it was ripe, husband and wife worked together at the harvest, gathering in the grain and bringing it back to the village for threshing. From the outset of harvest until it was all garnered, the woman might not wash any part of her body except her hands. When the threshing was finished and the grain was ready to be ground, the husband had to eat the first cooked meal of the new crop; then his family might eat, and after that anyone might partake.

As much grain as they thought to be necessary to keep the family in food until the next harvest season was stored away in granaries adjoining the house, and all that could be spared was set apart for making into beer.

BREWING

When the harvest was over, brewing began, an occasion which was greeted with joy by young and old, for it heralded the season of festivity. Some families had only sufficient grain for one brewing, whilst others might have enough for two or three.

First the grain was thoroughly dried in the sun; then some of it was taken and ground to flour and again dried in the sun for two days. The flour was gently baked in an earthen pot, being stirred the whole time until it was coloured a uniform brown, after which it was again exposed to the sun's rays to get rid of any moisture. Another supply of the grain was then taken, put into large pots, covered with water, and left until it sprouted, when it was drained and dried in the sun until hard enough to grind into coarse meal. This was mixed with the baked flour and the whole put into large pots. Cold water was added and the mixture left to stand a few hours, after which large quantities of boiling water were poured into it and it was allowed to cool. This beer was intoxicating; it was never freed from malt, and was drunk from gourd cups and never filtered or drunk through tubes.

Tobacco

Men smoked tobacco freely and sometimes chewed it; nearly all women smoked it when past middle age, but rarely chewed it; and young women seldom used it at all. It was also largely employed for barter with outside tribes in return for spears, hoes, and goats.

The tobacco was grown near the houses on the refuse-heaps, which were fertilised by the ashes from the wood fires and the sheep and goat droppings from the houses. When it was considered ready, the leaves were gathered, the mid-ribs cut out, and the leaves dried and pounded between stones. The pulped leaves were again spread out and dried in the sun before being stored in earthen pots ready for use.

Building

When a man was going to build he had only one taboo which had to be observed—if the fire in the house where he lodged died out during the night he would not go to work that day.

The type of hut formerly used by the tribe, which was built so that it could not easily be destroyed by enemies, fell, of recent years, into disuse, and the beehive-shape was adopted. The beehive hut with the grass roof was more easily and quickly built, requiring less labour and less timber than the old style; and therefore, when there was no longer the same danger of sudden raids, the people adopted it.

The old style of hut was oblong and flat-roofed, the walls being formed of poles some five feet long and not less than four inches in diameter, planted closely side by side in the ground and bound together. Posts were sometimes also planted inside the walls to carry stouter beams and help to support the roof. For the roof, poles some eight feet long and about the same thickness as those forming the walls were laid across from wall to wall projecting fully a foot beyond the walls to protect them from rain; then another layer of lighter timber was laid at right angles and bound to the first layer. The interstices were filled up with coarse grass, and a layer of damp earth about four inches deep was spread on the top and beaten hard. This earth was a little thicker in the centre than at the sides so that rain ran down and off the sides of the hut. A layer of mud was also plastered on the walls both inside and out and smoothed with the palm of the hand.

Only a few poles were required for building a beehive hut. The building was begun from the top, the apex being a few reeds bound to a small circle of grass some twelve inches in diameter. The workers built downwards from this, increasing their circle and raising the apex until the height and diameter required were attained. This basket-work roof was then raised on to its poles and thatched with grass. The only opening was the door-way, through which light entered and the smoke of the fire escaped.

No beds or stools were necessary, for the family slept on the floor with their feet towards the fire. A space was divided off for the goats and sheep, which were tied by the foot to pegs driven into the earthen floor. Calves were tied by the neck to the walls in the same part of the hut, while the cows went through it to another division, where they were left loose and not tied.

POTTERY

Pots were made either by men or by women, but they only made those which were used for cooking; water-pots were bought from other tribes, and milk-vessels were usually gourds. Their method of making the pots was the same as that of the neighbouring tribes—that is, they made the bottom and built up the sides with coils of clay laid on spirally and smoothed outside and inside with scraps of gourd shell. The pots were then baked in grass fires.

There were no special taboos observed in the making of the pots; but they preferred to bake them between new and full moon and not while the moon was waning.

IRON-WORKING

There were no smelters among them, for they bought their iron from other tribes ready smelted and prepared for use. The smiths of the Basabei made rough arrow-heads for use in hunting and war; but their chief work was the crude iron bracelets, anklets, and rings for fingers and toes which all the people wore. Hoes and spears the people bought from outside tribes, for none of the smiths were capable of making these. Knives they bought from outside smiths; but they also made some for themselves from rib bones of goats and sheep, which they scraped and rubbed down with stones to a sharp edge.

HUNTING

There were no professional hunters; but when anyone, feeling a desire for meat, proposed a hunt, a large number could always be got to join. They had to betake themselves to the lower slopes of the mountain to find game, for only isolated animals found their way to the higher plateaux and valleys.

When the game was such as antelope, zebra, or gazelle, a large number of people, armed with spears and clubs, formed a solid wall towards which a few others drove the game. There was generally no rule for dividing the meat, but when an animal was killed every one rushed upon it and tried to seize some of the flesh. Those who succeeded in getting meat would depart home, while the rest would go on hunting until they were successful or gave up the chase in exhaustion.

When the game being hunted was buffalo, three or four men placed themselves in hiding beside a path or in trees in positions from which they could spear the animals. Others surrounded the buffaloes and drove them along past the concealed hunters, who threw their poisoned spears at them.

The poison used was a very virulent one, and they stated that a wounded animal rarely managed to go more than a few hundred yards before it died. The poison was extracted from the tree *kyetit*, the bark being specially valuable, though the roots and branches also contained it. The parts were pounded to pulp and boiled until the water became thick, when it was rubbed on the spears and arrows. These were used for hunting big game and in war. Poisoned spears were attached by ropes to trees or to logs, so that if an animal rushed away after being struck, the spear was dragged out of the wound and was not lost, even if the quarry escaped into hiding.

When a buffalo was killed, it was flayed and the skin divided into two equal parts and taken to the fathers of the two men who struck the first and second spears into the animal. These old men made shields for their sons from the hide. The father of the man who first speared the buffalo was also given a leg as his share of the meat, the leader of the hunt was given the right shoulder, and the rest was divided among the others who took part. The head was eaten on the spot, the man who first speared the animal taking the tongue, while the wielders of the second and third spears took the remainder.

Should a herd of elephants be seen in the neighbourhood and a hunt be organised, a deputation was first sent to the house of a medicine-man. On reaching the house they elected one elder to go in and consult the medicine-man, who took auguries and gave advice as to the conduct of the hunt. When all was ready three men were chosen to secrete themselves in trees with poisoned spears, while the others, advancing openly upon the animals, drove them towards the place of concealment. The men in hiding speared them as they passed under the trees; usually one at least was hit and either brought down at once or died shortly afterwards from the poison. The tusks belonged to the man who first speared the animal, but one was given to the medicine-man who gave his blessing to the hunters. A shoulder was given to the chief huntsman, and the rest divided up on the spot amongst the hunters or carried back to the village and divided there. In former times little value was set upon the ivory, for which they had little use, though they were fond of ornaments made of it. More recently, however, they found a market for it and bartered it for calico, brass and iron wire, and beads.

Those members of the tribe who lived on the lower slopes of the mountain, near the rivers which feed Lake Salisbury, hunted the hippopotamus and ate its flesh. They seldom, however, went out for the express purpose of hunting; and it was only when a hippopotamus attacked a man that he speared it and called his companions to his assistance in killing the animal.

There were members of the tribe living near Lake Salisbury who gave some time to fishing and who ate certain kinds of fish, but this was not regarded as a regular part of the diet, and few people ate it at all. I· shallow pools fish were caught by the hand or in baskets, and some men used rod and line with bent iron hooks, or spears. Mud-fish and crocodiles were speared but never eaten.

WARFARE

The Basabei were not a warlike people. When their country was invaded, they preferred to retreat into the safe places of the mountains rather than to make a stand. Though at times they might combine to defend themselves against a common foe, they were as a rule too disunited to make any resistance. They sometimes made raids on the cattle of the Karamojo when the herds were sent with insufficient guards to pasture on the plains near the mountains; and the Karamojo would seek to capture the Basabei herds when they had to come down to the lower valleys owing to the scarcity of grass on the higher mountain slopes.

The Basabei came to the attack armed with spears, shields, bows and arrows, and heavy clubs. Should they find the cows well guarded, they might attack the Karamojo herdsmen, and, as the latter used only spears and small shields, the poisoned arrows were an effective weapon

If one of the enemy had been killed, the warriors on their return were all isolated from the other members of the village. They lived in a hut outside the village and for five days might not touch any food with their fingers, but used sticks to convey it to their mouths. The father of the warrior who had done the deed gave them a goat which they killed and ate. Strips of the skin were put on the right wrist and the ankles of the slayer and some of the contents of the stomach were smeared on him.

On the sixth day a medicine-man came, and, mixing various herbs in a pot of water, he washed the slayer and removed the skins from his wrist and ankles, throwing them into an isolated plot of land, where they were not likely to be found and people would not be contaminated by them. An old man, the father or clan-father of the warrior, came, bringing a pot of milk mixed with blood; he puffed some of this from his mouth over his son, and going to his house puffed some on the door-posts and, entering, puffed some over the house inside. After this the warrior came to the door, where an elderly woman met him and, taking his spear and shield from him, put them in their proper place in the house before he might enter. This ceremony prevented the ghost from following him into his house and doing him harm. All the warriors were then free to return home and resume their normal life.

A warrior who had killed a man was entitled to make keloids on one side of his chest; and when he had killed a second he might make them on the other side as well. These were marks of honour and were much envied by the man's companions.

DANCING

Among the Basabei, as in most African tribes, dancing was one of the great pleasures of life, and they indulged in it whenever a season of festivity gave an occasion for doing so. The chief festival seasons were marriage celebrations and the rejoicings after harvest, when beer was plentiful and the people gave themselves up to drinking and dancing.

The dancers arranged themselves in two lines, the men on one side and the women on the other, with a space of some twenty to forty feet between them. A woman had a small drum which she tapped with a stick held in one hand, silencing the vibration with her other hand when necessary, and chanting in a high monotone, while the crowd supplied a chorus on two notes without words, simply singing oh and eh. The result was a noise which resembled a cry of pain as much as one of joy.

While the music and song went on, dancers stepped out from the lines and hopped up and down with one leg extended in front. The men and women kept to their own sides and hopped along the lines at a rapid pace. The excitement among the onlookers grew and they all began to jump in the air, keeping the legs straight and stiff and springing from the toes. This went on for about ten or fifteen minutes and was brought to an abrupt termination by a shout of "Ah!" There was a pause of a few minutes and then the drums and songs began again and the same performance was gone through with fresh dancers in the centre.

Everyone joined in this dancing, from children who could just toddle to old folk who were too feeble to move about, but who took their parts in the songs and waved their bodies and arms to the rhythm.

The time for universal dancing was after harvest, when the new moon appeared; then the rejoicings went on night after night and the young people would travel many miles to take part. It was during these dances that young men and women met and arranged their marriages.

CHAPTER XI

BIRTH, INITIATION, MARRIAGE, ILLNESS AND DEATH

Sterile wives—adoption—birth—seclusion—birth of twins—bringing-out of twins—death of twins—dentition—initiation of boys—admission to clan-membership—initiation and admission of girls—arranging marriages—the marriage-feast—taboo on meat for a bride—fornication—treatment of illness—death—inheritance—suicide—death of women

BIRTH

As among other African tribes, a man was not looked upon as worthy of the name nor was a woman regarded as worthy of respect until they became parents, especially of a son. Should

a number of months pass after marriage and the wife show no
sign of conceiving, the husband would try various medicines
and different kinds of magical devices. Sometimes he summoned a medicine-man who would try by augury or by ordeal
to discover which of them was at fault and would direct the
treatment to be adopted; for sterility was seldom ascribed to
physical impotence, but to the action of some ghost which one
of the parties had offended. A husband rarely sent a sterile
wife away; but, if she believed that the fault lay with her
husband, she might go of her own accord and marry another
man. In such a case, the husband reclaimed the marriage-fee
which he had paid to her parents.

A man sometimes adopted a son of a clan brother when he
saw that he might not hope to have a son of his own. There
was no ceremony of adoption: the child simply went to live
with its new parents and was accepted as their son and heir.
Slaves were unknown, and when any children were captured
in raids they were admitted to the family and treated as sons
and daughters. When they grew to marriageable age a wife
would be found for a boy and the marriage-fee might be paid
for him by the foster parents, and a marriage-fee would be
demanded by them for a girl.

The only taboo which had to be observed by a pregnant
woman was that she might not eat the meat of any animal
that had died or been killed by a wild beast or in the hunt.

When the time of birth came, several women might be in
the house, but two of them were in charge, one being the
husband's mother. When the child was born, the mother-in-
law tied the umbilical cord and cut it with a knife, usually
when the after-birth had come away. The child was handed
to the assistant midwife, who washed it and started respiration, while the chief midwife attended to the mother. The
after-birth was taken out and buried in the cow-dung heap
or, if they had no cows, in the place where the heap would
have been. The child was named immediately after birth by
the husband's mother and other women of his clan, and it
was given the name of some deceased member of the clan.
For seven days after the birth the husband kept out of the

house and no other man was allowed to come in. Nothing was taken from the house during this time; and the fire was specially guarded, for it might neither die out nor might any outside person use any of it.

During her time of seclusion the woman wore only a waist-band and she was never washed. After seven days the medicine-man brought purificatory medicines for her. She was then taken out and washed, and the house was swept and the floor smeared with cow-dung. When the stump of the navel cord fell from the child it was buried near the wall of the house in a place where dogs or rats were not likely to find it and eat it.

On the eighth day the husband might come in and see his wife and child, but he might not come to her bed for four months. Should he have other wives, he had no sexual relations with her for a year after the birth. At the end of four months, relatives and friends came to see the child, and should the husband have had sexual intercourse with his wife before that time, he was vigorously abused.

The women were prolific, and when a man had one or at most two wives, it was quite common for each wife to bear ten children, while some were said to have as many as fifteen. As a rule, however, few of the children of these large families lived to grow up, and many died in infancy. Bronchitis seems to have been a common cause of infant mortality, for the mornings and evenings on the mountain were cold, and the children, who wore no clothes, suffered.

TWINS

When a midwife who was attending a woman in confinement, saw that there were twins, no one else might speak in the room until both were born. A medicine-man was then summoned and a woman who had had twins was sent for to cut the cord. The after-births were buried in the path by which the cows came into the kraal.

The mother and children lived in one part of the house and the husband in another, the rooms being separated so that husband and wife did not see each other. Neither was expected to go out during the day for four months; if for any reason the mother had to leave the house, she had to be careful not to cross a stream. The medicine-man gave the mother medicine, and no woman but the midwife was allowed to see her.

At the end of four months the father of the twins killed a female goat that was with kid. The unborn kid was skinned and the father wore a bit of the skin and the caul as a cap, while the body of the kid was put in a hole near the place where the after-births of the twins were buried. This hole was not filled up at once, but the husband and wife stood on either side of it, while the woman who had previously had twins and who had cut the navel cords stood beside the place where the after-births were buried. This woman had two pieces of iron which she clanged together to start the dance.

The brother of the husband, bearing a spear and a shield, and the brother of the wife, carrying a basket of grain, climbed on to the roof of the house in which the twins were born, and were given the irons, which they beat to keep the dance going. Beer was drunk freely by the people, who assembled in large numbers and danced and rejoiced all day.

On the next day, the husband took a pot of beer and sprinkled it on the land in all directions; and on the third day the wife came out with the children and, taking a pot of beer, sprinkled the land and the cattle. The brush end of a cow's tail was used to sprinkle with, and she had to be careful to direct some of the beer towards the rivers and the herds, for the rivers would dry up and the cattle cast their calves if she omitted them.

Should one or both of the twins die during the period of seclusion, they were buried under the eaves at the entrance to the house; and when another child was born and was six or seven years old, the bodies were exhumed and taken to a cave, where they were laid in a dry place. When the party returned from the cave beer was drunk and dancing and feasting took place. If the father was a rich man, he killed a bull, while a poor man would kill a goat that the relatives might feast and rejoice together. If one twin died, the one that survived was called *Kisa* (a blessing).

The cutting of a child's first teeth was watched with great anxiety, for if the upper teeth came first they brought evil with them. Should this happen to a boy, it was said that the father would die; and if to a girl, the mother would die. The parents and grandparents sat round while a goat was killed and offered to the god *Oiki*. The contents of the stomach were smeared over the parents and beer was blown or sprinkled over all the party, including the child. A medicine-man then broke out the offending teeth and thus saved the life of the parent.

When a child cast its first teeth, it was told to throw them up towards the sky, saying, "Give me new and better teeth." At puberty the two lower incisors were extracted and thrown on the roof of the house. At about the age of ten or twelve boys and girls pierced the lobes and the helix of the ears.

INITIATION

When boys attained the age of about fourteen, they were expected to come forward for the rite of initiation, which took place about every seventh year. They kept no record of age, and judged by the appearance of a boy when he was old enough to be reckoned among the adult members of the clan. The boys themselves were usually anxious to be considered men, and came forward to undergo the ceremony as soon as possible.

For a month before the ceremony the boys who wished to be initiated gathered together in companies of fifty or more and went about visiting the different villages and dancing. When the time for the ceremony came, the members of the different villages brought offerings of goats, and, if they could afford it, of cows. A number of the animals were killed and the contents of the stomach were mixed in a large bowl and smeared upon the boys, who feasted on roasted meat with boiled vegetables. Each boy then promised to be loyal to the tribe and clan and to adhere to the laws and customs which he had learned during the weeks of preparation.

The boys were made to stand in a line and a medicine-man stepped up to the first, pulled the foreskin out and cut it off with an ordinary knife to the end of the penis. He threw the foreskin down at the feet of the boy and passed on to the next. A second operator with an assistant followed. The assistant held the penis out to its full length and the operator made a cut along each side of the urethra, turned back the skin to the root of the penis, cut it off and threw it on the ground, leaving the strip of skin covering the urethra.

After the operation the boy danced, keeping his eyes turned up to the sky and his hands raised, and singing special words, until the next boy had been operated upon, when the first might sit down. A boy, however, often refused to sit until his father came and promised him a cow. Should a boy show signs of fear, he was so scorned and mocked that he would, unless restrained by some of the elders of the clan, commit suicide. Even a father would scorn a son who was timid, and would not prevent him from killing himself.

At the close of the ceremony the boys were divided into parties and sent to places near their own villages, where they could be nursed during convalescence. At each place a hut was built in an isolated spot for the boys to live in and people from their own village were appointed to look after them. The mother of each boy scraped up the blood and skin of her son from the ground where it lay and brought it in a bundle to the place of convalescence, where it was tied to the roof of the hut.

For six days the boys remained in the hut, and on the seventh they were brought out and were told the secrets of the clan and the medicines for healing various diseases. These secrets they were warned not to reveal to the women whom they might marry. During this time no woman might approach the boys and their food was brought into the hut by young men already initiated. When they left, the bundles of blood and skin were taken down and, with the hut, were completely destroyed by fire.

The boys were taken to another place where they remained six weeks longer: and at the end of this time, the elders of the clan gathered together in a remote place in the forest. A house was built and large quantities of fire-wood collected, and for a day the elders discussed the qualifications of the boys and agreed upon what should be said to them.

The boys were conducted to this hut, singing as they went, and near the place they met their companions from other centres. The boys of one party were told to crouch down; the boys of the other party stood in front of them and each aimed a blow at one of the crouching boys with a heavy club. As the blow was about to fall, the crouching boy made a leap to the feet of his assailant and evaded it, so that the club struck the ground. The first set of boys then stood up while the others crouched and were attacked in the same way. For this part of the procedure each boy carried a club, a shield, and a creeper twisted into a loop.

In the evening the boys were brought into the house to the elders, one by one, in the order in which they had been circumcised and the elders told them again of the clan customs and secrets and medicines, and impressed upon them that these things must never be revealed. Each boy had to bring to the elders a present of a fowl and some iron finger- and ear-rings.

When the youths were all assembled, some of the old men went out secretly into the grass and howled like wild beasts. The elders told the boys that there were beasts come to catch and kill them, and the boys had to go out singly and face the beasts in the dark. They went out into the grass to hunt the animals; but, as they had been instructed that they might bring something else if they could not find an animal, each returned with some plant which he said had cried out and was therefore alive. This plant or object was a guarantee that the boy had been some distance into the forest, and he had to be able, if required to do so, to take some elder in the morning to the place to which he had gone in the dark. This was the

last trial of bravery, and the boys on their return were admitted to the society of the men.

They were then allowed to rest for a short time, and in the
early morning when the first signs of dawn appeared, the
elders took them to the nearest stream and washed them in
cold running water. A party of men was sent to tell the
women in the chief village to boil water for the boys to wash
in. In due course the boys came to the village, when the
elders put certain herbs into the water and all the initiated
youths washed with it, in the order in which they were
circumcised, all using water from the same pot, which they
took out and poured over themselves in the usual way, for no
one ever thought of getting into water as into a bath to wash.

When all were washed, they were given food and were conducted to a prepared house where they met the elders from
the several villages to which they belonged, and were given
new names. The house was built a short distance off the main
village path in the grass or scrub, and a special track was
cleared to it. The initiated youths were escorted to the beginning of this new path, where they went down on elbows
and knees, covering themselves with cow-hides so that no
part of the body was visible. Each youth was accompanied
by a relative bearing ornaments which he would receive when
he got his new name. This man carried a stick and walked by
the boy's side as he crawled from the main path to the house;
if the boy allowed a hand or foot to be seen as he crept along,
the man struck him gently to draw his attention to the fact.
The boys crawled along, looking like turtles, this posture being
supposed to show respect to their elders. Each carried a staff
which he held vertically; and when they reached the house
they formed a line and lowered their staffs to the ground,
each gripping the ends of his neighbours' staffs on each side
so that they formed an unbroken line. One of the elders came
out, and, taking first a little milk and then a little beer into
his mouth from vessels placed ready, he puffed over each of
the boys in turn, saying, "Live long and excel my years."
The boys thanked him with a grunt. He then asked if they

wanted to retain their old names—a question which really meant, "Did they regret the step they had taken and wish to withdraw from the new conditions which had been imposed on them?" To this they signified their dissent by keeping silence. He next asked if they wanted new names, and they shouted "Yes." When he promised them these, they raised and lowered their sticks four times. The elder went along the line giving each a name according to the instructions received at the meeting of the elders. As he gave the new name he made a cross with fat on the back of each of the skin robes, and, pushing back the robe, laid a lump of fat on the head of the boy. He then took the ornaments from the attendant relative, placed them on the initiated youth, and put on him a new robe, pulling off the old one as he pulled on the new. When the last of the youths was thus robed they all rose to their feet, and, holding their sticks above their heads, jumped and sang, adding to the noise by hitting their sticks against their iron ornaments.

At the close of the ceremony they were given food and spent some five days in feasting and dancing, living during this time in a large house which had been newly built by the chief of the place, who put it at their disposal. When the five days ended the youths took their weapons and sticks and went off to find the Suk or some other enemy whom they might fight and plunder, thus proving themselves worthy to be clan members. If they could find no foe to fight, they threw their sticks into the grass as though spearing a hidden enemy, and retired with their spears and shields. On their return they were considered to be full-grown men and might marry.

Girls, like the boys, underwent a ceremony of initiation, and went through much the same course of preparation and instruction for membership of the clan. They were taken away to some isolated spot for instruction before the time of initiation, and a number of elderly women were chosen for the task of teaching them. They had their own particular songs and forms of dancing, which were conducted by women. The operation was performed on the girls about a week later

PLATE XIII

Women kneeling awaiting new names

Women kneeling in line covered with cow-skins

Initiation of Women at Sabei, Mount Elgon

PLATE XIV

Marriage assembly

Marriage dance

Sabei Marriage Ceremony

than on the boys, for they did not take so long to heal and both parties were expected to be ready for the dances and feasts at the same time.

When the time of the operation came, the girls were smeared with the contents of the stomachs of animals killed for the feast and ate the meat of them roasted, as the boys did. Two persons, both women, were required for the operation. The girls were arranged lying in a line a short distance apart, each lying on her back with her head turned towards the east and resting on her right hand. When the operator came, she placed her feet together sole to sole and drew them up until her knees were as far apart as possible. The assistant operator placed her hands on the genital organs and held open the large labia while the operator cut away the small labia and clitoris. A crowd of women always stood round watching for any sign of fear, and if a girl showed signs of timidity, even if her great toes twitched, she was branded as a coward. During the ceremonies and the healing no man was allowed near and other girls brought them their food. So far as it was possible to ascertain, death from haemorrhage rarely occurred, though no treatment was given in the case of either youths or girls. The wounds were left to heal without assistance, and almost invariably did so in about ten days.

When the girls were healed and ready to go out from their isolation, they were taken to a hut where they were to receive their new names. As in the case of the youths, when they reached the path which branched off the road and led to the hut, they went down on their knees and crawled on knees and elbows, with cow-skin robes over them so that only their staffs stuck out. A relative went beside each girl, bearing the ornaments which she would receive when she got her new name. As with the youths, this relative had to see that no part of the body was exposed during the crawl to the house. The girls were asked if they wished to retain their old names, and when they refused by their silence, they were offered new names, to which they agreed. As each was given her new name, she was clothed with a new robe and fat was put on her head.

A woman relative then put a large iron ring round the girl's neck and took the lump of fat from her head.

When both men and women were healed, dancing and feasting began, and they met and arranged their marriages.

MARRIAGE

This tribe differed considerably from their neighbours in their method of betrothal, for the couple concerned made their own engagement and asked the consent of the girl's mother. It was the mother's duty to consult her husband as to the amount of the marriage-fee, and when it was paid, she had the disposal of it.

Men and women usually arranged their marriages at the dances after the initiation ceremonies. If during a dance a man saw a girl he desired, he would offer her a cow, which she might accept or refuse. If she accepted she would go with the man to his house for the night, and in the morning he sent a hoe to her mother who, if she approved of the marriage, sent a messenger to inform him of the amount she required for the marriage-fee. If the mother refused to accept the hoe, the man had to return his bride to her home and seek another.

Sometimes, however, a young couple would simply agree at the dance to marry, and later the youth arranged for a number of his friends to go and seize the girl and bring her to him. They took her to the house of a clan relative of the bridegroom, and he joined her there. The boy's father then went to the girl's parents, told them where their daughter was, and arranged the amount of the marriage-fee, first giving a goat, a hoe, and tobacco to the mother. If she refused to accept these, the girl had to return home; but if all went well, the boy paid the marriage-fee, probably a cow or five goats, in addition to the present already given to the mother.

The bride's parents might not go to the wedding feast which was made by the bridegroom's parents, but three pots of beer were sent for them to drink with their relatives and friends at their own home. Members of both clans gathered at the bridegroom's home, where feasting went on for two days. Each guest usually brought a fowl, and there might be as many as forty fowls for the feast. The girl's parents made two pots of beer and sent it to the man's parents, who might keep it for a few days or drink it at once. After it had been drunk, the bride came out of her seclusion, had her head shaved, and took up her new duties. During the time of the bride's seclusion neither she nor her husband might see their parents-in-law, but when the beer had been drunk and she came out, this taboo ended.

For a month from the time of her coming to her husband, the wife might eat no meat. When this time was over, the husband killed a bull and sent a leg with the entrails, liver, and heart, to his wife's mother as a token of her daughter's happiness, and she was thus satisfied that her daughter was satisfactorily married. The bride's father then killed a bull and sent the back with the loin and kidneys to his daughter. From this time whenever either family killed an animal a portion had to be sent to the other; and when either brewed beer one or more pots were sent to the other household.

There was no restriction as to the number of wives a man might marry except his ability to pay the marriage-fee, and a wealthy man might have as many as ten wives. Each wife had her own house which her husband built for her either on his own or his father's land.

A wife during menstruation might not touch her husband's weapons or traps for game, but she might cook for him.

Fornication was at one time most uncommon, and if it existed at all was kept so secret that it was never heard of. Later, with tribal intercommunication, it became more common. Should a man have sexual relations with a girl who was still in her mother's charge, and the girl conceived, her parents forced her to tell the name of her seducer. Her father and some relatives then went and plundered the man's house and he had to come and plead his cause before them. They said, "You have dishonoured our daughter and must marry her," and the man was given no choice, but had to agree.

He had to pay two cows for the marriage-price and a third for the wrong he had done, and ten pots of beer.

SICKNESS AND DEATH

In common with other African tribes a wife would seldom undertake the responsibility of treating her husband even for colds or such simple complaints. The fear of being suspected and accused either of being in collusion with some person working magic or of working it herself made her as a rule seek the aid of some relative of her husband. If, however, an illness did not seem to be serious and a man desired it, his wife might treat him with remedies suggested by him, but should they fail she at once informed his brother, who called in a medicine-man and summoned some of the relatives to assist with the nursing.

Should the medicine-man find by augury that the cause of illness was a ghost, a goat was killed and a fowl was tied to the bed. The goat had to be with kid, and the caul and some fat were put on the sick man's head; the medicine-man puffed beer over his head, chest, and back, saying to the ghost, "There is your fowl. Go into that." When the sun was setting the medicine-man took the fowl, with the ghost now in it, into the forest, killed it, and threw the body away. This was the only form of exorcism practised by them.

When a man died there was no burial. The body was cast out upon waste land, and the widows remained in seclusion for four days, after which the members of the dead man's clan gathered and settled who was to be the heir.

If a dead man left property, a cow was killed for a feast at this gathering, but no beer was drunk. If the man chosen as heir was young and the widows old, an older man was appointed to take the widows and part of the property. If, however, the widows were young, the heir, though young, took them all to wife and took all the property.

If a man was struck by lightning, the clan members cut stout branches of trees, stripped them of bark, thus making them white, and planted them round the place to form an enclosure, in the centre of which was a post to mark the spot.

Suicides were simply thrown out on to waste land and left unburied, and the house was inhabited as before.

The bodies of women were also cast out on to waste land. If a woman died in child-birth, the husband had to give her relatives a cow; but if she died from another cause, her clan gave the husband another woman or five goats, or half the original marriage-price if this had been large.

CHAPTER XII

THE BAKAMA AND THE BATWA

Origin of the Bakama—smiths—differences from the Basabei—initiation—marriage—death—the Batwa—food and trade—beer

THE BAKAMA

ON one of the plateaux of Mount Elgon people were found who were called the Bakama, and who were regarded as a clan of the Sabei tribe. On investigation these were found to be one of the agricultural or artisan clans of Kitara, who came to Mount Elgon from Buruli about the time Kamrasi reigned in Kitara, and who took the name Bakama because of their former allegiance to the Mukama of Kitara. Their totems were *nkima*, the black-faced monkey, and *kisanki*, the grass used for thatching houses; and, as they understood smelting and general iron-work, they were important additions to the Sabei tribe, whose customs they to a large extent adopted.

The clan numbered some six hundred, and included some purely agricultural workers as well as smiths. The iron-workers all taught their sons, who followed their trade, so that the art was confined to certain families. They never made hoes, but only weapons and ornaments.

They retained their old superstitions and gods, but have added and still continue to add to them by adopting the religious ideas of the people whom they have joined. In certain customs, however, they differed from the Basabei. When twins were born they and their parents were secluded for two months, during which goats and other food had to be collected for a feast when they were brought out. If the father had to go out himself to collect this material he had to find a substitute to remain in his place in the hut and to be with his wife. Should one or both of the twins die, the body was buried in the vicinity of the home and the husband and wife had to leave the hut to attend the burial. At the end of three years, the bones were dug up and carried to a dry cave in the mountain, where they were laid in a safe place. To leave them in the earth to moulder away would prevent the women of the clan from giving birth. At the time of the removal relations and friends came together and rejoiced with beer-drinking and dancing.

In the past, when the tribe inhabited its old country, mutilations were avoided, with the exception of the extraction of six teeth in the lower jaw; but when they had migrated, parents found that their children could not marry into the tribe they had joined. Clan exogamy was their rule; and, in order to obtain husbands for their daughters and wives for their sons, they adopted the Basabei customs of initiation, and all the present generation have been circumcised. They followed the customs of the Bambei, the second division of the Basabei, which varied slightly from those of the Basabei in that the girls were caught and taken in marriage during the dance which followed the circumcision ceremonies. If the bride's mother accepted the youth, the marriage-fee, which was five goats and a bull, was paid. In earlier times girls who were marriageable lived together in a special house, and a man who wished to marry one of them spent the night with her there. The next day he sent a hoe to her parents, this being the usual token by which he asked for their daughter in marriage. If the hoe was accepted, the marriage-fee, which at that period was five or six goats, was arranged and paid; and the bridegroom sent for the girl, who came to him accompanied by some twenty companions. These remained with her seven days to dig her new garden, and on their departure were given iron bracelets, necklets, and finger-rings. Should the bride's mother reject the hoe, the man had to seek another maid in marriage, leaving his first choice to some more acceptable suitor.

The dead were simply thrown into waste ground in accordance with the Sabei custom, until the British authorities ordered the chiefs to see that they were buried.

Another small agricultural clan, the *Bagweri*, who lived near these Bakama, were also immigrants from Kitara.

THE BATWA

A report that there were a number of people called Batwa living on the higher peaks of Elgon aroused much interest, as the name is that given to the pygmies who live in the Congo districts to the west of Lakes Albert and Edward. One or two diminutive Bagesu were even pointed out as being of the type of these Batwa of Elgon. It was difficult to find any members of the clan on the lower mountain slopes, but after some trouble a few were found in forests and on the higher peaks, and were persuaded to come and be interviewed.

The meeting, however, was disappointing, for they were found to be tall men who claimed to be members of the Sabei tribe, who had separated from them and given up all agriculture to follow hunting and trapping, especially of rats and a species of mole. They were few in number and lived scattered over the higher parts of the mountain. They kept a few cows, sheep, and goats, which they herded on the mountain, but they lived mainly on wild animals, which they trapped, and upon young and tender shoots of bamboo, wild honey, and milk. They seldom hunted any game larger than hares, but they trapped rats and moles, which they roasted in their skins, merely removing the entrails. These animals they regarded as a great delicacy. What meat they could spare from their catch they dried and bartered with the other clans for grain, pots, and sheep- and goat-skins for their girdles and shoulder robes.

They visited recognised spots which were known to the agricultural people as market-places for the sale of their products.

They ate the young shoots of the bamboo as vegetables, using only the tender tips; but they dried some ten inches more, which they brought down to the lower parts of the mountain and exchanged for grain. The people who purchased these dry bamboo shoots cut them up and used them, boiled, as a relish with other food.

They brewed a kind of beer from honey, which they extracted from the comb and strained through grass to remove wax. This extracted honey was put in pots and hung on trees for about ten days to ferment, after which it was again filtered through grass to remove any remaining comb; and formed a drink more intoxicating than the millet-beer used by other tribes.

All the customs of initiation and the clan ceremonies of the Basabei were observed as before their severance from the main body. They may therefore be regarded as an offshoot of the tribe.

CHAPTER XIII

LANGUAGE OF THE BASABEI

Relationships—divisions of time—counting—currency—vocabulary

RELATIONSHIPS

Father, baba.
Mother, yoyo.
Brother, yayanyenyu.
Sister, gayenenyu.
Husband, boyondenyo.
Wife, gorogo.
Son, sekwa.
Daughter, sekwa.
Father's mother, gugo.
Father's father, gugo.
Mother's mother, kameti.
Mother's father, gogo.

Father's brother, babausi.
Father's sister, senge.
Mother's brother, mama.
Mother's sister, mama.
Father's brother's wife, yoyonyo.
Father's sister's husband, bubo.
Mother's brother's wife, gogo.
Mother's sister's husband, buba.
Father's brother's son, sewekino.
Father's brother's daughter, kye-minyo.
Father's sister's son, mujugoliti.

Father's sister's daughter, mujugo-liti.
Mother's brother's son, kasenya-ndeti.
Mother's brother's daughter, kase-nyandeti.
Mother's sister's son, mama.
Mother's sister's daughter, mama.
Son's son, gugo.
Son's daughter, gugo.
Daughter's son, gugo.
Daughter's daughter, gugo.
Sister's son, lekwenyu.
Sister's daughter, lekwenyu.
Brother's son, lekwenyu.
Brother's daughter, lekwenyu.
Wife's father, kabigoi.
Wife's mother, kyabiyorakabigoi.

Wife's brother, kabikoi.
Wife's sister, kabikoi.
Wife's brother's wife, karoga lwa-lekweti.
Wife's sister's husband, bugo-tyenyo.
Husband's father, baba.
Husband's mother, lwekwenyu.
Husband's brother, karogo.
Husband's sister, yaiyenyu.
Husband's brother's wife, harawe.
Husband's sister's husband, hara-we.
Son's wife, eyonyo.
Daughter's husband, sandeta lwa lwekwenyo.
Elder brother, katini nyene.
Younger brother, katini nyini.

Seasons

These people had no means of marking dates though they could give a general idea of the time of an event not more than a year old. When a child was born, its age might be remembered for a few weeks but, beyond that, age was judged by the appearance of the person—by the size of the breasts in girls and by the signs of adolescence in boys. For their own purposes they divided the year into moons which were named:

August, Mugeyo.
October, Tamwa.
December, Teriti.
February, Wagiabureti.
April, Lalabehi.
June, Sundetabureti.
September, Tedere.
November, Watukob.
January, Wagitiabutai.
March, Labutoi.
May, Sundetabutai.
July, Silwona.

The beginning of the year was *Togo*, or *Kenyini*. The season of the lesser rains (*kenyino*) was *Dumbi* and the heavy rains were *Bengati*. The season of the hottest sun was *Kimei*. *Kyawalaseti*, the rainbow. *Katulili*, thunder. *Ela* or *elet*, lightning.

Counting

1. *Agenge*, index-finger extended.
2. *Ayenyi*, index and second finger extended.
3. *Simoko*, index-finger bent in and others extended.

4. *Mweni*, four fingers extended in pairs.
5. *Muntu*, closed fist.
6. *Muntunekagenge*, closed fist and index-finger of other hand put to it.
7. *Muntuagayene*, two fingers laid in the other hand.
8. *Muntuasomoka*, three fingers of the left laid in the right hand.
9. *Muntuangwe*, closed fist and four fingers of the other hand extended.
10. *Tamani*, two closed fists.

For the higher numbers they brought bits of stick for each ten.

CURRENCY

Two cows=a woman.
Twenty goats=a female cow.
Ten goats=a young bull.
Twenty fowls=a female goat.
Fifteen fowls=a male goat.
Five rats=a bunch of plantain.
Ten rats=a basket of grain about 20 lbs.

VOCABULARY

All, tokole
arm, out
arrow, kotet

Back, runget
bad, miat
be, to, unyoto
beast, kyonito
beautiful, natebon (i.e. *perfect, good*)
believe, kajam
bird, gogele
bitter, nywe
black, nyetuwi
blood, koroti
body, oluta
bone, kawet
born, to be, kirikwet
bow, eyanda
breath, itit
bright, ayosit
burn, kabere

Carry, kusut
chief, munongotya

child, lehweta
club, koroita
come, jo
command, kayaroriki
cut, kateri

Dance, tumuto (*sing*)
dark, komoye
die, kami
do, isiet
dream, ilwotegi
drink, kiye

Ear, ititi
earth, tenyek
eat, kyokyamu
enemy, mihati
eye, konyita

False, kiberabera
fear, nyogor
few, minini
fight, bori
fire, mata
fish, buburunik
food, oniki

PLATE XV

Man of the Batwa tribe. Mount Elgon

PLATE XVI

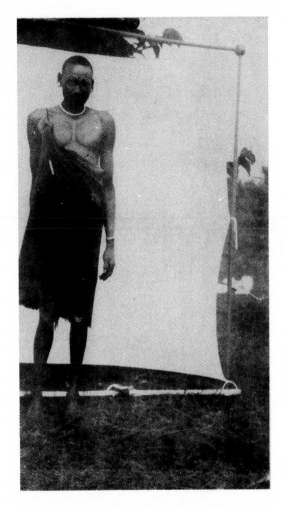

Man of the Batwa tribe, Mount Elgon

foolish, minyi
foot, kerengeti
forest, samita *or* wogeti
friend, jolwa

Ghost, oike
give, kikono
go, yau
good, natebon (*beautiful*)
green, ata

Hair, kurore
hand, auti
hard, nyewahi
hate, katai
head, mititi
hear, kalimi
heart, muguliito
heavy, nigisi
high, tarat
house, kwota

I, aninyo
it, kinigyo

Kill, kabala
know, karim

Large, kyamos
leg, aita
lie down, to, eru
light, koskos
live, pabani
liver, augutani
long, koi
loud, kwanangarhusi
love, gyamike
low, lingit

Man, muroni
many, bagalai
marry, kamutu kurogo
moon, awareti
mountain, legamet
mouth, kotati

Nails, bulo
neck, katit
new, kalai
no, katai *or* kutai
nose, siruti

not, buliegi

Old, boyo

Palm, tabesta
part, muroro

Quick, lawkar

Red, ara
river, ainet
run, ogonyi

Sea, ainet (*river*)
see, kukasi
shadow, atotoeto
she, anenya (*thou*)
shield, longet
short, onwak
shoulder, leet
sing, tumuto (*dance*)
sit, tebinguyi, burunguyi
skin, rihondeti
sky, talati
sleep, rungunyi
slow, kiomoti
small, kisiki
smell, samisi
soft, bunubun
sorcerer, wologoyo
soul, mugule
speak, ngowo kumwo
spear, ngotit
stand, ionyi
star, ogelek
stone, lwandet, lwondo
strike, kumiri
sun, asisista
sweet, anyingot

Take, sutwe
taste, ngoranyi
tell, jokumo
that, onyin
they, birine
thing, terekwo
think, tunuwo
this, onyi
thou, anenya (*she*)
tongue, eleta

tooth, kaleke
touch, bulyokonani
tree, kitiki
true, kuromsgota

Ugly, mietini

Walk, yabucheki
war, borei, setetwa
water, bego
we, ajek
which, kinegyo

white, nyerere
who, ngomere
whole, tegutukole
wise, netinyarek
wish, kajamekuwo
woman, kurogo
word, nalek

Yes, kajamu
you, wenyo
young, kisiki

PLATE XVII

Teso granaries

THE BATESO

CHAPTER XIV

A NILOTIC TRIBE

Clans and totems—government—robbery—murder and suicide—the cattle—agriculture—clothing and ornaments—rain-making—birth—training of children—marriage—adultery and fornication—death—mourning—inheritance

THE following notes are supplementary to those given in the *Northern Bantu* and give in some cases customs which differ from those described there.

This tribe was a large one and the villages, which were numerous, seemed prosperous. The cattle, which were of a kind with a hump, were plentiful and in good condition. The tribe was divided into clans which were totemic, though I have not been able to find many of the totems. The clan divisions were used to settle marriage questions, for the tribe practised clan exogamy. The names of the clans were:

Magoro, totem *mpeyo*=kind of antelope.
Yatekoko.
Iraraka.
Inyakoi.
Igolya.
Ipalama.
Iyale.
Nyakwe, totem *ngabi*=kind of antelope.
Gwarimota, totem *nyana*=calf.
Emesina, totem *nyonyi*=bird.

The clans were often at enmity and fought each other frequently, the warriors carrying spears and shields.

GOVERNMENT

There were no chiefs who had any extended authority, though here and there a man might make himself the head of several villages. As a rule, however, each village had its own head-man who settled all disputes in it, and there was no possibility of appeal to any higher authority. There was no taxation, but the village chief might call men to build or to dig for him, and in payment gave them meat and beer.

Robbery was not common, but there were certain men who were known to be expert thieves and who were hired by others to steal for them. They took auguries by the *ngato* leathers (*v.* p. 108) to find out where and how to do the required work, and were often tracked afterwards by their footprints. If one was killed, the man who had hired him had to pay one or two cows to the relatives of the dead man, and had to supply his father with a girl who might bear him another child to take the place of the dead son. Should a thief be captured and brought to trial, he was punished by a fine.

If a murderer escaped, the offended clan killed some member of the murderer's clan and were satisfied.

If a man wounded another while out hunting, they would most probably settle the affair on the spot by a free fight during which some men were sure to be killed.

A man who committed suicide was buried by his relatives in the ordinary way.

OCCUPATIONS

Cows were numerous, for even a poor peasant usually possessed four or five and women also kept a few. The cattle of a village were kept together in a stockade at one side of the village, though sometimes they were kept in it.

When a cow calved, the milk was left to the calf for three days. The cow was then milked and the milk cooked until it formed a solid cake, which was eaten by members of the owner's family before the milk might be used in the ordinary way.

The small millet, called *bulo*, was the staple food, but other millet was also grown and from it beer was brewed. Sorghem, sweet potatoes, ground nuts, and semsem were also grown and of late years Europeans have settled in the country and are growing cotton.

CLOTHING

Fifteen years ago when I visited this people they wore no clothing at all, though they wore ornaments of different kinds. Young women pinched up and pierced the flesh of their chests and threaded in the holes rows of fine iron rings about the size of finger-rings. The more wealthy people wore wire or strings of beads or cowry-shells round their waists, necks, upper arms, and wrists. The ears were pierced from the lobes right round the helix and small brass or iron rings were inserted. A few girls wore aprons, some six inches broad and four deep, of plaited fibre decorated with beads or cowry-shells, but even these were regarded as ornaments, not as covering.

Of later years, however, the steady influx of Indian traders and settlers has altered the people's outlook, and garments of cotton and calico are generally worn, with the addition, in most cases, of ornaments.

Religion

The only religious ceremonies seemed to be those of rain-making. When rain was wanted the people took branches and danced round some hill or rock singing to *Edeke* who was the creator. They splashed water about and prayed for rain and good crops.

Birth

When a woman conceived, she informed her mother, who came and stayed with her until the birth and the period of seclusion were over and the woman was able to go about again. The mother acted as midwife during the birth. The cord was cut with a knife and the placenta was buried, by the midwife in the house, on the far side from the bed. The mother was isolated for five days, after which she was brought out to be purified and the house was swept out and fresh grass laid on the floor. During the time of seclusion no fire or fire-wood might be taken from the house, but there was no other taboo.

A child was named at birth, and at six months old it was made to sit up. The mother usually nursed it for from eighteen months to two years.

Little boys were taught to herd calves, and at about the age of seven they went out with the herdsmen and learned how to look after the cows. At about the age of seven also the girls began to learn to dig and do the other work of women.

At puberty both boys and girls had the two lower incisors extracted. It was unheard of for anyone to refuse this, and boys and girls were usually eager to have it done in order to be considered grown-up.

MARRIAGE

The usual clan exogamy prevailed among these people, and as marriages were arranged by the parents, questions of relationship and clan membership seldom presented any difficulty. Boys and girls were betrothed in infancy and never thought of rebelling against the arrangement made for them. Most men contented themselves with one wife, though there seemed to be no restriction as to the number of women a man might marry.

When a marriage was arranged, the boy's father gave a cow to the girl's parents as a pledge, and the acceptance of this was the agreement to the marriage. When the girl grew up her mother brewed beer and summoned the prospective husband to come and drink and settle the marriage-fee, which amounted to from ten to twenty cows.

When he had succeeded in obtaining the required number of cows, the bridegroom, with a companion, took them in the afternoon to the bride's home and brought her away, timing their journey to reach her new home about four in the after-noon. Four girl friends accompanied the bride and remained with her for two days. Before they departed the bridegroom gave them a sheep, or, if he was a poor man, a fowl. On the day of her arrival the bride brought in water and cooked a meal. The newly-married couple lived with the bridegroom's parents until the bride had dug her field and grown enough food to support her husband and herself. The husband then built his own house near and they moved into it. If a man married more than one wife he built each a house in his village.

When a man committed adultery, the aggrieved man called

together his friends and they attacked the offender's house, carrying off all his goods and despoiling his field. To redeem his possessions he had to bring a cow and five sheep.

When a girl was found to have gone wrong and to be with child, she was beaten by her parents until she confessed the name of the guilty man. He was then accused and fined a cow and five sheep. The child was looked upon as the child of the woman's husband whether she married the seducer or another.

DEATH

When a man died his widow or widows slept beside the body for two days before it was buried. They threw all kinds of grain upon the body in the grave and also threw in the first earth. A cow or bull was killed and the body wrapped in the skin, while the meat was eaten by the mourners during the days of mourning. The grave was dug in the house where the man had died and mourning went on for five days, the people wailing each morning at four o'clock. On the third day a second cow was killed and eaten by the mourners, and on the fifth day they departed to their own homes.

The widows remained in the house and mourned for some five months. It used to be customary for widows to commit suicide by ripping up their stomachs or by hanging themselves, but they were guarded and might even be tied up to prevent this. There was no purificatory ceremony after the mourning, and the widows themselves arranged how long they would mourn.

The first time beer was brewed after the death, a little was thrown on the grave.

When the heir came to take possession of the house and property, he killed a third cow or bull and brewed beer. He then summoned the members of his clan to eat and drink with him, which was the last ceremony of the funeral. The heir took possession of the widows, but if one chose she might return home if the original marriage-fee was repaid. The house was kept in repair and the people continued to live in it as before.

Inheritance

If a man had a son old enough to manage his property, he was usually the heir, but if he had no grown-up son, a relative, usually a brother, was appointed to inherit. If there were several sons in the family, the eldest took the house and the widows, but the others received each a share of the cattle. Sometimes a man gave his wives presents of cattle during his lifetime, and in that case, the widows retained possession of these when they became the wives of his heir.

BUSOGA

CHAPTER XV

THE PEOPLE AND THE GOVERNMENT

Early condition and later subservience—effects of rule of Kitara—
taxation by Buganda—training of chiefs—clan land—chiefs—the
great chief—lesser chiefs—right of appeal—the clans and their totems
—taxation—punishment—murder and suicide

THE people of Busoga who were examined were purely
negro in type, though of a somewhat higher development
than the Bagesu on Mount Elgon. They were of the same class
as the peasants of Kitara or Bunyoro, with broad noses and
thick lips. At one time they formed a collection of small
independent family groups, whose only connecting link was
the intermarriage rendered necessary by the laws of clan
exogamy. In later years, however, the Bakitara, or Banyoro,
became overlords of the country, and the scattered family
groups were united into districts governed by chiefs. These
chieftainships were hereditary; but disputes often arose as to
which son should inherit, and such questions were settled by
the king of Kitara. The people of Busoga called the Bakitara,
Baduli, and their country, *Buduli*. Later the Baganda began
to encroach upon much of the land which belonged or was sub-
servient to Kitara; and by degrees the whole of Busoga, with
the exception of one district, came under the rule of the
Kabaka, or king, of Buganda.

The effects of the rule of Kitara are still plainly visible, for
the people follow in many ways the customs of the Bakitara.
For example, at puberty they extract the six front teeth in
the lower jaw, and many of their ceremonies, especially those
connected with death and mourning, are similar to those of
their former overlords. Their language, too, was much influenced by Lunyoro and when contact with Buganda became

close, the combined effect was such that nothing is now left to show what the original tongue was.

Under the rule of the king of Buganda, the Basoga were not subject to any fixed taxation, but messengers were sent into the country each year to collect a tax, and the king, if he found himself in need of animals or slaves, would send into Busoga and demand to be supplied with what he required. The tax in itself was not heavy, but the messengers sent to collect it seized the opportunity and demanded as much as they liked, keeping the surplus for themselves. It was this additional burden which caused the chiefs of Busoga, in later years, to ask that the British would free them from the yoke of Buganda.

Another effect of this subservience to a neighbouring kingdom was that the sons of chiefs were sent at one time to the court of the king of Kitara and later to that of the king of Buganda. This was not only a method of educating the sons of the chiefs, but it ensured that these boys would succeed to the chieftainships of their own country and rise to high positions there. Each of the greater chiefs of Busoga had a small estate in Buganda, which was looked after for him by a steward. He was thus enabled to visit Buganda and remain there for some considerable time, living on the products of his own land.

LAND

The clans of the Basoga did not keep themselves entirely separate or confine themselves strictly to their own localities, but to a certain extent they scattered and mixed. Each clan, however, had land which belonged to it, and the head of the clan was known as the *Mutaka* or freeholder. This land could never pass from the ownership of the clan, and a clan member who was granted land by the head of the clan could not be deprived of it. There was always plenty of land, and a clan member who desired to possess some had merely to apply to the head of the clan, who would allocate to him a certain defined portion. A member of another clan might be allowed to cultivate land, but only as a tenant (*musiga*) whose land

might be taken from him if it was required for a member of
the clan to which it belonged.

The paramount chief, or *Mwami*, in each district was also
the head of the clans in that district, the office being hereditary. He was regarded as the owner of all the land, and could
grant to any man a piece of ground which would become the
freehold of his family. The *Mwami* gave the man a tree which
he planted on the ground, and when he died, his son buried
him in this ground and claimed it as his by virtue of the tree
and of his father's grave. If, however, a man buried his dead
in any place without the sanction of the *Mwami*, and later
became owner of another piece of land, he might be ordered
by the *Mukungu*, or secondary chief, to remove his dead,
even of two generations, and bury them in his own land.

The members of each clan were careful to see that their
rights of property in land were not infringed. The possession
of land was a frequent cause of disputes and fighting between
clans and tribes. The members of two clans would often fight
the matter out, and the stronger side took possession of the
disputed ground. At times, however, the clan which had
transgressed beyond its own boundaries would consent to
withdraw and allow the matter to be settled by arbitration.
When the matter concerned two districts, it was left to the
Mwami, or paramount chiefs, to arrange.

THE CHIEFS

The superior chief or *Mwami* in a district was regarded as
the owner of all the land in that district and as the head of
the clans there. He tried any cases which were referred to
him from the lesser chiefs, and might refer them in his turn
to the king of Buganda, but there were no regular court fees.
The names of the chiefs of the districts at the time of my visit
were: Wakole of Mukama, Kitimba of Mukama, Luba or
Mutabula of Mukama, Zibondo of Mukama, Kisiginya, Miro,
Zimba of Mukama, Tabingwa of Mukama, Menya of Bugwire
of Mukama.

When a chief left his district to visit friends or to go to

Buganda, he appointed in his place someone in whom he had confidence. During the chief's absence this man was regarded as the chief, and for anyone to treat him with disrespect or abuse him was a criminal offence punishable by a heavy fine.

The first great chief was said to have been a prince of Kitara, called *Kitimbo*, who came with his brothers *Musali* and *Ngobe* from Kitara and ruled Busoga. His descendants, who succeeded him and were chiefs of western Busoga with the official title of *Kitimbo*, were Mawarara—Nadiope—Kagoda—Gabula—Kajumbula—Mutilwa—Naika, who was deposed by the British—Nadiope. These chiefs, who claimed to be descendants of Kitimbo, were considered of greater importance than all other chiefs. Should any person commit adultery with a wife of one of them, he and his whole clan were put to death and their lands and other property were confiscated. The mother of such a chief was known as Namasole, and possessed land in her own right, where she had complete power, trying cases through her own prime minister or *Katikiro*. No other woman in the land possessed property. The sister of such a chief or of any district chief, was an important person and invariably married some chief in the same district, having due regard to the rules of clan exogamy. She possessed no property and her position after marriage depended on that of her husband.

The second grade of chiefs were known as the *Bakungu* and they, with the third grade, the *Bamitale*, formed a council to assist the superior chiefs when required. The *Bamitale* were appointed by the district chiefs or *Mwami*, who had the right to appoint any man to one of these posts, regardless of clan, and to depose him. Usually another man of the same clan as the former holder succeeded to such an office, but this was not a binding rule. Below the *Bamitale* was yet another rank of chiefs who were known as the *Wakisoko*.

When a cause arose which had to be settled by law, the litigants probably appealed to the chief who was in direct touch with them, but they had also the right to appeal to the higher courts of the superior chiefs, who in turn might carry cases to the king of Buganda; this, however, was rather an expensive proceeding, for not only must they take presents of cattle to the king, but they had to be prepared to give handsome presents to any Muganda chief through whose lands they passed on their way to the court of the king.

THE CLANS

The following is a list of a number of the clans of the Basoga given at this time:

CLAN	TOTEM
Baise mbupi	*Njazi*, antelope
,, magaya	*Ngonya*, crocodile
,, ndigo	*nfumbe*, monkey, and *nyonyi*, a bird
Basubu	*musisi wa bulo*, chaff of millet
Baise nulondo	*nkima*, monkey?
Bakose	*musisi wa bulo*, chaff of millet
Baise kidugu	*mamba*, lung-fish?
Banangwi	*mbuzi*, goat
Baise musobya	*nkobe*, large monkey?
,, mwasi	*ndaza* (? *njazi*, antelope?)
,, muchwa	*ndiga*, sheep
,, muiri	*mpindi*, beans
,, ngobe (chief)	*ngabi*, bush-buck
Basoko	*mpongo*, antelope?
Baise musoswe	*mpisi*, hyaena
Bakoyo	*nabibalu*, or *mamba*, lung-fish?
Baise kisigi	*nyonyi miweba*, a bird
Bapina	*nkofu*, guinea-fowl
Baganza	*mbuzi wa kubuli*, goat that cast its young
Baise ndasi	*mpewo*, antelope
,, kaboza	*mpindi*, beans
,, sanga	*nkofu*, guinea-fowl
,, mukaya	*mpanda*, ground-nuts
,, egaga	*musisi wa bulo*, husks of millet
,, bagaya	*nyonyi*, bird
,, kisukwe	*butiko*, mushroom? (*tabitantyo*, a vegetable?)
,, ngwa	*mbuzi*, goat
,, semakika	*mbogo*, buffalo
,, rungu	*nyangi*, white bird
,, nkwanga	*njovu*, elephant

TAXATION

The chiefs had no power to impose taxation for their own benefit, but the people would bring them gifts of animals and

vegetable food at times by their own free will. The king of
Buganda, however, imposed regular taxes and sent his own
messengers to see to their collection. These tax collectors took
up their abode with different chiefs and made known the
amount of the tax which had to be paid. The people were expected to bring their share of the tax to the chief's house,
where the total amount was gathered together. There was no
legal method of assessing the tax, and the people, by bribery
or other methods, made the best bargain they could with
the collector, who not only wished to take to the king as
much as he could in order to be commended and rewarded,
but tried to obtain something beyond the king's requirements, which he could keep for himself. It was this method of
tax-collecting which made the rule of Buganda obnoxious to
the Basoga, who on the arrival of the British asked to be
relieved therefrom. The tax was usually paid in slaves, cattle,
and bark-cloths which were specially made for the purpose
and brought tied in bundles of fifty. The chief in whose place
the collection was made received some of these and the rest
were conveyed to Buganda.

CRIME AND PUNISHMENT

The usual method of punishment was by fines, which were
often so heavy as to necessitate years of hard labour before
the man was free from debt. Imprisonment in the stocks was
used more as a method of detention until a case could be tried
than as a means of punishment, though for adultery or theft
a man might, in addition to being heavily fined, be flogged
and put in the stocks until the fine was paid or someone was
found to stand surety for its payment. The greatest hardship
of detention in the stocks was the difficulty of obtaining food,
for there was no prison fare and the person had to depend on
the pity and generosity of friends. If, however, a man was
convicted of being a confirmed stealer of vegetables from the
gardens or of animals, or of making a practice of breaking
into houses by digging under the walls, he was put to death,
usually by being speared.

Murder was not a common crime and it was usually not difficult to discover the murderer, for men seldom wandered beyond the range of their own village and friends. When a murder was committed, it was the duty of the dead man's clan fellows to seek out the murderer and avenge the death. Fear of the vengeance of the ghost, which might punish them with illness or even death for negligence, made the clan members eager in their search for justice.

If a man killed another of the same clan, he himself was caught and killed, unless he succeeded in taking refuge with some other tribe. In that case he allowed some four or five years to pass, and, when the bitterness had died down, he returned and paid a fine of a cow in settlement of the affair. Even if the murder was accidental, the man fled from his home and lived in some secret place until the fine had been paid and the matter settled. Any man who had killed another had to live and eat alone until he had atoned for his wrong and been reconciled.

If a man murdered one of another clan, the relatives of the murdered man raised the alarm, whereupon the clan rushed to arms and prepared for war. The chief might succeed in restraining his people while he went to the chief of the other clan to demand the person of the murderer. If he was given up, he was killed and the matter ended, but if the chief refused to give him up, the two clans fought until a few deaths and some wounds induced the injured clan to consent to a settlement by arbitration.

A man, however, who killed another in battle was treated with respect, received presents from his chief and was feasted and praised by all. In this case there was no separation from his friends nor was any purification required.

Should any man spit upon another, the injured man might kill him without being accused of murder.

A man who committed suicide was never buried, but the body was cast out on to waste land. Should the deed have been done by hanging on a tree, the tree was cut down, cast on to waste land near the body and burned. A house which was the scene of a suicide was also destroyed by fire. The idea evidently was to dislodge the ghost from the place lest others might be induced to commit the same crime.

CHAPTER XVI

RELIGION

Sacred places—the gods—ghosts—removing illness—worship of dead chiefs—rain-making—auguries by the *ngato* leathers—workers of evil magic—the new moon—earthquakes—water-spirits—tree-spirits

THOUGH the religion of the Basoga was polytheistic and the gods had their temples and their priests (called, as in Kitara, the *Bachwezi*), there was no definite or systematic form of worship, though certain requests were made through the priests at the temples of the gods. In some places there were sacred hills and rocks which were said to be animated by spirits, and to these the people went in time of need. They built small shrines and made offerings to the spirits of the place, calling upon them for help. At these places as at the temples there was no ordered form or stated time of worship, but offerings and prayers were made when the need arose.

The names of the gods were:

Lubare, the creator. He had numbers of shrines in different parts of the country to which people went with offerings and requests. The priest presented the offerings to Lubare and then killed fowls in front of the shrine and divided them. One-half went to the people who had brought the offerings and the other to the priests.

Lubanga, the god who healed sickness.

Kintu, the helper of women in child-birth.

Walumbe, the god of the dead. To him all the departed souls went soon after death to report themselves. Singularly, *Walumbe* was also the god who gave women children. Each

newly-married woman went to ask his blessing in order that
she might bear children. If a wife of a chief had no children,
he sent her with offerings to this god.

Watambogo, the god of the hills and of gifts.

Musisi, the god of earthquake.

Kiwanuka, the god of thunder.

Each family adopted one of these gods as its special deity
to whom the members might turn in times of extreme need.
The priests were known as *Bachwezi* and might be either male
or female. They dwelt in the temples and acted as inter-
mediaries between the people and the gods. They had mediums
who communicated directly with the gods and through them
the people received oracles.

As a rule only men approached the priests in order to appeal
to the gods, but a man might on occasions send his wife,
accompanied by a suitable escort. Sometimes women who
were childless would stand on ant-hills and call upon the gods
to help them, promising substantial gifts in return for a child.
They would also sometimes steal away to the priests and
pray for help to have a child. When a child was born after
such a visit, the woman and her husband visited the shrine
and gave a gift of a goat and fowls. No children were ever
given to the gods for the temples.

The gods, however, concerned the people much less directly
than the ghosts of their ancestors. The ghosts were regarded
as phantoms and spoken of as air, but the people built shrines
for them and were convinced of their power to help or injure
the living. Though invisible, they dwelt in the vicinity of
their living relatives and their influence could be felt.

When a man died, he was believed to remain among the
plantains near the place where the body lay, to watch what
was done, for the treatment of the body affected the future
of the ghost. The body was always buried in the earth and a
mound or ridge of earth, sloping to the ground all round and
rising to a height of about eighteen inches, was made over
the grave. This mound was beaten hard and had to be kept
in good repair and not allowed to crumble away, for it was

the roof of the grave and served to keep it dry. At the head of the grave a shrine was built, which in the case of a peasant took the form of a small hut, while that at the grave of a chief was quite a large building in which his widows resided during the mourning and where one of them took up her residence to guard the grave. The grave was guarded and kept in repair sometimes for as long as eight years, for any neglect would annoy the ghost, which would cause illness or trouble in the 'family.

Offerings were made to ghosts of the family and also to important ghosts of the clan. These usually took the form of cattle, which were killed at the shrine and eaten in communion with the ghost. The ghost of one of its ancestors became the guardian of a child, though it was never supposed to enter into it as its animating spirit.

No shrines were built for women, and as a rule no attention was paid to their ghosts; but offerings might be made to the husband of a dead woman by members of the clan when there was illness among the children of the clan, and he would be requested to entreat his wife's ghost to spare the children.

Ghosts which were said to be causing illness had to be prevented from passing from one place to another, and for this purpose bark-cloths were hung on trees; beer was poured out at the roots and a pot was put under the tree. Passers-by were thus freed from the danger of being caught by the ghost. When, however, a hostile ghost succeeded in catching a man as he passed along a road, the man soon fell ill and had to send for the medicine-man to find out the cause. When the medicine-man discovered the presence of the ghost, he sang and made enchantments until it came out, when he caught it in grass, put it in a pot, and carried it away. For this work he had to be paid a goat, which he took home with him and either ate it or added it to his herd as he wished.

The bodies of great chiefs were treated differently from those of ordinary men, for the skull or sometimes the jaw-bone of a dead chief was removed and decorated, after which it was placed first in the shrine in which lay the skull or jaw-

bone of his predecessor. After a number of years, sometimes
as many as ten, a new shrine was built near the former one
and the latest skull was placed in it for worship. The time of
erecting this shrine was a season of public rejoicing; cows
were killed for food and much beer was drunk. There was a
high priest in this shrine whose office was confined to one clan.
When a priest died, many months were often allowed to
elapse before the election of a new holder of the office.

The common people regarded these skulls with much reverence, but they did not pray to them. The chiefs alone sent
an annual offering of a cow as well as many other offerings of
girls, cows, goats, or sheep, whenever there was any trouble.
The girls thus dedicated were used to dig on the estates of the
dead chief, and if one wished to marry, her clan might redeem
her by sending another girl to take her place. In return for
these offerings, the high priest consulted the oracle and gave
information connected with the civil and political affairs of
the country. He never concerned himself with personal
matters.

When people wanted rain, they might apply to a chief, who
demanded presents from them. He then sent to the high
priest and made known their wishes. As a rule, however,
when rain was wanted, the chief applied to certain medicine-
men known as *Basawa* who were important chiefs themselves.
The chief provided an animal, usually a bull, and called the
medicine-man to come with his fetishes. A fire was made
before the fence of the chief and prayers were offered for rain,
after which the bull was killed. The medicine-man took some
of the liver and heart of the animal killed, cut them up,
cooked them, and threw the pieces about for the ghosts,
who in return caused the rain to fall. The meat of the sacrifice
belonged to the medicine-man. People sometimes tried to
bring rain for themselves. They made large fires upon which
they threw damp grass and leaves so that dense clouds of
smoke arose, and they beat drums to imitate thunder. They
called upon the ghosts of their fathers and offered them beer
which they drank in communion with them.

Auguries for discovering a theft or other crime were often taken by means of the *ngato* leathers, which were pieces of leather, nine in number, made of thick cow-hide, and measuring five inches by three. The medicine-man threw these along a strip of leather and by their position read his augury. The office was hereditary and each man taught his skill to his son, who succeeded him.

There were certain men, the *Basizi*, who made magic for evil purposes and who were dreaded and if caught were burnt to death without mercy. They were said to come by night and dig up dead bodies from which they made medicine. They sprinkled this on gardens and cursed the place and people. When the owners of a garden found that such magic had been used, they left the place in terror and it was allowed to become waste. The *Basizi* were also said to be able to make fire by clapping their hands. Thus the whole population of a village might be made to flee from the place, which soon became a wilderness.

The new moon was always hailed with delight and people believed that it brought blessing. Mothers took their babies out and tried to make them look at the new moon, for that ensured health and rapid growth.

When there was an earthquake, a woman with child tied a band tight round her waist and all animals with young had bands tied round them, lest the young should be startled and made to jump and bring about premature birth.

When streams had to be crossed, coffee beans were scattered to appease the water-spirit. A woman while menstruating was never allowed to enter a canoe to cross a river, for the canoe would certainly be sunk by the water-spirit. The water-spirits had to be appeased before the body of a drowned man could be taken from a river, as is described later in the section upon Death (chapter XVIII).

All big trees were feared because they were the abode of spirits, and the members of a clan were afraid to cut down any big trees on their land. To overcome this difficulty they called in peasants from another place to come and fell the tree and cut it into boards. A goat or a sheep was tied to the tree and was then killed, and the men who had been sent for ate the meat in communion with the tree-spirit before they began to fell the tree. These spirits of trees and of water were of quite a different order from the spirits of men, but though they were not ghosts, they possessed superhuman power and were able to injure people if offended and to make them prosper if pleased.

CHAPTER XVII

OCCUPATIONS OF THE PEOPLE

The cows—milk restrictions—milk-pots—crops—plantains—millet—the first-fruits—brewing beer from millet—sowing maize—other crops—semsem—preparing food—clothing—preparation of bark-cloth—ornaments—building huts—taboos while building a new house—building canoes—canoes and tree-spirits—pottery—amusements—bands—hunting—taboos of hunters—care of dogs—fishing—warfare—arms of warriors—killing an enemy—treatment of wounds

CARE OF THE COWS

IN Busoga each man was the real owner of his cows and no one had the right to deprive him of any, though his chief often succeeded in obtaining some by the imposition of fines. The cows of Busoga were smaller than those in most parts of Uganda; they were black or black with white markings, and had a small hump and short horns. In many respects they were closely allied to the buffalo and were uncertain in temper and rather wild. There were no large herds, for even the chiefs had only a few animals; but every peasant, however poor, kept at least one cow, while some had as many as ten.

The cows were taken out to pasture during the day and were tied to posts in the houses by night. Men or men and boys herded them, and sometimes they were looked after with the goats and sheep by children; but women were not allowed to herd or to milk, though they might help to drive the cows into the houses at night or to let them out in the morning.

Boys were taught at an early age to look after and take entire charge of the cows and they acted as herdsmen to their fathers or hired themselves out to other men. Should a boy offend his master he might flog him or dismiss him, and the boy himself was free to leave his master whenever he felt so inclined. No regular payment was made for service, but a boy who was quick and a good worker was sure of promotion and might in time become a chief.

Milk restrictions were few and chiefly connected with the birth of calves. Among some clans, when a cow calved, the owner appointed a boy, his own son if possible, to drink the milk for three days. If he had no son he had to choose a boy over whom he had control, in order to be sure that the boy did not eat or drink anything which might, by sympathetic magic, injure the cow or its calf. When the umbilical cord dropped from the calf the owner might also drink the milk, and after that the taboo was ended and anyone might drink it. In other clans the boy chosen for the purpose took the first lot of milk and put it in some place of safety. The second milking might be drunk by anyone. When the milk of the first milking was clotted, the boy summoned some companions and shared it with them. Women might never drink the milk from a cow which had just calved.

Milk was drunk fresh or mixed with salt and cooked. Men drank it freely, but as a rule after any work or after a meal they refreshed themselves with beer. Milk-pots were made either of wood or of clay and were shaped rather like those of Kitara. They were washed with water by the women, who also churned any milk they could spare, the butter being used for smearing on the body and on weapons.

AGRICULTURE

The people said that they brought millet and plantains with them when they came into the country, but they learned to grow and use other food by contact with neighbouring tribes.

Plantains were the most important crop. For many years Busoga was looked upon as the finest plantain-growing district in the Uganda Protectorate. The groves extended without a break for many miles and supplied the people with abundant food. The men cleared the land, removing the trees and scrub, after which the women planted. The men also gave some assistance in the later work, such as pruning the trees, which, if properly attended to, would grow and bear freely for generations in the same place. The only instruments used in agriculture were the large knife for pruning the plantains, and the hoe.

The plantain was used both for food and for beer, the kind for beer being the "male," *mbide*, which was artificially ripened for the purpose.

The small millet (*bulo*) was the chief grain sown and it was used both for food and beer, though beer made from the large millet was preferred. A field was sown with millet for two or three seasons only and was then planted with sweet potatoes, while new land was found for the millet crop. The men cleared the land for the women, who then dug it and sowed the seed. Before sowing, however, both the land and the seed had to be blessed by a medicine-man, and while sowing the woman might not speak to anyone until she had finished. The fire which she took to the field to light her pipe was sacred, and no other person might take a light from it. There was no taboo on the woman while she was digging the field.

Two women, or sometimes a woman and her husband, sowed the seed. The husband went in front with his hoe, making holes about two inches deep, and the woman followed, dropping two seeds into each hole and pushing back the earth with her foot. If both the plants grew they were not thinned out, but were allowed to grow together. Sometimes four or five grains were planted in one hole, and as the millet grew it was thinned out by the men and the young plants were either cooked and eaten or replanted. The men often built huts in the fields and lived there to protect the crop from the ravages of wild animals, and they also helped at the time of harvest.

In some clans, the women would not allow anyone to eat

of the crop until their husbands had partaken of the first-fruits. In other clans there was no restriction as to this, while in others again, a woman took the first of the crop to her own father who ate it either raw or cooked, thus removing the restriction.

Millet, when used for beer, was roasted, ground, mixed with malt, and left for one night. The next day it was filtered, the malt being kept for use in the next brewing, and the liquid formed a slightly intoxicating drink, favoured because of the ease with which it was prepared.

Maize was grown in small plots and used as a luxury but never regarded as food for a meal. Sweet potatoes were cultivated in large quantities and were left in the ground until they were wanted for change of diet or to eke out the millet during the dry season. Beans were grown and, to a lesser extent, peas, which were eaten along with plantain. A little cotton was also grown.

The small oil-yielding plant semsem was grown by some of the more diligent women, whose husbands made the frame on which they dried it. If the husband himself was absent, he sent his representative to make this frame. The semsem was pounded to extract the oil and the pulp was made into cakes which were eaten with plantain in the place of meat. With this, as with other of the less important foods, it was not necessary that the husband should eat the first-fruits, but he had to eat some of the first ripe crop.

As a wife's part in the cultivation of food was so great, idleness or inability on her part was a common cause of strife between husband and wife, and bad cooking was also sufficient reason for a man to drive his wife away and send her back to her parents.

FOOD

Another of the duties of a wife was to cook food, which she did twice daily, at noon and again in the evening, the latter being the chief meal. The food was cooked in one large pot, the different kinds being made into packets and placed on green plantain fibre. A little water was added and the whole covered with leaves. A small fire would keep this food cooking and a child was left to watch the fire and keep it burning. If, however, a man wished to go on a journey and had to have a meal in a hurry, his wife cooked a little food in a small pot for him. If there were no guests, a man would eat with his wife, but if a guest appeared, the men ate together while the women and children ate apart from them.

Men might eat fowls and eggs but women were generally forbidden to do so. Women also avoided mutton, for they believed it would cause old age and decrepitude to come prematurely upon them; goat mutton, however, they ate freely. Various kinds of fish were common, but women were forbidden to eat them.

Clothing

The national dress was either bark-cloth or goat-skin, but most of the people preferred skins either of domestic or wild animals because of their durability and freedom from vermin, which increased rapidly in bark-cloth.

Bark-cloths, however, were still largely used, and were taken from the same trees and prepared by the same methods as in Buganda. A description of these methods will be found in my book *The Baganda*. After the bark-cloth had been beaten and dried, it was dipped in the boiling juice of the root of the *musasa* tree and then in a pool of black mud in a swamp. When dry this bark-cloth was quite black, which was a distinctive feature of the Busoga bark-cloths. Bark-cloth robes were worn by men like a mantle, tied up into a point at the back, while the women wrapped them round their bodies under their arms and wore a loin cloth as well. Bedding was always of bark-cloth.

Women wore necklets, bracelets, and anklets of brass, copper, or iron, which could be used for barter if necessary. They also sometimes cut scarifications, called *njalo*, on their bodies, but men never did so.

BUILDING

The huts of the Basoga were bee-hive in shape, like a large inverted basket of reeds or elephant grass, supported on poles which were firmly imbedded in the ground. The huts were carefully finished and the floors were made of earth, smoothed and beaten hard, and smeared with black clay mixed with cow-dung, which gave a hard smooth surface.

There were a few taboos to be observed when building. When the man gathered the grass for the thatch, his wife might not come near it or see it until it was on the house. When the dwelling was ready, a girl was sent to bring fire from some house near. She entered the new house with this, and, having lit the central fire, she rushed out with the smoke clinging about her. This was supposed to make the smoke in future go out of the house and not hang about to stifle people. No food might be cooked in a new house nor might anyone live in it until the wife had visited her parents and brought from them a fowl which she cooked there.

A man sent for his friends to help him in the building, and other friends brought food which his wife cooked. The workmen were supplied with this food and beer, and the work might take as long as the man wished.

When people entered a new house, the husband went first with his shield and spear and placed them on the right side of the doorway. The woman then came, bringing with her semsem prepared for a meal. She sent for a neighbour, who carried in the stones on which the pots had to stand while cooking, and put them in their place.

Canoe-building was one of the important industries of Busoga, and at one time the Basoga canoes were the best and largest on Lake Victoria. I have described the method of building in *The Baganda*, p. 283.

There was a strong belief in tree-spirits and the spirits of large trees were especially feared. A man, therefore, could not cut down a tree to make a canoe until he had made an offering, which generally consisted of a goat or a sheep, while

PLATE XVIII

Busoga hut

a string of cowry-shells was often tied round the trunk of the tree. When going to make the offering the man was accompanied by a priest, who went through a form of prayer or incantation, begging the spirit not to be annoyed and to allow the tree to be cut down and made into a canoe. As the spirit was supposed to accompany the boards which formed the canoe, offerings were made to it from time to time whenever a fishing expedition or a long journey was contemplated. When the canoe was finished beer and coffee-beans were put in it before it might be put into the water. Before launching, too, an offering of a fowl or a goat was made to the spirit and the blood was poured into the canoe at the bows.

OTHER INDUSTRIES

Smithing was seldom attempted, for all iron goods, spears, hoes, knives, etc., were purchased from the Bakitara, who brought them into the country and exchanged them for goats and sheep.

Pots were made by the women, who used the spiral method, that is, they made the soft clay into long rolls which they coiled round to form the sides of the pot, shaping it and smoothing it with the fingers and then with a piece of gourd shell. The pots were thick and heavy and little attempt was made to decorate or polish them. They had to be baked when the moon was increasing lest they should break. This was done in an open place where the fire could be kept up without fear of burning any house. Only light brush-wood could be used, for anything heavier would crush the pots.

AMUSEMENTS

Few games were indulged in, though at times men would meet together and feast and drink beer, after which they had a sham fight. These fights would sometimes become serious, for the men became too excited and clubbed and speared others as if they were really enemies.

The chief occasion for such feasts and games was when two neighbouring chiefs took an oath of friendship. A dog or a goat was then taken to some place agreed upon, and the two chiefs held the animal, one by the front and the other by the hind legs, while the priest cut it in two with one stroke of a knife. The two parties then had a feast and some games before separating. At such times bull-fights were usual, the animals being incited to attack each other until one was gored or driven away.

The appearance of the new moon was a time of universal rejoicing, when people gathered together and dancing continued far into the night, with much beer-drinking. Men and women danced separately, the men on one side and the women on the other, and they danced either standing up or crouching as they preferred.

The Busoga bands were famed all over that part of the country and were even sent for by chiefs of Buganda to go and play on special occasions. They would go to the chief's residence and live there for about a week, playing daily for him. The bands consisted chiefly of wind instruments like trumpets, made of gourds or horns, some quite short and others from twenty to thirty inches long. Two or three drums to beat the rhythm and ten or twelve of these trumpets composed a band, and the men marched round the dancers as they played.

Harps, too, were sometimes used. A wooden bowl some ten inches long by eight wide and four deep formed the sounding board. This was covered with lizard-skin, and to it were attached two sides of a frame some fourteen to eighteen inches long. A cross-piece was fixed to the end of this frame and the strings were attached to pegs passing through the cross-piece so that they could be turned and the strings loosened or tightened for tuning.

HUNTING

Busoga was not an elephant country, and it was only when herds passed through on their way from one grazing ground to another that a hunt was possible. Until recent years no value was placed on the ivory and hunting was only for the sake of the meat, so that few men cared to run the risks attendant on the sport. Lately, however, the people have learned to place a value on ivory, and men have taken to hunting for the purpose of securing it.

The most common method of killing elephants was by spearing them from trees. The hunters climbed into trees along a path by which the animals went to the water. As an elephant passed under one of the trees the hunter hurled his spear down, aiming at its back between the shoulders. Another man then waved something to attract its attention and as it charged at him it had to pass under another tree, in which a man was concealed, and another spear was aimed at it. This was kept up until the elephant fell. Weighted spears were sometimes fixed in trees and a trap arranged so that the animal in passing under the tree released the spear, which fell on to its shoulders or back. Men had to lie in wait and follow the animal, which might die soon if the spear had been well placed, but might wander for days before it died or could be killed.

Another method was to dig a large pit and conceal it carefully. This was a safe method, for the animal, once it was in the pit, could easily be killed, but it was very difficult to conceal the pit in such a way that the elephant's suspicions would not be aroused.

One tusk of a slain elephant went to the chief hunter and the other to the man who first speared it. The Baganda and other traders who came into the country bought the tusks, giving in exchange brass, copper, iron, calico and prints.

One leg was given to the chief hunter and the rest of the meat was divided among all the men. The head was taken to the home of the chief hunter, who built a shrine to the ghost of his father, if he was dead, and offered the head to him, thanking him for his help and asking that he might have the good fortune to kill another. The heads of elephants and buffalo were the only parts of animals which were treated in this way. The chief hunter had to settle any disputes which arose among the men.

Buffalo were usually hunted with dogs, which kept an animal at bay while the hunters surrounded and speared it. Smaller game was hunted with nets which were used either to trap the animals or to stay them in a rush. The man who first struck an animal with his spear claimed both legs, one of which he had to give to his chief. The man who was second took a shoulder, and all the rest was divided up among the men who took part in the hunt.

When a man was going to hunt he had to be careful that neither he nor his weapons came in contact with his wife or any other woman during the night before the hunt. He therefore took his spear with him and slept in the open. If on setting out in the morning he met a woman before meeting a man, he would turn back. Hunters had always to leave any dead animals on their path and follow up the living.

Most men kept dogs which were taught to hunt and were rewarded, after a kill, with the offal. At other times they were fed on potatoes and plantain mixed with milk. A dog with puppies was specially cared for and fed. Big puppies could be sold in the market for a goat apiece, but the smaller ones were given away to friends. It was believed that young puppies would open their eyes if a death was mentioned in their presence.

Along the Nile and on the lakes many men occupied themselves with fishing. Large baskets and intricate traps with an entrance which was almost invisible from the inside were used for deep water, while many men went out in canoes and fished with lines or nets. When a man was making a line or a net no woman might approach him. He lived apart from his wife and might not wash nor eat salt, butter, or fish until he had tested his net or line. If he caught no fish he took a cow and cast it into the lake as an offering. When he caught the first lot of fish with the new line or net he ate some of it as a sacred meal, sent some to his chief, and might sell the rest.

WARFARE

Warfare on even a moderate scale was scarcely known, but some fighting took place, generally as a result of some man's

PLATE XIX

Musoga, showing dent in forehead from a stone thrown in battle

encroaching on land of another clan. If he refused to retire, the drums were beaten for war, but the chiefs would attempt to settle the affair without recourse to arms and a boundary might be arranged. If arbitration failed, the fighting might last from one day to two months. Warriors carried two or three spears and a shield and slings for stones were also used. When one clan felt that it was getting the worse of the fight, three or four men would be sent to meet representatives of the stronger side and make a settlement. A boundary would then be fixed, and the warriors returned to their homes.

The dead were never mutilated, and a man who had killed an enemy was not separated from his fellows or regarded as in need of purification, but the members of his clan and his friends came to see him, bringing presents of sheep and fowls, and tied cowry-shells on his wrists.

A wounded warrior was nursed by some male relative. Some members of the tribe had attained to great surgical skill and treated wounds and broken bones with success. Wounds in the head from stones were common and the medicine-men were expert at removing the splinters of bone, after which the wound was dressed with pounded herbs.

CHAPTER XVIII

BIRTH, MARRIAGE, ILLNESS, AND DEATH

Importance of a son—care of a pregnant woman—birth—the after-birth—seclusion of mother and child—bringing-out and naming a child—cutting the first teeth—birth of twins—bringing-out and naming of twins—blessing from the new moon—cutting a child's hair and nails—training of boys and girls—extraction of teeth—taboos of a menstruating woman—polygamy—clan exogamy—forbidden relationships—arranging a marriage—divorce—adultery—fornication—causes of illness—death and burial of ordinary men—mourning—inheritance—death of great chiefs—temple of the chiefs—inheritance of chiefs—death of women—death by drowning

THE all-important object of every woman was to become a mother, especially of a son, for not only would she then be regarded with respect as having added another man to her husband's clan, but she would have supplied her husband with someone who would care for his ghost when he had left this world. Whenever a woman, therefore, realised that she was pregnant she had to take many precautions lest by food, by some action, or even by hearing or seeing something, she might injure the life she was giving to her husband and his clan. Some female relative of the husband was appointed to 'see that the woman followed all the necessary rules and ate suitable food. Other women of the husband's clan might also take part in guarding the expectant mother, for it sometimes happened that a wife who had a grudge against her husband would seek to kill her child. Should she fail to do this before birth she would try to do it during birth by crushing or sitting upon the child, the crouching position adopted during delivery affording opportunity for doing this. Should she succeed in killing her child at birth, members of her husband's clan would flog and abuse her and would carry off the husband's goods, for they considered him responsible for his wife's action and said, "You have killed our child."

A woman during pregnancy had to be especially careful to avoid eating salt and beans, and cooked plantain might not be eaten hot but left until almost cold. No man might use the woman's seat or step over it, nor might she drink from a pot which a man had used. Members of her husband's clan might come to her house, but she avoided sexual intercourse with them. The husband, however, though he avoided his wife during her menses, might approach her while she was pregnant and also while she was nursing a child. When the time for birth drew near, the woman was careful not to go far from her house lest the child should be born in the field. This was especially to be avoided because if it happened that there were twins, they could not be moved after birth until a special medicine-man had been sent for and brought to the place.

When the birth took place three or four women of the husband's clan were present to assist. If it was during the day the woman went into the garden among the plantains, but if it was at night she remained in the house. The cord was cut by a girl with a strip of reed fastened on a hoe handle, for the midwife might not cut it.

Should a child be born feet first, it was regarded as a serious matter and a medicine-man was consulted as to the medicine to be given to remove the evil, which, if left, might cause the death of the parents and bring all sorts of misfortune on the child. The Basoga declared that the Bakitara killed children born by feet presentation, but the Bakitara would not confess to this.

When a case was one of cross birth, a medicine-man was sent for and he and the midwife usually succeeded in turning the child. If, however, this was impossible, they would dismember the child and try to save the woman.

The midwife buried the after-birth by a plantain tree, covering it with bits of pot so that the earth could not touch it. The umbilical cord when it fell from the child was thrown at the root of a plantain tree where the dust from the house was also cast. The plantains from this tree were eaten by the woman and her husband during the period of seclusion which followed a birth, and no one else might partake of them.

After the birth, the mother was taken to her bed where she remained for four days. During this time a bright fire had to be kept up in the house and none of it might be taken out of the house until the child had been brought out for the inspection of the relatives. When the four days were ended, the woman was taken out to the back of the house where she was washed and shaved; while this was being done, the house was swept out and friends might look at the child, though they might not touch it.

The parents gave a child a name when it was born, but when it was four or five months old, the father brought his friends and made a feast, during which the mother's head was shaved. On the following day, the child was given a name by the father's parents and after that time people were allowed to touch it.

The cutting of a child's first teeth was anxiously watched, for in almost all clans it was considered dangerous if the upper teeth appeared before the lower. Some clans, however, did not regard this omen. When the teeth appeared a feast was given by the parents, and the midwife then made the child sit upright, for until this time it had been kept lying on its back.

When a child's head was shaved for the first time it had to be done by the midwife, who received a bark-cloth as payment.

When twins were born, they might not be moved from the place of birth at once nor might the navel cords be severed. Their eyes, ears, and mouths were washed out and respiration set up, and the mother lay beside them and nursed them until a special medicine-man had been summoned. When he arrived, he gave his permission and the cord was cut. The afterbirths were put into earthen pots which were sealed with clay and buried in a heap of ashes near the house to keep them safe until the bringing out of the twins.

The midwife announced the birth to the father and the members of the clan, and a representative of the father was appointed to make arrangements. A hut was built or set apart for the mother and children, who remained in seclusion sometimes for two months and sometimes for as long as four months. The father had to inform his wife's parents of the birth, and during the seclusion he and his representative collected food for the feast which took place when the twins were brought out and shown to the relatives. The father was distinguished by wearing a circlet of cowry-shells on his head.

The cord of each child when it fell was wrapped in bark-cloth and shaped like a doll. When the child was nursed, the doll containing its cord was held to the breast as if it were also being fed. When the children were weaned the cords were preserved by the mother.

At the time appointed for the bringing-out of the children a large company of relatives came together in the evening and the father and mother of the twins shaved their heads, pared their nails and washed them. In some clans this purification was done in the early morning, which was the arrangement common to most other tribes of this region. In some clans the hair and nails were kept for some time and were then taken as secretly as possible into the country of some other tribe and thrown away so that any evil from the twins and their birth might be deposited there. In some clans the hair and nails were simply thrown down in the house in which the mother lived and later were swept up with the dust from the house and thrown on an ant-hill.

During the night the relatives of the father and of the mother kept apart from each other, forming two camps, and danced and sang until early morning. Among some clans the mother and father came out of their house naked before sunrise and ran round the house in opposite directions, which was supposed to bring strength to the twins. The mother then ran into her house and the man who had been chosen as the father's representative in making the earlier arrangements was allowed to follow her, but a rope was tied to his leg and when he attempted to embrace her he was pulled back. Her husband had then to go in and have sexual relations with her to perfect the twins.

The pots containing the after-births were then taken with ceremony to the forest and left there, and on her return from this duty, the mother brought out the children, who were given presents of cowry-shells and were named by the father's mother. The names for twins were Waiswa and Nabiri if they were boy and girl; if both were boys the second was Tengwa, and if both were girls they were Wada and Nabiri. People always preferred to have one twin of each sex and should both be of the same sex, the parent whose sex was missing was derided.

While the twins were out the house was swept and the sweepings were taken and put on an ant-hill where, among some clans, the after-births were also deposited. After this there was general rejoicing, which lasted all day, and when it was over, the father and mother spent several weeks in paying visits and dancing. Their presence at this time was supposed to bring blessing to people, cattle, and crops, and their visits were therefore welcomed. Special attention was paid by them to those people who had given presents of food for the bringing-out ceremony.

When a baby was about a month old, the mother took it out when the new moon appeared and tried to induce it to look up at the new moon, for she believed that this would bring it blessing and ensure satisfactory growth.

A woman who was nursing her child did not live apart from her husband, but should she conceive again she had to cease nursing and the child had either to have a foster mother or to be fed on artificial food.

When a mother had several miscarriages or her children died in infancy, she was given medicine, and the medicine-man also tried by augury to discover what ghost was causing their deaths and what it wanted. He then made offerings to appease it.

When a boy's hair required cutting, he went to some female relative of his father who shaved his head, gathered up the hair, took it to some place of safety, and hid it there. She also cut the boy's nails and hid them to prevent anyone from using them for magical purposes.

When a child began to walk a feast was made for which a goat was killed. One leg had to be given to the midwife.

At about the age of five a boy began to go out with the herdsmen of the goats and learn their work, and later he was sent to learn to herd the cows, after which he might hire himself out to some chief or cattle-owner. Boys were active and rejoiced in sham-fights and racing, while wrestling was also a favourite form of amusement. At about the age of five girls also were expected to begin to be useful and were taught by their mother to dig and to carry water and fire-wood.

When boys and girls reached puberty they had the four front teeth in the lower jaw extracted. Should one be afraid and refuse to have this done, he was called a Muganda and taunted with being like a dog. The extracted teeth were thrown away and not preserved.

As a boy grew up he built his own house near his parents

and lived there until he married. Sometimes several boys would live together in one hut. Unmarried girls remained with their parents and had a place curtained off where they slept.

When a girl first menstruated, she slept near her mother and avoided all men; even her father and brothers might not touch any of her things. At such a time a married woman must get some other person to peel her plantains for her; she might not eat in the presence of others nor might she prepare food for her husband, and he might not approach her.

MARRIAGE

The Basoga were a polygamous tribe and the only limit to the number of wives a man might have was his ability to pay for them; polyandry, however, was forbidden. The clans were exogamous, but a man, though he avoided women from his own clan, might take several wives who belonged to the clan into which he married, indeed they might be sisters. In such a case, the wives, if they agreed, lived together in one house, but if they did not get on, the husband built them separate houses. As a rule each wife had her own house and her own field. The laws as to forbidden degrees of relationship were strict. First cousins and even second cousins were forbidden to marry and children of the same mother by different fathers were regarded as brothers and sisters and thus might not marry each other. A man generally married a second wife when his first proved to be sterile. He would, however, first procure from a local medicine-man some drug for her. If this did not act he would marry another woman, and the first wife, unless she had some hold on her husband's affections, became little more than a slave and was kept to dig and do rough work.

As a rule when a youth wished to marry, he got some friend or relative to go to the girl's parents and ask for their consent. He might, if he thought best, go himself to visit them and plead his cause. The parents then took counsel with some of their relatives, and should there be no objection to the youth, they settled the amount of the marriage-fee, which varied, according to the position of the youth, from one to three cows. In some cases when the parents gave their consent to the marriage, the youth took two or three pots of beer, the drinking of which confirmed the agreement, and sometimes a feast was made and a goat was killed; this, however, seemed to be a custom introduced recently from other parts. A father might arrange a marriage for his son and pay the marriage-fee for him.

There were times when a young couple would agree between themselves that they would marry. The girl then escaped from her home and betook herself to the house of the youth's brother or of some friend, where he joined her and they lived together for some days. The girl's parents sought their daughter; but when she was discovered they did not punish her, but simply set to work to settle the amount of the marriage-fee, which would probably consist of two or three cows and two or three sheep or goats. The young husband might be given as much as six months to procure it, and during the time he lived with his wife. If at the end of that time he was unable to pay, he might be fined or his wife might be taken from him and held as a hostage to spur him on to greater diligence.

There was no ceremony about marriage, but the woman remained in seclusion for four days after she joined her husband, and he had to give her a bark-cloth, a hoe, and water- and cooking-pots as tokens of her position as mistress of his house. When her seclusion ended she went to see her parents, taking with her a bark-cloth and a goat for each, as presents from her husband. She remained with them two days and then returned to her husband bringing presents of food, probably a fowl or a goat, salt and semsem.

There was no taboo on seeing or speaking to relations-in-law. Unlike the custom in many parts of Uganda, a man might meet and speak to his mother-in-law freely and might even visit her, and a father-in-law might speak to his daughter-in-law and give her gifts.

If after marriage a woman failed to agree with her husband,

she might leave him and return to her people if they consented to return the marriage-fee, but otherwise she had no alternative but to remain with her husband. Divorce might take place at any time if the marriage-fee were restored, and the husband always kept possession of the children, who belonged to his clan. If a man found cause to blame his wife for idleness, he might beat her; and if she did not then improve he might sell her into slavery. A woman might call the witnesses of her marriage to help her if she felt herself wrongly punished, but she seldom obtained satisfaction by this method and as a rule bore her punishment in silence. A woman's father rarely interfered in the domestic disputes of his son-in-law's house except to insist upon his daughter's obeying her husband.

Adultery was generally punished by a fine. If a man found that his wife had committed adultery he endeavoured to find out the offender and accused him to a chief. The fine imposed usually consisted of a cow for the judge, a cow for the injured husband, and a goat for each assistant chief who took part in the trial. If, however, the husband actually caught another man with his wife, he might put him to death on the spot. If a man was convicted of adultery with the wife of a great chief, he was put to death.

If a girl had a child before she was married, her father brought the cause before the chief, who ordered the man who had seduced her to marry her, and to pay a fine equal to the amount of the marriage-fee and also a fine to those who tried the case. Should he refuse to marry the girl, she went to his home and was cared for by his mother until the child was born, when she returned to her own home. At times, however, severer punishment was meted out and both girl and man were driven from the clan, no fine or reparation of any kind being accepted. This was only done when it was believed that some ghost was offended by the act and was preparing to bring evil upon the clan.

ILLNESS

As with all these primitive peoples, serious illness and death were regarded as natural only when they came to old people;

if young persons fell ill and died some supernatural cause had
to be discovered. If a man's illness, however, did not appear
to be very serious, his wife and relatives would try what effect
home treatment might have on him, and only when that failed
would they send for a medicine-man, who was often also the
head-man of the clan, to find by consulting his fetishes the
cause of the illness and to direct the treatment. The medicine-
man had to be paid with a fowl or a goat according to the
circumstances of the patient. Illness might be caused either
by magic worked by someone who had a grudge against the
patient or by a ghost, either one belonging to the same clan
as the patient, which used this means to call attention to some
infringement of the clan rules, or one belonging to some hostile
clan. It was also possible that illness might be caused by some
god; and in that case, if the patient was a wealthy man, a
cow was given to the god and the patient was smeared over
with its dung to secure a blessing. In cases of smallpox the
patient was isolated and someone who had had the disease
nursed him and fed him, pricking the pustules and sponging
away the pus.

DEATH

When a man died, his wife and any relatives who might be
present prepared the body for burial. The body was washed
and laid out straight with the legs extended together and the
arms lying along the sides, after which it was wrapped in
bark-cloth and the face was washed and oiled. Burial took
place on the same day as the death and the members of the
clan gathered to assist in the ceremony and to choose the
heir, which was done before the body might be buried. The
heir came into the house and in the presence of the mourners
rubbed butter or oil on the forehead and face of the dead man
and covered it, after which he remained to be present at the
burial. If the dead man was of importance, his grave was
either dug in a house or a house was built over it, but ordinary
men were buried outside their houses, in their gardens or
fields. The grave was five or six feet deep and was lined with

bark-cloths, and the body was laid in it, a man on his right side and a woman on her left.

If there was any suspicion that the death had been caused by magic, the chief wife of the dead man caught a little of the earth that was first thrown into the grave, and made it into a ball which she threw over some tree near. This act freed the ghost of the dead man which might otherwise be held in bondage by the person who had caused the death. When the grave had been filled in all those present washed their hands beside it and threw the sponges on to the mound which was raised over it.

When the grave had been filled in, mourning commenced and continued for any length of time from four days to three months. During this time the men and women lived in different houses and remained strictly apart, even husbands and wives being separated, and they had to avoid any excesses either of food or drink lest the ghost should be annoyed and visit its wrath upon the culprit or some other member of his clan. Twice a day, at sunrise and at sunset, the mourners visited the grave and wailed and lamented. In order to keep up the wailing for some time they did it in relays, several at a time throwing themselves upon the grave and calling to the dead and weeping for him. When the sun had risen they returned to their houses and spent the day in talk. They might not wash or shave or cut their nails, and they wore wreaths of dry plantain fibre round their heads and girdles of the same round their loins. They watched each other, and should one commit any act which might annoy the ghost, he was tried and fined and the others fled from the place of mourning lest the ghost should wreak its vengeance on them. The ghost during this time was supposed to be in some tree near, where it was watching all that took place. When the mourning was over it retired to the uncultivated land, the home of the ghosts.

The heir supplied food for the mourners and beer for them to drink, and he decided when the mourning should cease, showing its termination by bringing a goat and a special pot of beer. Some of the beer was poured upon the grave and the mourners ate the goat and drank beer. They then washed and shaved all the hair from their bodies, and the hair was taken and deposited in some neighbouring country. This had to be done secretly, for the hair was thought to bring death and if discovered would almost certainly lead to war. After the mourning the house in which the man died was deserted and allowed to fall to pieces.

When the mourning was over, the property of the dead man was divided. The heir was almost invariably the eldest son, though if he was absolutely unsuitable he might be passed over and another chosen. The heir, however, whoever he might be, only received a share, often less than a quarter, of the whole of the dead man's property, and one or two of the widows. The headman of the clan received a large portion and the other sons and daughters had to be supplied with something, the daughters' share being always meat or other food and never anything that could be kept and passed on, for no woman had the right to possess property nor could she hand any on to her children, who could inherit only from their father. The widows were divided, some going to the heir and some to other members of the clan. A widow might, if she so desired, return to her own family if they consented to return the marriage-fee which had originally been paid for her. The personal property of the dead man, that is, his water-pot and special food-pot, with his mats and bed, went to the heir.

The people bought slaves from surrounding tribes, a man being bought for one cow and a woman for two, and they passed on by inheritance like other property. Though the lot of these people was not hard and they were often treated like members of the family, a slave might not inherit property, even if his master gave him his freedom and adopted him as a son. If a male slave married, his children were always slaves, but the children of a female slave who married a free man belonged to her husband's clan and might inherit his property.

A man's grave was always covered with a mound of earth

beaten hard, which had to be kept in good repair as a shelter for the grave. At the head of this was built a shrine, which in the case of a peasant was a miniature hut only three feet high, but in the case of a chief might be a large house enclosing the grave. The ghost was supposed to visit this shrine, where offerings were made to it from time to time.

The procedure at the burial of a great chief was different from that at the burial of ordinary men and the lesser chiefs. The grave was not completely filled in, but a shaft was left reaching down to the head. Under the head also a space was left in which a basket was placed. A bell was attached to the head so that when it fell off the bell sounded, warning the men who guarded the tomb. These reported the fact and the jaw-bone was then taken up, cleaned, wrapped in the skin of a goat, decorated with beads, and put into a bag. This bag, in a wooden vessel, was placed in a hut or temple where a woman and some men chosen from the clan guarded it. When the jaw-bone of the next chief was brought to the hut, the woman guardian was given a goat or a sheep and left the place taking with her the jaw-bone she had guarded. She visited some house where she passed one night and on her departure left her bag with the jaw-bone in it behind her. The people, realising what it was, deposited it in some place where it would not be disturbed. In some tribes the whole skull of the chief was treated in this way, and when a new skull was brought, the former was taken to a place where it was customary to deposit them and left there without further attention.

The temple of the departed chiefs had, in addition to the woman guardian, priests who consulted the dead for information desired by the reigning chief. In return for this the reigning chief sent offerings of cattle and at times of girls, who became slaves of the temple and worked in the fields which belonged to it. In times of drought, offerings were made by the priests in the temple and they prayed for rain. The building of a new temple was always a time of rejoicing. In some parts of Busoga widows and slaves were buried with a chief, but as a rule the body was buried alone.

During the mourning for one of the great chiefs, the sub-chiefs lived in huts near the place of mourning and directed the affairs of the district. The heir of a great chief had always to be the eldest son whether he was the most suitable member of the family or not. When the mourning was ended, the heir brought a sheep and a cow and killed them with a spear, and the meat was distributed among the mourners. Messengers were then sent to the king of Kitara and to the king of Buganda to announce the death, and the appointment of the new chief. They took with them numbers of bark-cloths, and the king of Kitara in confirming the appointment sent presents of hoes.

A woman was always buried in the open and a hut was built over her grave, where she lay on her left side.

When a woman died in child-birth, her husband declared that she must have caused the mishap by unfaithfulness. Prolonged labour and cross-birth were also accounted for in this way. The woman's parents had to assist her husband to bury her and her relatives had to provide him with another wife for whom he gave a present of one cow. When a woman died in child-bed before the husband had paid the full marriage-fee for her, he had to pay the full fee for the new wife who was then provided for him by his deceased wife's relatives.

Rivers were not bridged; and as the usual way of crossing them was by jumping from root to root of the papyrus, there was a considerable amount of risk, for if a man slipped into the water, he was easily drawn under the roots and drowned. Very few men learnt to swim as their fear of the river-spirits made them avoid lakes and rivers except when obliged to cross them during a journey. When a man fell into a river and was drowned, his clan fellows, both male and female, came to the place. They offered a fowl to the river-spirit by throwing it alive into the river. Each drank a little water and, drawing some more, they cooked a meal on the river bank and ate it in the presence of the spirit. Not till then might they take the body from the water and bury it.

APPENDIX

Counting

1. *ndala*, extend first finger.
2. *ebiri*, extend two fingers, first under second.
3. *esatu*, extend second, third, and fourth fingers, with first held down by third.
4. *ena*, extend four fingers, in two groups of two.
5. *etano*, extend closed fist.
6. *mukaga*, extend three fingers of each hand.
7. *musamvu*, extend four fingers on one hand and three on the other.
8. *munana*, extend four fingers on each hand.
9. *mwenda*, closed fist and extend four fingers of other hand.
10. *ekumi*, two closed fists.
20. *abiri*.

From 20 to 100 they used the Luganda words.

100. *kikumi*.
200. *bibiri*.
1000. *lukimi* and also the Luganda word.
10,000. *kakumi*.

Seasons

Mutweigo =March to September.
Musambya=September to December.
Endwozi =January to March.

In some parts the seasons are:

Kaleminiri=time for preparing land.
Kusiga =time for sowing.
Kukola =time when the crops grew.
Kulkul =time for harvest and for rest.
Mwezi =month of thirty days, or moon.

Times of the day

Kibambya =cock-crow.
Kyankyo =sunrise.
Kanyuka =time for women to rest.
Kafumbe omusana=midday cooking, about 11 a.m.
Bakalia musana =eating at noon.
Bawate egulo =time for evening cooking.
Balye ekiro =evening meal, at sunset.
Nkoko ziingire =fowls go to roost.
Buire =night or midnight.

Currency

Five cows bought a wife.
Thirty goats bought a cow.
Fifty fowls bought a goat.

Salutations

Kojea or *Kodeo?* (pronounced with a slight lisp)=Are you all well?
Answer, *Balio*=All are well.
Balio?=Are all well? Answer, *Balio*=All are well.
Agufayo?=In your home is all well? Answer, *Tulio*=We are well.

Relationships

Father, lata, aifwe or wange.
Mother, mama.
Brother, muganda.
Sister, mwanyina.
Husband, ba.
Wife, mukazi.
Son, mwana or mutabani.
Daughter, mwala.
Father's mother, jaja.
Father's father, musange.
Mother's father, musange.
Mother's mother, jaja.
Father's brother, lata muto.
Father's sister, songa.
Mother's brother, jaja.
Mother's sister, makaisi wange kaidi.
Father's brother's wife, mukaisi wange.
Father's sister's husband, lata.
Mother's brother's wife, mukazi wange (*my wife*), denotes possibility of marriage.
Mother's sister's husband, lata.
Father's brother's son, muganda.
Father's brother's daughter, mwanyoko.
Father's sister's son, muganda.
Father's sister's daughter, mwanyina.

Mother's brother's son, jaja.
Mother's brother's daughter, mukaisi wange.
Mother's sister's son, muganda.
Mother's sister's daughter, mwanyina.
Son's son, musangi.
Son's daughter, mukazi wange (*my wife*).
Daughter's son, musangi.
Daughter's daughter, mukazi (*wife*).
Brother's son, mutabani.
Brother's daughter, muwala wange.
Sister's son, muganda.
Sister's daughter, mwanyoko.
Wife's father, muko.
Wife's mother, muko.
Wife's brother, muko.
Wife's sister, mukazi.
Wife's sister's husband, musangi.
Husband's father, nyazala.
Husband's mother, jajawao.
Husband's brother, muganda.
Husband's sister, mwala.
Husband's brother's wife, muka muganda mulamu.
Son's wife, muka mwana
Daughter's husband, muko.

Vocabulary

All, bona
arm, mukono
arrow, miti

Back, mugongo
bad, kibi (*ugly*)
be (to), kinabawo
beast, nsolo
beautiful, kirungi (*good*)
believe, kukurizi
bird, noni
bitter, kika
black, kidugavu (*dark*)
blood, musai
boat, lwato
body, mbiri
bone, egumba
born (be), azaire
bow, buta
breath, muka
bright, kitangala
burn, kuwokya

Carry, tuike
chief mwami
child, mwana
cloud, kiri
club, mwigo
come, idya
command, kulagira
cut, kusala

Dance, kina
dark, kidugavu (*black*)
day, kasana
die, afire
do, kola
dream, kulota
drink, anyuwa

Ear, kutu
earth, etaka
eat, alya
enemy, antazi

False, mukobi
fear, bukyere

few, batone
fight, kulwana
fire, muliro
fish, byakulira ebyenyanza
food, matoke
foolish, musiru
foot, kigere
forest, kibira
friend, mugonzi

Ghost, muzimu
give, kuwa, kumuwa
go, golola
god, lubare
good, kirungi (*beautiful*)
green, kiragala

Hair, muviri
hand, kifunsi
hard, kikebangofu
hate, kutala
he, oyo
head, mutwe
hear, wulira
heart, moyo
heavy, kizito
high, walieri
house, endyu

I, nze
it, ekyo

kill, kuita
Know, kutegera

Large, kinene
leg, mugulu
lie, galamirira (*to lie down*)
light, kyangu
lightning, lukuba
live, mulamu
liver, mani
long, kirei
loud, mwogezi
love, yagala
low, wansi

Man, musaiju
many, bange
marry, kubaiza
mountain, lusozi
mouth, munywa
moon, mwezi

Neck, nkoto
new, luwiya
night, buiri
nose, nyindo

Old, mukaire

Part, kitundu
priest, mulaguzi

Quick, mangu

Rain, madi
red, kikunyukunyu
river, mwiga
run, lumukaku

Shadow, mpombia
she, oyo
sea, nanza
see, ku-moga
shield, ngabo
short, kimpi
shoulder, ebega
sing, yasubaga
sit, tyama
skin, luwo
sky, waigulu
sleep, kutenduka
slow, kugayazi
small, katona
smell, myuka
soft, kiwolu
sorcerer, muyiga
soul, moyo
speak, yogera
spear, efumu

stand, imirira
star, munyenyi
stone, ibare
strike, kukuba
sun, kasana
sweet, kirungi kiwoma

Take, tola
taste, gezako
tell, kukobera
that, ekyo
they, bo
thing, kantu
think, kulooza
this, kino
thou, iwe
thunder, lukuba
tongue, lulimi
tooth, maino
touch, gemako
tree, muti
true, wamazima
to be, kinabawo

Ugly, kibi (*bad*)

Walk, tambula
war, lutalo
water, madi
we, ifwe
which, ki
white, jeru
who, bani
whole, byona
wind, mpewo
wise, magezi
wish, kwagala
woman, mukazi
word, kigambo

Yellow, kivuvu
you, mwe
young, muto

PLATE XX

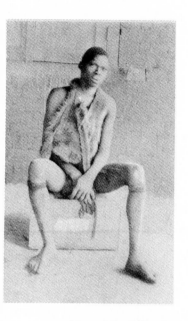 

Man of the Bakonjo, a cannibal tribe of Ruwenzori

PLATE XXI

Man of the Bakonjo tribe

THE BAKONJO

CHAPTER XIX

THE PEOPLE

The country and the people—clans and totems—villages—government—agriculture—millet—other crops—domestic animals—cannibalism and hunting for meat—fishing—warfare—counting

THE Bakonjo were a small tribe inhabiting the eastern
slopes of Mount Ruwenzori, or, as the natives of the
region frequently call it, Luenzori[1]. The tribe seemed to be
native to that region and numbered only a few hundreds.
In appearance they were short and sturdy but of a low
and degraded type of countenance. They were to be found
generally on the upper plateaux of the mountain, where they
made small clearings in the scrub, built huts, and grew their
crops.

They were a totemic tribe, divided into a number of clans
which followed the usual custom of clan exogamy. There is
little doubt that each clan had a secondary as well as a
primary totem, but during the short visit of the expedition
to that region, it was not possible to discover it. The names
of the clans with their primary totems were:

Baswaga,	totem	*njoju*,	elephant
Ahera,	,,	*ngabi*,	antelope
Abaswi,	,,	*ekisuba*,	heron
Abakira,	,,	*mpunu*,	pig
Abahambo,	,,	*nseri*,	crocodile
Abasukari,	,,	*mbogo*,	buffalo

The clans did not live apart but intermingled, forming
villages of from three to twelve huts. When a man married
and felt that he required more room, he left his own village

---

[1] The snow-capped peak is called *Mbalagala*, shining hill, and this name
is more generally known to the inhabitants than Ruwenzori.

and made a new clearing where he built his hut and settled. Other men joined him, and in a few years his settlement might have become a village of some eight to a dozen huts. The man who first settled in a place generally became the head-man of the village, and to him matters of local disputes and questions of land were referred, and he acted as the mediator between the other members of the community and the superior chiefs of the clans and tribe. Anyone who wished to cultivate a new plot of land had to get the permission of the head-man of his village.

The people grew enough millet to keep them in food, and they also kept a few goats and sheep for the purpose of barter and the purchase of wives. The animals were of a poor breed and little or no attempt was made to improve them. People aimed at increasing the number of their animals but cared nothing for their quality.

AGRICULTURE

The tribe was purely agricultural and their staple food was the small millet, *bulo*. This kind grew more easily upon the ridges of the mountain and required a shorter period to ripen than the larger kinds of millet.

Both men and women worked in the fields, though women claimed the plots as theirs and were responsible for them and for the supply of food for the household.

When new land had to be re-claimed from the wild, the man had the first of the work, felling trees and shrubs, cutting down the coarse grass, and burning them. He might then help with the digging if time pressed, but this was generally done by the woman, who used a short hoe. When a field was dug for the first time they did not go deeper than about six inches, but the second year and afterwards it was necessary to dig to a depth of some twelve inches. There was no knowledge of manuring or of rotation of crops, and when land had been under cultivation some years and showed signs of being exhausted, it might be left to run wild again while new land was used. Land was plentiful, and all a man had to do was to get the permission of the head-man of the village to break up new ground. The old plot remained the property of its original owner, who would return to it after a few years.

Millet was sown soon after the beginning of the rains. The land was dug as soon as the sky began to show signs of the coming of rain, so that when the rain began it was ready for sowing. September and October were the months for sowing, and the millet was ripe by the end of January. While ripening it had to be guarded against wild animals and birds, and scare-crows and rattles were used to protect it. It was often necessary to build huts in the fields and remain there by night to keep off the pigs, which might destroy the crop.

When ripe the millet was cut and beaten from the husk with short sticks, after which it was winnowed by being poured from a basket held at a height of some four to five feet. It was stored in granaries made like large baskets and resting on stones or stakes. The lids of the baskets were thatched, and projected on all sides to keep off rain. Each wife had her own granary near her house, from which she took grain as she required it. The millet was ground with a small stone on a flat slab of stone some two feet long and eighteen inches wide. This was tilted, and at the lower end a basket was placed to catch the flour as it was ground and allowed to slip down the stone slab. From this coarse meal a kind of porridge was made.

Maize was grown to some extent, and those who planted it got their crops in November, for it was used while still young and tender. Potatoes when once planted bore nearly the whole year, though during the dry season they were tough and stringy. Beans were freely grown, and were never eaten young, but always dried and stored for use during the dry season when crops could not be grown.

Men and women as a rule ate apart, and a woman and her children generally had their meal after the husband had finished.

Domestic Animals

Goats were the animals most frequently kept, for they throve on the high places of the mountain, but they were

not of a fine kind. Both men and women ate goat flesh freely.
The goats from two or more villages were taken out to pasture
together, and were herded generally by boys and girls, though
the latter only did this work if there were no sons in the family
and until they were old enough to dig.

Sheep were not so commonly kept. They were of a small
kind and did not seem to thrive on the mountain herbage.
Women had various taboos which often prevented their eating
mutton. The chief use of goats and sheep was to pay the
marriage-fee to the parents and relatives for a wife.

A small kind of fowl was kept, but they were not cared
for nor fed and had to fend for themselves, so that they often
fell a prey to birds and wild animals and did not increase
rapidly in number. Fowls were often eaten and might be exchanged for goats, but they were mostly used for the taking
of auguries and for offerings to ghosts. Eggs were eaten on
rare occasions and were more frequently left for the hens to
hatch.

Most men possessed dogs which they fed sparingly and
which acted as the village scavengers. A woman had to be
most careful not to injure her husband's dog, for that would
bring evil. If a dog had puppies it had to be fed and more
carefully looked after.

HUNTING

In the past I found these people much addicted to
cannibalism; and though they asserted that they buried
their dead, there is reason to believe that they ate them,
but these things have now to be kept secret. Most of
their meat was obtained from hunting, and they would eat
almost any kind of animal, even rats, wild cats, and leopards.
They hunted with nets or traps, though at times they would
surround an animal and hunt it from side to side until it was
exhausted, when it was speared or clubbed. The owners of
dogs took them with them to assist in the hunt.

The dwellers near the rivers or on Lake Albert caught fish,
which they ate either fresh or dried.

WARFARE

The Bakonjo were not a warlike people, and were for many years the vassals of the Banyoro, who treated them as slaves. Now and again they rebelled against their masters and fled to the higher forests on Ruwenzori, but after a time they returned and submitted again.

When they had to fight they carried leaf-bladed spears and small oval shields of wicker-work. When a village was suddenly attacked by an enemy, they would use ivory horns to sound the alarm, and call to their assistance the inhabitants of neighbouring villages.

Counting

1. *Embe*, index-finger extended.
2. *Biri*, two first fingers extended while third and fourth were bent inwards.
3. *Satu*, the index-finger bent in while the three others were extended.
4. *Ena*, four fingers extended and thumb bent in.
5. *Etano*, index-finger placed under the thumb.
6. *Endatu*, index-finger on each hand placed under thumbs.
7. *Ebisinda*, four fingers on right hand extended while on left the index-finger was bent under the thumb.
8. *Munane*, all four fingers extended on each hand.
9. *Mwenda*, right hand laid upon the fist of left hand, while the fingers were extended.
10. *Kumi*, the two fists placed together.
20. *Amaku abiri.* 30. *Asatu.* 50. *Endata.*
70. *Abena.* 100. *Enjana.*

CHAPTER XX

BIRTH, MARRIAGE, ILLNESS, AND DEATH

Care of a pregnant woman—birth—seclusion and purification—making a child sit up—cutting teeth—training of children—clothing—clan exogamy—arranging marriage—marriage ceremonies—treatment of illness—death and burial—mourning—inheritance—ghosts and spirits

A WIFE, realising that her strongest claim to her husband's esteem lay in bearing him children, made known the fact as soon as she realised that she had conceived; and her mother, or, more often, her husband's mother, came to look after her until the child was born. The duty of the woman in charge was to see that the prospective mother took the medicine which was considered necessary and did everything possible to ensure the birth of a healthy child.

One or two women came in to assist at the actual birth, which took place in the house, the mother crouching on grass laid down near the central post. When the child was born, the midwife cut the cord with a strip of reed and the child was handed to an assistant who washed its face, cleaned its eyes and mouth and started respiration. The midwife attended the mother until the afterbirth came, when it was buried outside the house near the door.

If the baby was a boy the mother remained in seclusion for four days, and if it was a girl for three. During this time the husband was the only man who might enter the house, though women might come to visit the mother. On the fourth day, the woman's head was shaved and she was washed; the house was swept out and new grass laid on the floor. When this purification was over, friends might come in freely to see the mother and child.

The midwife, generally the husband's mother, then went home for three months, and until she returned the child was kept as much as possible lying on its back. After three months she returned, and made the child sit up on the floor. A feast was made for the relatives to celebrate this step in the child's progress.

The cutting of a child's first teeth was anxiously watched, for should the teeth in the upper jaw appear first, offerings had to be made to the gods to avert evil. A child which cut the upper teeth first was called *Kitenda* and offerings were made to the gods to remove their displeasure, lest evil should ensue. When all went well and the lower teeth appeared first, relatives came to congratulate the parents, and the father killed a goat and made a feast.

A child was always nursed by its mother for fully three years, and during this time the mother avoided sexual relations with all men.

At an early age a boy went out with the goat-herds, and soon learned to do this work himself. Later he had to learn to build and to hunt, and by degrees took his place as a man of the clan. Girls were expected to help with domestic duties and were first given the task of keeping the fire burning under the cooking-pot. Then they carried water and fire-wood and later were taught to dig and to take their part in the other duties of daily life.

Children wore no clothing nor did they trouble about washing. When a girl showed signs of maturing, she wore a small bit of goat-skin as an apron, and that was all that was considered necessary until she married.

MARRIAGE

The rules of clan exogamy were strictly observed and the marriage of near relations was avoided. There were no restrictions as to the number of wives a man might have, but as a rule men were too indolent to procure the wealth necessary to purchase more than one.

When a youth desired to marry, he would confide in his parents or in some friend. The youth would probably know of some girl whom he wished to marry, and his confidant went to see the parents and ask them to agree to the marriage. If the union was not forbidden by the laws of relationship and clan exogamy, the parents seldom made any objection, and the messenger returned to the youth, who had then to prepare two pots of beer. This he took to the parents of his bride and both father and mother generally collected some of their relatives, so that two pots of beer, each containing some two gallons, were necessary. The drinking of this beer formed the pledge of both parties to the engagement, and at this meeting the amount of the marriage-fee, which was reckoned in goats and varied from five to twenty-five, was settled.

When the marriage-fee had been paid, the woman was sent to her husband without any further ceremony, and on her arrival she remained in seclusion for two days before taking up her ordinary duties. When she had been with her husband for two months she returned to her parents and spent one or two days with them. When she left to go back to her husband, her parents gave her some uncooked food of every kind they grew. This food was carried for her by some friends; and on her arrival at her husband's house she cooked it and made a feast, as a sign of her contentment with her marriage and her ability as a cook. Should a wife be unhappy with her husband she did not return to him after going to her parents, and the marriage-fee had to be repaid.

ILLNESS

In cases of slight complaints such as colds and fever, a wife would treat her husband or a husband his wife without appealing to the medicine-man, but when an illness appeared to be more serious the medicine-man was sent for. His first step was always to find out by augury the cause of the illness, for until that had been ascertained it was of no use to apply remedies. A fowl was generally used for the augury; the head was cut off and the flow of blood noted, or at times the head was cut off sharply and the headless fowl allowed to run about, the way in which it ran and fell in death being noted. After death the lungs and intestines were examined.

When magic was found to be the cause of the illness, it had to be overcome by stronger magic; but when the cause was a ghost which had to be propitiated, a fowl was cooked and offered to it. When the cause had thus been dealt with, the patient was treated according to the symptoms of his disease, bleeding being the favourite treatment for almost every trouble. The medicine-men were acquainted with many herbs which they employed in treating their patients.

DEATH

When death occurred, the first step was to place the body in the correct position for burial, and in many cases the at-tendants did not wait until the man was actually dead to do this. When they saw that he was dying, they would bend up his legs and cross his arms in front of him so that he might die in that position. After death, however, the arms were bent up and the hands placed under the right side of the head for a man and under the left side for a woman. All ornaments were removed from the body, which was wrapped in bark-cloth. The grave was dug by relatives and friends in the ground near the hut, and a layer of grass placed in it. The body was laid on this on its right side if it was a man and on its left if it was a woman, and covered with grass before the grave was filled in. Those who took part in the funeral then washed their hands and faces, shaved their heads, and cut their nails at the grave, and poured the water they had used upon it.

Mourning went on from the time of burial for some two months, but if the dead man was an important member of the clan it might last for as long as six months. The mourners were supplied with cooked food and beer by friends, and they danced, drank beer, and wailed. During mourning they might not wash or shave or cut their nails.

The heir, who was the son of the dead man, ended the mourning by bringing a goat to the grave, where he killed it, and the mourner ate it as a sacred meal in the presence of the ghost. The mourners shaved their heads, eyebrows and bodies of all hair, pared their nails and washed; the hair and nail parings were placed on the grave and the water was poured over it. When the mourning was ended, the house in which the man died was deserted and pulled down, and the materials used for building elsewhere.

The widows became the property of the heir, but were free to return to their own homes if their relatives would refund the marriage-fee which had been paid for them.

GHOSTS AND SPIRITS

After the death of a man, the ghost was supposed to reside in the house, and the occupants, whether the man's widows or his heir, placed food near the main post for the ghost's use. Shrines were not built to ghosts, but fowls were sometimes offered to them in the house by the relatives. Children were named after departed ancestors so that the ghosts might care for and help them, and protect them against other ghosts and against magic.

Little was known about other kinds of spirits, but certain places in rivers where there was a swift current were feared because of the water-spirit in them which occasionally destroyed people.

A man who was found making magic was fined the value of a woman because his deeds were dangerous to the community; he might pay the injured party the value of a woman in cattle or purchase one and pass her on to them.

PLATE XXII

 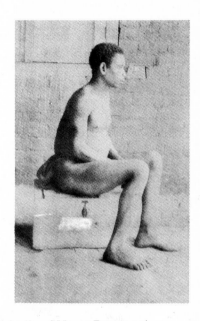

Man of the Bambwa, a cannibal tribe of Mount Ruwenzori

PLATE XXIII

Man of the Bambwa tribe

THE BAMBWA

CHAPTER XXI

THE PEOPLE AND THEIR OCCUPATIONS

Subservience of the Bambwa—cannibalism—clans and totems—
government and the land—religion—agriculture—domestic animals—
artisans—fighting—hunting—food—seasons—counting

THE Bambwa were a mountain tribe living on the western
slopes of the Ruwenzori range. They were a turbulent
people and were never completely subdued, though in the past
they were regarded as free-men under the king of Kitara.
Their subservience, however, though nominally the head-man
of a clan was accountable to his over-lord, only meant that
from time to time small presents and submissive messages
were sent to Kitara or sometimes to Toro.

Neighbouring tribes declared that the Bambwa were can-
nibals; and though the people themselves denied this, the
evidence pointed to the truth of the assertion. In fact when
I visited the western slopes of the mountain some twenty-two
years ago, I found them actually using human flesh. They
were also in the habit of filing their teeth to points, which was
said by their neighbours to be a sign of cannibalism.

The tribe was divided into a number of totemic clans which
in most cases seemed to use the name of their totem as the
name of their clan:

1.	*Engo*, leopard.	11.	*Njaza*, antelope.
2.	*Nkende*, a kind of cat.	12.	*Njojo*, elephant.
3.	*Ngeye*.	13.	*Nsumba*, cat.
4.	*Nko*, a cat.	14.	*Musu*, rat.
5.	*Nsugu*.	15.	*Omwaga*.
6.	*Ntale*, lion.	16.	*Mbuku*.
7.	*Mpuru*, pig.	17.	*Kapude*.
8.	*Nsenge*.	18.	*Kabebe*.
9.	*Mbogo*, hippopotamus.	19.	*Kakereme*.
10.	*Mpara*, red buck.	20.	*Kigasi*, monkey.

Clan exogamy was practised, no man being permitted to marry a woman whose totem was the same as his own.

GOVERNMENT

Each clan had its own head-man, who not only settled the affairs of his clan but acted as intermediary when negotiations with the over-lord in Kitara or Toro were necessary. The members of a clan usually dwelt together, forming a small village, and all disputes were brought to the head-man. He had power to imprison men for refusing to perform some duty or to pay some fine which was demanded of them; but this was rarely done, and his principal task was that of judging questions of the possession of land.

Though land which had never been cultivated was free to all, a piece of land which had been dug and had been allowed to return to its wild state, still belonged either to the man who had originally planted it or to some member of his family; if anyone took possession of such land, objections might be raised by the real owner and the head-man had to intervene. Unless the usurper quitted the plot or the matter was satis- factorily arranged, quarrels and bloodshed would certainly ensue. When a man wanted help in a matter of this kind or permission to occupy certain land, he paid the head-man four or five goats, and in return a field and a site for his house were granted to him.

Matters of debt, generally in regard to the payment of marriage-fees, had also to be brought before the head-man of the clan or village.

RELIGION

The Bambwa acknowledged the existence of a creator, but paid him no worship and made him no offerings. The only supernatural beings which were regarded as having any real influence on their lives were the spirits of the dead, which became ghosts and had occasionally to be propitiated with offerings. After death ghosts of both men and women returned to their own clans, those of women who had married returning to their original homes and not to the clans of their husbands.

Ghosts were always careful to promote the welfare of their own clans, but would cause illness or trouble among the members if they had been in any way offended or neglected. Illness or death might, however, be caused by a ghost of another clan which had been influenced by an enemy of the person affected. It was therefore necessary in a case of illness to send for the medicine-man to discover by augury what ghost was responsible and what method should be used to deal with it. The methods generally adopted will be described in the section on Illness (p. 153). The medicine-man had to be paid for his services from one to five fowls or a goat, according to the wealth of the patient.

Children were called by the names of.their ancestors because the ghosts became their guardians, those of men looking after boys and those of women after girls.

OCCUPATIONS

The Bambwa were an agricultural tribe, and, as usual, the main work of cultivation was done by the women, though the men cleared new ground of trees, shrubs and rough grass, digging up the tree roots and burning all the rubbish. The women went over the ground with their hoes, digging some ten to twelve inches deep and raking the earth towards them, picking out from it the roots of weeds and grass which would grow again if buried; these were burned with the other rubbish.

The small millet, *bulo*, was the principal food, and was stored in basket granaries raised on three stumps of trees so that a clear space of some two feet was left underneath. A conical lid with a layer of thatch and a smearing of cow-dung inside protected the granary against rain.

Sweet potatoes, beans, peas, and marrows were also grown, and of recent years plantains have been largely cultivated on the lower mountain slopes.

Goats and sheep were fairly plentiful and fowls were kept, for the people ate both fowls and eggs. Most men kept dogs which they trained to help in the hunt. Women had trouble in keeping the dogs from stealing food, but they had to be

careful in their treatment of them, for if a woman killed a
dog, her husband would divorce her and demand the return
of the marriage-fee from her family. When a dog had puppies
the owner fed it with the best food he could procure, for
puppies were of value and one might be exchanged for
a fowl. If the death of any person were mentioned in the
hearing of a new litter of puppies, it was believed that they
would at once open their eyes.

There were a few smiths in the tribe, but their workmanship was poor and showed no sign of skill nor any evidence
of artistic taste. They had crude methods of smelting, and
worked the metal up into spears, hoes, knives and other
implements. Carpenters made rough stools and vessels, and
pots were made by the women, though the men brought clay
to them from the swamps in the lower parts of the valleys.

It was evident, from the precautions taken to secrete food
and their preparedness for hurried flights up the mountain,
that they were little accustomed to fighting. Their weapons
were bows and arrows, spears, and shields. There was no
order in their battle array, and their methods of attack were
individual and extremely primitive.

Hunting was of importance, for the people would eat almost
any kind of bird, beast, or reptile. Dogs were used in the hunt,
and the bones, entrails, and offal of the animals killed were
given to them, the dog which had been of most use receiving
an extra share of the food. Fish were caught in the rivers
and were an important item in the diet. Some were dried and
smoked, but as a rule they were eaten fresh.

Men and women never ate together. Food was usually
eaten in company, the men and the women of a village collecting in separate places for their meals.

SEASONS

They had no means of fixing the beginning of the year,
which might be earlier or later, being reckoned from the
commencement of the rains. The year fell thus into two parts,
drought and rains:

> *Manya gwira* or *kyanda*, drought and sun
> *Ndula soki*, rain.

The year consisted of about six months, though the two rainy seasons were distinguished, the greater rains being the time for sowing the principal crops and the lesser rains the time for sowing those of quick growth.

The next division was marked by the new moon, and each new moon was greeted with songs and dancing. At the time of new moon the potters, who were almost always women, did not make any pots. No special superstitions were attached to the waning moon.

COUNTING

1. *Moti*, the index-finger extended.
2. *Bota*, two fingers extended.
3. *Salu*, index-finger bent in and three fingers extended.
4. *Ena*, four fingers extended in open formation.
5. *Tano*, hand closed over thumb.
6. *Nkaga*, second, third, and fourth fingers of each hand extended, index-fingers held under thumbs.
7. *Musanvu*, four fingers of right hand extended and laid on three of left, which has the index-finger bent inwards under the thumb.
8. *Nane*, four fingers on right hand extended and laid on four of left hand also extended.
9. *Sobi*, right hand laid flat on the inside of extended left hand, one thumb extended.
10. *Kumi*, the thumbs of both hands laid along the index-fingers and the hands clapped together, making a hollow sound.

20.	*Mwe simoti.*	70.	*Bwe sanvu.*
30.	*Bwe salu.*	80.	*Bwe nane.*
40.	*Bwe ena.*	90.	*Bwe sobi.*
50.	*Bwe tano.*	100.	*Bwe kumi.*
60.	*Bwe kaga.*		

CHAPTER XXII

BIRTH, MARRIAGE, ILLNESS, AND DEATH

Birth of a child—seclusion—making a child sit up—birth of twins—training children—exogamy and polygamy—obtaining wives—the marriage-fee—treatment of illness due to ghosts—death and burial—mourning—murder

A WOMAN never hid her condition when she expected a child, for it was a matter for general rejoicing among her husband's clan-fellows and relatives. There were no special taboos to be observed by a pregnant woman and she was at liberty to eat or to refuse different kinds of food as she wished. Her mother came to care for her and acted as midwife at the birth, which took place in the hut, the woman crouching beside one of the posts and supported by a friend.

If the child was a boy the navel cord was cut with an arrow, while if it was a girl, a strip of reed was used. The after-birth was buried in the house near the door and the mother remained four days in seclusion. At the end of the four days she was washed and shaved, after which she might do her household work such as cooking and bringing fire-wood and water, but she might not go to dig in her field for a month. Her husband, however, went about his usual work during the whole of the time.

When the stump of cord fell from the child, the mother shaved the child's head and buried the hair with the cord in the house. A fowl was killed and eaten to mark this ceremony.

At the end of a month, if the child was a boy, the father made it sit up on a little cut grass laid on the floor; if it was a girl the mother did this. The father's father named a boy and the father's mother a girl. The mother continued to nurse the child for some two years or until she found that she had conceived again, after which she might not nurse it any longer.

Twins were sacred, and when a woman bore them she was secluded from all people. The father's mother was sent for to cut the cords, and the women who were helping in the house had to be careful not to quarrel with each other. A fence was built round the house and only the husband and the midwife might enter. For about four months the mother remained in seclusion.

After the birth of twins a medicine-man was sent for and was given a goat, which he killed, sprinkling the family and any friends who had gathered for the occasion with the blood and making a feast of the meat. For four days dancing went on and drums were beaten day and night. The husband had to see that the people were kept supplied with food and beer, which he collected from his relatives. During all this time he had to be careful not to quarrel with anyone or to lose his temper, for that would be harmful to the twins. After four months the mother might go among her friends again and return to work.

When a boy was about five years old he began to accompany the boys who took the goats out to pasture, and in a short time he was regarded as a goat-herd himself. A girl was taught by her mother to dig, to cook, and to perform other household duties. There were no rites of initiation at puberty either for boys or for girls.

MARRIAGE

Among the Bambwa, clan exogamy was strictly followed and polygamy prevailed. A man was always anxious to have as many wives as he could procure, especially because of the extra food he was thus able to obtain. There was always a great desire to grow more grain than was required for food so that it might be used for beer-making. When visitors came to spend a night with a man, they were not allowed to sleep in his house but an empty hut was placed at their disposal.

Wives were as a rule obtained by exchange, and if a youth had sisters it was an easy matter to obtain wives. He would arrange with his parents to give one of his sisters to some man of another clan, who would arrange with his parents to give one of his sisters in exchange. The girls went to their husbands and took their places as wives without any ceremony or formality. When a man had no sister to exchange, he got the permission of some man and woman to marry their daughter and promised in return a number of goats. The fee might amount to as many as twenty goats, but it was not paid at once, though the girl was given to her husband without delay. If after a reasonable time the husband had not paid the animals promised, his wife was taken from him and given to another man.

ILLNESS

When the cause of a man's illness had been found by the medicine-man to be a ghost of his own family, the ghost had to be appeased by the offering of a goat, which was killed by having its throat cut near a shrine built at the spot where the ghost was supposed to have taken up its residence. The blood was allowed to run on the ground by the shrine, and prayers were made to the ghost that in return it would refrain from causing further trouble. The meat was cooked and eaten near the shrine, only relatives of the sick person being permitted to partake.

If, however, the ghost was of a hostile class, different tactics had to be adopted. The medicine-man killed a fowl, allowing the blood to flow over various medicines which he had brought and spread in front of the sick man. He then proceeded to make incisions in the flesh of the sick man's chest, arms, legs, and back and, powdering some of the medicines which had an irritating effect in the palm of his hand, he spat on his thumb, dipped it into the powder and rubbed it into the incisions. A small hut was built near and the patient laid in it, after which it was set on fire. A strong man was deputed to stand near and as soon as the patient was in danger of burning, he was snatched out. By this time the ghost was supposed to have fled from the fire. The medicine-man then took the fowl, pounded the meat and made it into a savoury dish which he offered to the ghost, praying to it not to injure the man again.

When a man was suffering from abdominal troubles, he was given an enema of hot water and was carried outside to defecate, being treated afterwards with other remedies.

Death

When a man died his legs were bent up and his hands were crossed in front of him with the arms straight. This was sometimes done before death and the limbs were tied lest they should be stretched out and become rigid in that position. All ornaments were removed from the dead man. The grave was dug in the hut, the body placed in it on an old sleeping mat in a sitting posture, and the grave filled up with earth. A woman was buried outside, lying on her back with her legs bent up and her hands on either side of her head.

The brother of a dead man took possession of his widows at once, but one widow was left in the hut for a month to guard the grave, and the mourners also remained there for a month, during which they carried out a daily programme of mourning and wailing. At the end of the month, a goat was killed and the head placed on the grave. The mourners ate the meat, washed, shaved their heads and cut their nails. The hair and nail parings of each person were tied in a bundle and fastened to the roof of the hut. They then left the hut, the posts were cut and the hut fell on the grave. This ended the mourning and no further notice was taken of the place, though the ghost was supposed to hover near it.

When one man murdered another, no quarter was shown and no compensation was accepted, but the dead man's relatives hunted down and killed the murderer.

KATWE IN TORO

CHAPTER XXIII

THE SALT-WORKS

Hot springs—the salt-works at Kasenya Nakalongo—purifying salt—
salt-workers—their village—carrying salt—salt at Katwe

THE salt-works at Katwe have long been known to the
inhabitants of the Lake region, and purchasers come from
long distances to buy the salt. In the Katwe district and
along both sides of the Ruwenzori range there are to be found
streams, flowing to the rivers and to the lake, which leave a
saline deposit on their banks. Most of these streams rise from
springs which are hot, and one of the largest rises on the
western side of the Semliki valley, where the spring forms a
large pool fully twenty feet wide drained by a stream which
meanders into the Semliki river. In all these places the inhabitants know how to extract the impure salt by washing
the sand and evaporating the water.

The best salt was not obtained at Katwe proper, but from
a small lake, or rather a depression with a pool in the bottom,
a few miles to the north of Katwe at a place called Kasenya
Nakalongo. I visited this place and saw the work in process.
The depression was some three to four hundred yards in
diameter, almost circular, and some thirty feet deep. The floor
was lined with a dark grey clay or mud, and the pool was
foul-smelling and had a dirty-looking scum on it. In the dry
season the pool was small and shallow and sometimes dried
up entirely and the salt-workers scraped up the deposit left
and washed from it the salt. In the clay surrounding the pool
the salt-workers dug dozens of shallow pools some ten feet in
diameter and cut gutters connecting these with the main pool.

PLATE XXIV

The salt-pans

Huts of salt-workers

Katwe Salt Works

The water from the main pool was allowed to fill one of these salt-pans, and the inlet was then stopped and the water left to evaporate in the heat of the sun. The crust or scum left behind was scraped up and carried to the village, where it was spread upon the hard ground to dry before being packed up for salt. When I visited the place some of the pools were dry and the scum had been removed, others had just been filled, and on some the scum was rapidly hardening as the water evaporated. When a better salt was wanted, the scum was washed in pots which were perforated in the bottom with fine holes. The washing water was then evaporated, the resulting salt being cleaner and whiter than that got by simply drying the scum, but not so good as that obtained from Kibero on Lake Albert.

The depression was intensely hot and had a foul sulphurous smell. The people there declared that the pool did not rise from a spring but was filled by the rains, and that the saline properties came from the ground; but there is probably a hot spring, as in so many places in this district.

The workers at the salt-works were almost all of the Bakonjo tribe, but were called *Munyampaka*. Their village was about half a mile from the salt pool and there they had their drying grounds and boiling pans and stores. There were huts in which the people who came to buy salt might lodge, and a large shed in which they sat to bargain and where they made up their bundles. Purchasers came from various parts of Ankole and from Toro. The ferry to Ankole did a great trade in conveying buyers, who paid a few cents to cross the river, which was here about half a mile wide. Each day as we journeyed from Ankole we must have passed anything up to one hundred traders, and each man carried at least eighty and some a hundred pounds of salt. On the Toro side we found many of the Bambwa tribe carrying salt to the north. They tied their loads to slings which they put round their foreheads, resting the loads upon their backs according to the method adopted by Nilotic peoples and by the people on Mount Elgon and the Masai tribes.

At Katwe proper the salt was of a coarser kind and was largely used for cattle. No attempt was made to purify it, and it was scraped up, dried, and used without any effort to get rid of the sand and other impurities which were mixed with it. During the rainy season there was so much water that salt could only be obtained by evaporating it.

THE BAKUNTA

CHAPTER XXIV

ORIGIN AND CUSTOMS OF THE PEOPLE

Descendants of a man of Buganda—clans and totems—agriculture—
marriage—illness—death—inheritance

THIS small tribe was found on the shores of Lake Edward.
The members claimed to be descendants of a man Ndeki,
who fled from Buganda with a number óf companions. This
was in the earlier days in Buganda, when a new king did not
put all the princes to death at the beginning of his reign, but
left them to live with chiefs who were responsible for their
behaviour and welfare. These princes often rose in rebellion
against their brother, the reigning king, and endeavoured to
wrest the kingdom from him. If the king was killed in the
fight, the man who did the deed was handsomely rewarded
and raised to a position of authority and importance at the
time, but when later any misfortune or illness attacked
members of the royal house, the priests would declare that
the ghost of the last monarch desired vengeance on his
murderer, and the dead king's successor would be persuaded
to arrest and kill the man whose act had put him on his
throne. If it was the rebellious prince who had been killed,
the same treatment would be meted out to his slayer, for
none might shed royal blood with impunity.

The chief Ndeki had killed a prince in this way and was
forced to flee for his life, because the priests insisted that he
was the cause of misfortune in the land. He took with him
some companions and they passed through Ankole, settling
finally on the shore of Lake Edward. The company consisted
of a few men belonging to two or three of the Baganda clans,
with a limited number of women, and to build up their

numbers these men formed alliances with the women of
various tribes in the district. Their customs naturally became
somewhat modified to suit their altered circumstances. Ndeki
and his sons were the recognised leaders of the tribe, though
various clan elders ruled under them as heads of their own
clans. Recently all the sons of the chief, Munyankomi, a
descendant of Ndeki, died, but his daughter bore a son, called
Petero Kayanhu, who became the leader. They called their
country Bunyampuka.

The names of the clans with their totems were:

1. Mamba,   totem *mamba* (lung-fish).
2. Mamba Basonga,   „   *mamba* (lung-fish) and *butiko* (a fungus).
3. Bagahyi,   „   *nseri* (frog).
4. Bakulungu,   „   *ngobe* (monkey).
5. Nsenene Basonga,   „   *nsenene* (grasshopper).
6. Abaitiri,   „   *nte* (cow that had been with the bull).
7. Bayangwe,   „   *nkuni* (antelope).
8. Abaluwha,   „   *njovu* (elephant).

AGRICULTURE

As in Buganda, the women did the work in the fields and
the men built and fought. A man would cut down the grass,
shrubs, and trees for his wife, but all the digging was left to
the woman. They lived mostly on plantains, but also cultivated
millet, both the larger kind called *mutama* and the smaller
bulo, peas, beans, a little maize, and various kinds of marrows
and edible roots.

MARRIAGE

In marriage ceremonies they followed the customs of
Buganda, but combined with them a few of the Banyankole
customs. A marriage-fee had to be paid by the man before
he could claim his bride, and it amounted to two cows and
ten goats. The bride was treated as in Ankole, being fattened
and secluded before marriage and carefully guarded, but after
marriage she might permit any of her husband's friends to
share her bed.

ILLNESS AND DEATH

Illness was treated as in Buganda, that is, it was attributed to magic or to ghosts and the medicine-man was summoned to discover the cause. If it was a ghost it had to be propitiated, and if it was magic it had to be overcome before ordinary remedies were used.

When a man died, his limbs were straightened, his hands crossed on his breast, and the body was wrapped in bark-cloth or cowskin. He was buried near his house and the mourning continued for four days. The eldest son was always the heir, and inherited the widows as well as the property.

THE BAKYIGA, PEOPLE
OF KIGEZI

CHAPTER XXv

THE COUNTRY AND THE PEOPLE

Position and scenery—the people—hostility of clans—villages—elders of the village—land—language—clans—clothing—food—slaves—seasons—*Nabinge*, god of earthquake—magic and ghosts—amulets—superstitions

THE district of Kigezi occupies the southern part of the Ruwenzori range of mountains, bordering on Lake Edward, stretching south to the Ruanda district and west to the Belgian Congo, and bounded on the east and north by Ankole. The equator lies to the north, but so near that Kigezi may almost be said to be on the equator.

The climate is an excellent one, and the district with its tropical fertility and its wonderful mountain scenery is certainly the finest in Eastern Africa. The mountains vary in height from five to thirteen thousand feet, and seem generally to be arranged in horse-shoe-shaped ranges or in circles, so that it is impossible to enter some parts of the country without climbing over a range nine or ten thousand feet high. Enclosed by these ranges are large expanses of country, often dotted with hills of considerable height. These valleys, with their luxuriant growth of trees, shrubs, and flowers, their brightly-coloured birds and insects, their many wild animals, and the splendid waterfalls which here and there dash from the heights of the mountains, make a spectacle hardly to be equalled[1].

Though the Bakyiga were a fairly large tribe, the inhabitants of the district numbering well over a million souls, their land was so large that all the traveller saw of them was a few scattered groups of huts at long intervals. Round these

[1] In some of the valleys there are beautiful lakes of clear, cool water, some of the largest being two miles long and a mile wide. These lakes have forests of splendid timber round them, the foliage of the trees having wonderful colouring. Water lilies in the lake and flowers on the sides add to the enchantment making the scene appear almost too beautiful to be real.

villages extended plots of cultivated land where each woman possessed a large field, and where the cows, goats, and sheep were pastured. The members of each village claimed as their own the sides of the hill on which their village was built, and any intrusion by strangers was fiercely resented and often led to strife and bloodshed. As each man in a village might have several wives and each wife had to have a field of her own, the hills surrounding the villages were ... all cultivated.

The people were of the Bantu stock and were mostly agricultural, though a few pastoral clans might be found on the lower slopes of the hills where the large plateaux afforded excellent pasturage. The Bakyiga were a wild race who in the past resisted all attempts to bring them into subjection, and are only now being brought into some sort of order by the British Government. Life was of little value among them, and they murdered friends, relatives and enemies indiscriminately. The men were of average height, the tallest being about five feet ten to six feet, while the women were slightly shorter. Both sexes were strong and well built, and the mountain life made them muscular. The women were deferential to the men, but not servile, and no marked affection was shown between husband and wife or between parents and children.

There was no supreme chief, but the tribe was divided into clans which were ruled by their own elders and lived completely isolated from each other; they were even hostile, for one clan would not associate with members of another and it was unsafe for a man to travel alone beyond the boundaries of his own clan land. When going on a journey two or three men always travelled together, and they went completely armed.

There might be several villages belonging to one clan, for men might build for themselves a little apart from the first village. If anyone wished to join one of these groups, he had to bring the leader a sheep in order to get permission to build in his village. Such a village was called *Ekilolero*, and the head-man was a *Mukungu*. As the members increased, men were chosen as elders of the village to assist the *Mukungu*, who, however, retained the right of final decision in all matters. No judgment of a case was valid unless it had been set before these elders of the village, and a man had always the right to refuse to accept any other means of trial. When a man wanted land he applied to the head of the village for it, and an annual rent of a pot of beer was often imposed. Land thus granted was handed down from father to son and anyone who intruded on it or questioned the owner's right to it ran a grave risk of being speared down on the spot.

The language was allied both to Lunyoro and to Lunyankole, so that communication between these places and Kigezi was possible without much difficulty.

I managed to obtain the names of some forty-eight clans, but only in a few cases could I find out their totems, though there was every reason to believe that each clan had one.

CLANS

1. Basige (totem, *ente ngobe*, a cow with short straight horns. If such a cow was born in a man's own kraal, his people might drink its milk and eat its flesh, but if it was born anywhere else they had to avoid it).
2. Abageyho (totem, *epu*, meaning uncertain, possibly a kind of antelope).

3. Abatimbo.	26. Abachuchu.
4. Abawungule.	27. Abazingwe.
5. Abahimba.	28. Abainiki.
6. Abahesi.	29. Abasogi.
7. Abahubwa.	30. Abatabalwa.
8. Abafumbira.	31. Abanyakazu.
9. Abazigaba.	32. Abasonde.
10. Abalundo.	33. Abalihi.
11. Abalihira.	34. Abatendula.
12. Abawiga.	35. Abasyiaba.
13. Abayunorulo.	36. Abakoko.
14. Abakongwe.	37. Abakonjo.
15. Abasakuru.	38. Abagunga.
16. Abakimbire.	39. Abalere.
17. Abanyabutumbi.	40. Abanewiru.
18. Ababitira (totem, *epu*).	41. Abagaru.
19. Abasaka.	42. Abasanza.
20. Abalitu.	43. Ababaizi.
21. Abanyangabu.	44. Abasuku.
22. Abageri.	45. Abagala.
23. Abagabira.	46. Abakongola.
24. Abazubikhi (totem, *epu*).	47. Abajija.
25. Abasingola.	48. Abanyonyi.

PLATE XXVI

Man of the Bakyiga, Kigezi

PLATE XXVII

Man of the Bakyiga, Kigezi

CLOTHING, FOOD, AND HOME LIFE

The skins of animals formed the only clothing worn by either sex. Boys and men wore a goat-skin, hanging from the right shoulder by a sling of two legs tied together, and passing under the left arm. Girls until about the age of seven went nude and when they showed signs of maturing they wore a small skin round their loins. Women wore two skins round the loins, one in front and one at the back; and they put their children in slings of sheep-skin on their backs, so that they could carry them with them as they went on with their work.

Goat-skins were valued and bought for clothing. A wealthy man who hired peasants to look after his goats might give them the meat of killed animals as payment, but he used the skins for clothing for himself and his family. An elder of a village might have as many as seventy goats and sheep. Poorer people contented themselves with sheep-skins for clothing. They generally shaved the wool off and, after drying the skin, stamped upon it until it was soft. Sheep-skins were always easily obtained, for sheep were often killed for sacrifices and the taking of auguries.

Men and women generally ate together unless the meal consisted of goat or sheep mutton, which no woman might eat. In that case a woman and her daughters ate together, apart from the male members of the family. Frogs and tadpoles were caught and eaten by some clans on the shores of the lakes.

In the house a special place was reserved for the husband, who sat near the fire where he could see out by the doorway. His seat was not the stool cut from a block of wood which was used by most tribes, but it was made like a bed, with four legs and side pieces to which a woven or plaited seat was attached. Women and children sat on the floor near the fire.

Slaves used to be common, and were bought for a cow or a sheep, but for some time the presence of the white man has prevented the holding of the slave-markets.

They had no fixed names or divisions of seasons, but

regarded the year as being about six months, divided into the
dry and the rainy seasons. The length of these seasons varied
in different years.

RELIGION

It would hardly be correct to say that there was no religion,
for there were many objects of reverence and there was an
imperfect idea of a creator, who, however, was not in any
sense worshipped.

Of recent years much attention has been paid to *Nabinge*,
the god of earthquake, but this god was introduced from a
southern tribe and was formerly quite unknown. When plague
or other illness broke out, it was attributed to *Nabinge*, who
must be appeased. The head-man of the village built a shrine
and called upon the people to bring offerings of goats and
sheep. These were exchanged for a cow or cows according to
their number. One cow was killed at the shrine and the blood,
which was allowed to run on the ground, with the heart and
liver, which were placed in the shrine, were the portion of the
god. Some of the meat was cooked and eaten on the spot, and
the people carried the rest to their homes.

Magic was greatly feared; but the chief objects of reverence
and dread were ghosts, to whom offerings were made in any
case of trouble or illness. When a man fell ill, a medicine-man
was sent for to decide what ghost was causing the trouble and
what offerings should be made to pacify it. An augury was
taken by the medicine-man and his assistant over some
animal, generally a fowl or a sheep, and the medicine-man
was then able to announce whether it was necessary to destroy
the ghost entirely or whether it should be pacified by some
offering. Auguries were also sometimes taken by sprinkling
grain and watching how it fell and spread, or over water upon
which the powdered leaves of herbs were sprinkled; according
to the shapes the powder formed the interpretation was given.

Amulets were the chief objects in which men placed their
faith, and a man would pay as much as a large sheep for one.
They were made from wood or horns of sheep or antelope;

and herbs and other ingredients, which had been blessed by the medicine-man who made them, were put into them. They were worn on the neck, arms, and legs to ward off illness, attack by wild animals, and every other evil to which man is subject.

When a house was burnt down and there happened to be salt in it, people kept away from it and might not even allow the heat of the fire to reach them.

When lightning struck a man, his whole village ceased work until offerings had been made, with prayers that no more might be killed.

CHAPTER XXVI

OCCUPATIONS OF THE PEOPLE

Agriculture—ownership of land—guarding against attack—preparing a field—millet—the firstfruits—death of the owner of a field—other crops—cattle—birth of calves—milk and milk-pots—goats and sheep —fowls—dogs—bee-keeping—honey—brewing—smiths—carpenters —potters—hunting—warfare—causes of battle—weapons—killing an enemy

AGRICULTURE

THE people of Kigezi were diligent workers in their fields; and though they could not start work in the higher parts until about nine or half-past nine, owing to the cold mists of the morning, they worked steadily until about five o'clock in the evening with only a short pause for rest, when they would eat some cooked food, which they had brought with them from their homes, and smoke their pipes. They always carried a few embers with which to start a fire in the field so that they could light their pipes.

Men and women worked together in the fields, for a husband was expected to help each of his wives in turn to cultivate her plot of ground. Each woman claimed the produce of her field for herself, but she was expected to do her share with the other wives in supplying her husband with food. What she could spare after her household needs were satisfied she bartered for goats and sheep, which in turn she exchanged for cows. In this tribe women might possess property and might even pass it on to their children.

A man probably inherited some property from his father, and if he had any daughters he used the marriage-fees he obtained for them to swell his wealth. Each man kept a plot of land for himself in addition to the fields with which he supplied his wives, and they had to assist him in its cultivation. The crops from his field he used for his own purposes, brewing beer or bartering grain for sheep, goats, and cows with which to procure wives. His wives had to supply him with food, so that the whole of his own crop was set free for other purposes.

The fields were sometimes quite half an hour's walk from the village, for naturally those immediately surrounding the village were soon all occupied. When working in these distant fields, men went in companies of three or four and took with them their weapons, keeping them near so that they might seize them in case of alarm or sudden attack. If an attack was made and the men were killed, the women who were with them were spared, but were taken captive and kept until ransomed by their husbands or clans.

When a man and his wife set to work to prepare new land for sowing, they first cut down the trees, shrubs, and tall grass, which were carried to the lowest boundary of the field, for the fields were in practically all cases on the sides of hills. The rubbish from the field was heaped up and burned, the burned trees and stones and earth forming a barrier against which more earth was washed when the rainy season came, so that by degrees the hill-sides became terraced with the cultivated plots.

The staple food was millet, which was ground into flour between stones and used as a kind of porridge. When going to sow millet, a man made a charm of the leaves or seeds of various shrubs which were prolific in growth, and placed this with his seed that it might impart its qualities to it. There were no ceremonies or fetishes for guarding growing crops, but when harvest had ripened the owner had either to eat the first-fruits himself or to carry the first head of grain gathered to his father or mother, after which the crop might be used by all.

Should a man who had planted a crop die before harvest, a clan-brother took his place; but before he might begin to reap the grain, the father of the dead man brought a stone and some cow-dung which he laid in one part of the field. The reapers then left the corn uncut for a few feet round this spot. After the rest was reaped, the father came and cut the corn on this plot, which he kept for himself. This ensured the ripening of the millet and made it wholesome for the family to eat.

In addition to millet, beans and, more especially, peas were largely grown, and were valued because it was possible to raise two crops of them to one of millet. This was the only place where I saw the edible pea with blossoms of various colours. Potatoes were also grown and a little maize, which was never ground or pounded but was roasted whole in the ear.

ANIMALS

Cows were of importance, not so much for their milk, which was looked upon as a luxury and not a necessity, as because they were the means of obtaining wives and of purchasing other things, for prices were fixed on the standard of the value of a cow. Cows were seldom killed except to celebrate some special occasion such as a wedding, or in the event of an offering made to some ghost. Animals were too valuable to be killed to gratify cravings for meat.

The cows were smaller than those of Ankole and had short horns, though here and there might be found a few of the long-horned cattle of Ankole. All the cattle belonging to members of the same village were herded together; and when it was necessary to send them for pasturage to any distance, herds from several villages of a clan might be gathered together and the men of the different villages took it in turn to go with them. Should a man be unable through absence or illness to take his turn, his unmarried daughter might take his place if necessary; but no married woman might herd cows, and no woman was ever allowed to milk. The owner of the cows went out to meet the herds on their return in the evening, and drove his own cows home. Each village had a strong stockade inside which the cattle were gathered for the night. The calves were herded by small boys and girls, and were kept in the houses by night.

When a cow bore a calf, the first milk was boiled with peas and raspberries, and a little flour of the small millet was added. A boy and girl of the same mother ate this, and afterwards the cow's legs were tied as though it was about to be milked and the boy and girl crawled under it. This freed both cow and milk from any further taboo. No notice was taken of the navel cord from the calf, which in other tribes was watched with interest.

When a cow bore twins, the members of the owner's family who were at home drank the milk and used any butter churned, for it might not go out of the village.

When a cow had mated, the owner might not on that day consult any medicine-man or augury. Should he be compelled to do so for any special reason, he might not drink milk from that cow that night.

Milk was not regarded as an essential part of the diet, but it was freely used. Men drank it either warm from the cow or clotted; while women rarely drank it fresh, and preferred butter-milk or clotted milk when possible.

The milk-pots were of wood, and were washed and hung on sticks to dry, but never fumigated as in Ankole. Little milk was churned, for butter was hardly used; but both men and women might churn, though only women might wash the milk-pots.

Goats and sheep were to be found in large flocks, for all those in a village were sent out to pasture together in the charge of children. Goats were more valued and their skins were prized for clothing, but sheep were more numerous, as they were considered to be hardier. Sheep were used for offerings to the spirits, and the poor people used their skins for clothing. Both goats and sheep were excellent animals with good coats, and the aim of a woman was to sell the produce of her field for goats and sheep, which she later exchanged for cows. Men also bought goats and sheep with the crops from their own fields.

A few fowls of a small kind were kept, but they were not numerous and were used chiefly for taking auguries.

Dogs of the common yellow colour were plentiful, for every man liked to possess one for hunting. They were as a rule of little use as watch-dogs, though cases have been known when one would protect its master. In the hunt, however, they were very useful in "putting up" the game, and the scarcity of their food made them eager in the chase. Ordinarily they received little food and had to exist on what scraps they could find; but if a dog drove game which was killed, that dog's owner claimed the kill and gave his dog a share of the entrails and some scraps of the meat.

When a dog had puppies, the owner drew blood from a cow, mixed it with milk and gave it to the dog. The owner might not approach his wife until the puppies had opened their eyes.

It was believed that if a woman killed a dog that was about to have puppies, she would lose as many children as the dog would have had puppies in the litter, that is, as many as five or seven, before she would bear a child which would live.

Bee-keeping

Bees were kept by many men who handled them without fear. A man might have as many as three or four hives placed round about his house. The hives were often merely logs, split in half, hollowed out, and the halves lashed together. Sometimes, however, a hive would be made of plaited papyrus. This was cylindrical, some four feet long and about twelve inches in diameter. In most cases the hive was lodged in the fork of a tree, but sometimes a man would make a stand of logs.

When a man was going to take the honey from a hive, he had to keep apart from his wife for a night. The next day he smoked the bees, driving them to one end of the long hive before he opened it and removed the honey. Young bees were eaten and were looked upon as a delicacy.

The people ate honey, but a woman who was menstruating had to refrain. The chief use of it, however, was to mix with beer. It was added to pots of beer which were then covered· so as to be air-tight, and left for a week. When thoroughly fermented this was the most intoxicating drink the people knew, and its use often led to quarrels and fighting.

BREWING

Beer was generally brewed from the large millet, which was not so sweet as that called *bulo*. The grain was put into pots, covered with water, and left a few days until it sprouted. It was then thoroughly dried and ground into a coarse meal which was boiled. A little freshly ground millet meal was added and the whole allowed to ferment, when it was ready for use. Honey was sometimes added while it was standing to ferment, and added greatly to the strength of the beer.

When a man was brewing he was careful not to sleep with his wife, though he might hold ordinary converse with her, and he avoided all other women. He was also careful not to cross any water and especially not to carry a water-pot across a river, until the beer was ready for drinking. If he neglected these observances the beer would not ferment and would have no more strength than water.

There was much beer drunk and drunkenness was common. A man when going to drink with a friend would often take his wife with him, that she might look after him and see him safely home.

SMITHS

There were men who had a certain rude knowledge of smithing. They collected their own iron-stone where it lay on the surface of the ground and smelted it, following the Ankole methods, which were rough and inferior to those of Kitara. The chief things made were hatchets, knives, and hoes, but warriors also required arrows, good axes, and one or two spears.

CARPENTERS

Carpenters were few and much less expert than those of Ankole, and the articles they turned out were not in the least artistic in shape or well finished. People generally made what they required themselves, and there were few or no professional wood-workers. A rough kind of pot and a few stools, some of them cut from solid blocks of wood some ten or twelve inches high, were practically the only things made.

POTTERS

The art of pottery was also in a very primitive state. The vessels were thick, brittle, and of a clumsy shape. Both men and women did the work. They found white clay in swampy soil, brought it home to their houses, and dried it in the sun. This was then beaten to powder, and mixed with water and a little grit from a broken pot or from pounded stone. There was a little decoration round the necks of water-pots and near the rims of cooking-pots. This consisted of cross-markings made by rubbing the pot with plaited straw, first in one and then in the opposite direction, making criss-cross patterns of lines two or three inches long.

While at work the potter might not spit, for that would weaken the pot. A woman might not make pots while menstruating, for they would crack in drying or when being baked. During the months of July and September no pots were made, for the strong winds which prevailed at these times dried the pots too quickly and cracked them.

Special pots with two mouths were made, originally for some sacred purpose connected with one of their own gods. Recently, however, these pots have been set apart for *Nabinge*, the god of earthquake.

HUNTING

As a result of the enmity between clans, the possibilities of hunting were limited; but when an animal was known to be in some place where it would be safe to go, a company soon surrounded it, and it was clubbed or speared to death. Nets were sometimes used and the game driven into them.

Pigs have only recently found their way into these districts and their flesh is not eaten but given to the dogs, while the skins are used for sandals and shields. The skins of domestic animals were used for clothing, while those of antelopes, leopards and wild cats were used for the aprons worn by warriors and for rugs in the houses.

WARFARE

Though the Bakyiga were a wild and unruly people they were not aggressive, and only once or twice within living memory has there been an occasion when the clans combined to meet and resist some invasion of their country. Such an invasion would come from the Ruanda direction, and, though the clans combined, each clan fought under its own leaders and kept as near as possible to its own part of the country. The clans boast that they have never been overcome by any tribe; but during the expedition places were passed which, though deserted, bore signs of recent occupation. These the people said had been vacated during raids made by the pygmies.

Inter-clan wars were fairly common, for clan would rise against clan for some slight cause, the fight would be short and sharp, and the clans would soon return to their normal life. The commonest cause of clan fight was intrusion upon clan land. When a stranger took possession of clan land, there would first be a fiery dispute with the real owner, who would then appeal to his village for help in expelling the invader. The stranger's clan would come to his aid, and the result would be a short battle when one or two might be killed and a few wounded. If the clan who felt themselves injured were worsted, they might patch up a truce which would hold good until they had recovered their strength sufficiently to make another attempt to set the matter right.

Another cause for clan warfare was murder, for if a member of a clan was murdered by someone of another clan, a common

PLATE XXVIII

Bakyiga warriors

occurrence, the murdered man's relatives would strive to rouse the clan to arms to avenge him.

Marriage by capture also sometimes led to fights. A man might lie in ambush and steal away a girl from another clan. When he reached a place of safety he would call to the parents of the girl and inform them of what he had done, saying that they could have the marriage-fee if they sent for it. There was thus no real cause for fighting, but the girl's brothers would sometimes wish for a fight and would refuse to accept the terms.

Even when working in the fields men had always to have their weapons near, for the opportunity of a man's being occupied and off his guard was often taken to attack him. This was one of the easiest methods of retaliation, and if a man had been murdered his relatives would watch the murderer until they caught him off his guard, and fall upon him before he could defend himself. A woman was never attacked in a fight, but she might be captured, and her husband had then to ransom her.

The arms carried by warriors consisted of small wooden shields, a bow with a few iron-tipped arrows, barbed but not poisoned, and two spears. A fight was usually hand-to-hand between individuals, but archers remained in the back-ground and shot at the enemy from a distance.

When a man slew an enemy in fight he took one finger from the dead man to mark the deed. When a man slew his first enemy, the members of his clan gave him a pebble to swallow and guarded him during the first night after the deed. In the morning a medicine-man gave him a purgative and a fetish to wear and he might then return to his wife. The spear or arrow with which he had killed the man was also purified with special medicine to prevent any harm coming to the owner. No rewards were given for bravery, but a man who had killed an enemy was praised and feasted by his clan fellows.

When a man was wounded, he might be looked after by friends; but no one paid much attention to him.

CHAPTER XXVII

MARRIAGE, ILLNESS, AND DEATH

Initiation—fornication—arranging a marriage—arrival of the bride—
marriage by capture—polygamy—relations between wives—care of
the sick—causes of illness—death and burial—armistice during mourning—offerings to ghosts—murder and its punishment—inheritance of
property and widows

AMONG the Bakyiga there were no initiation ceremonies before
marriage; but a boy at adolescence was instructed by his
father or one of the clan-elders in the duties pertaining to
married life and also in the clan customs and beliefs. He was
also told what clans it was necessary to avoid in the search
for a wife because of some special cause of enmity, and where
he would be wisest to choose his bride. Girls, too, were instructed by their mothers in the duties of married women,
and were given advice as to what kind of men they should
accept or refuse as husbands.

Prior to marriage the morality of a girl was strictly guarded
by her parents, with whom she generally lived until she
married. As there was no communication between clans, if
a girl went wrong it was with some man of her own clan and
therefore one who was regarded as her brother. She would
not, however, be condemned unless she conceived, but in that
case she would be driven away from her home and clan and
would have to find a home with some other clan. When her
child was born she would kill it and strive to find a husband
for herself. The harsh treatment meted out to a girl who conceived before marriage was due to the fear of ghosts, for her
deed would anger the dead of the clan, who might cause illness
among the living if the crime was not thus severely punished.

The rule of clan exogamy and the constant enmity between
clans made it impossible for a young couple to know each
other before marriage; and a girl's only opportunity of seeing
and judging of the man who proposed to marry her, was after
the proposal had been made. In some cases she was brought

face to face with the man before anything was arranged, while
in other cases she would hear about the man and might dislike
what she heard. She was then at liberty to refuse to marry
him. The common custom of capturing a wife made the relationships of married people often doubtful; but as a girl was
brought up in the belief that her husband was to be her lord
and master and that she had no choice but to submit, she
generally settled down to her married life without great
difficulty. It was also impossible for a man to learn much
about the girl he proposed to marry, for he had no communication with members of her clan, though he might hear
something from other women of the girl's clan who had
married men of his own. Women at times visited relations
who had married into other clans, but this took place very
rarely.

When a youth wished to marry, the regular and legal procedure was for his father to make arrangements for him. The
father got into communication with the parents of the girl by
sending one of his wives into their village to arrange a meeting
somewhere outside, for it was not safe for him to go there.
To this meeting each side brought one or two friends; and
they at once settled the amount of the marriage-fee, which
varied from three cows to twenty in the case of a rich man,
who might also be asked to add a few goats. This was paid at
once and the bride sent to her new home without delay,
though at times a meeting between the bride and bridegroom
might be arranged so that the bride had an opportunity of
objecting if she so desired.

The bride had to walk to her new home, for, as it was not
safe for men of her clan to go there, she could not be carried.
She was accompanied by her father's sister and by a younger
sister of her own, and was veiled with cow-skins. When her
husband met her at the gate of his home, he took her hand
and struck it with a stick, saying, "Speak!" At this point,
should she object to the man, she simply turned and walked
out of the place. There was no discussion, as this made it clear
that she would not accept him. If she remained, the stick was

put in the bedroom as the witness of the marriage, and the bride retired there while the friends of the bridegroom danced and feasted outside. A goat was killed to provide meat for the feast, and beer was supplied. During the first night the bride's aunt or sister slept in the bed with the married couple, and next morning this visitor was given a sheep and returned home. The bride then commenced her new life as a married woman.

Though the foregoing was the more formal and legal method of marriage, it was also common for a man to obtain a wife by capture. A man sought the aid of a few friends and together they pounced upon some unprotected girl and carried her off. When they had reached a place of safety, the man sent messengers with the cows and sheep for the marriage-fee to some place near the girl's home. The messengers called out to the girl's father, "Your daughter has become the wife of so-and-so. Here are the animals for the marriage-fee. Come and fetch them." Should the father on examining the fee be dissatisfied, he entered into negotiations about the matter, which was usually settled peaceably. At times, however, as was mentioned before, the girl's brothers would be anxious for a fight and would refuse all overtures until they had fought the matter out.

There was no limit to the number of wives a man might have except his ability to pay for them. Many men had three wives, while a few had as many as five, and only a poor man contented himself with one. Each wife expected to have a house and field of her own and would not live in the same house as another wife. The houses of the wives might be in the same compound and their fields close together; but there was seldom any close friendship between them, and the children of the different wives did not regard each other as brothers and sisters. Should a wife die, leaving young children, it was seldom that another would do anything for them. There were cases when a close bond of friendship existed and one wife would look after the children of another who had died, but such cases were very rare. The care of children usually

PLATE XXIX

Young married woman of Kigezi

PLATE XXX

Old woman of Kigezi

devolved upon the father or upon older members of the dead woman's family; and cases of young children being left to die after the death of their mother were quite common.

ILLNESS

Illness received but little attention and nursing seemed to be entirely unknown. If a man was too ill to go about he was left at home to manage for himself, and his wife's care consisted in offering him his usual food at the usual times. If he could not eat it he went without, and his wife left him while she went to work in her field as usual. A mother seldom remained at home to look after a sick child. If it was too big to be carried with her, she placed a little food beside it and went off to her work.

A man who could afford it, however, would send for a medicine-man to divine the cause of the illness and prescribe its cure. The medicine-man used the usual methods of divining, taking his augury either over the entrails of a fowl or other animal, or by sprinkling powdered leaves of the *kirikiti* tree on water, or grain on a mat, and watching the shapes formed by the powder or by the grain.

If the medicine-man decided that the illness was caused by a ghost, an offering was made at a shrine and the patient was then given medicine. If the cause was magic, the medicine-man was expected to make more powerful magic to overcome the first. If there was no improvement, a second medicine-man was sent for to add his strength to that of the first.

DEATH

When a man or a woman died, the relatives dug the grave in the vicinity of the house and prepared the body for burial by bending up the legs and raising the arms. In the case of a man both hands were brought over the right shoulder and put under the head, and in the case of a woman they were brought over the left shoulder. Any valuable anklets and bracelets were removed; and a reed-mat was wrapped round the body, which was then carried to the grave. The mat was taken off and the body laid in the grave naked; turf was laid upon it with the grass downwards, and the grave was then filled up with earth and a small mound the length of the grave heaped over it. A fence was built round the grave to keep children and cattle from wandering over it and annoying the ghost, and the mat and a few of the dead person's bracelets were put on the fence. The people who had buried the body washed their hands and feet and poured the water on the grave. The members of the household mourned four days and at the end of this time they shaved their heads to signify that the mourning was ended. A short time after a death, the house in which it took place was pulled down and a new one built, care being taken that the fence enclosing the new house excluded both the site of the old house and the grave.

Even after a woman was married and thus belonged to another clan, she would, if she heard of the death of her father, her mother, or of a sister or brother by the same mother, attend the funeral. She was permitted to bring her husband with her and he was given a cow, sheep, or goat, according to the wealth of the dead person. When the funeral was over, he was allowed to return unmolested by the members of his wife's clan, who at any other time would kill him if he ventured amongst them.

Should the ghost of a dead person become troublesome, his family built a small shrine near the grave and made an offering. A goat or a cow might be killed and the blood poured on the ground. A piece of the meat was cut into small portions and placed in the shrine, and the rest was eaten by the family in the house.

MURDER

The Bakyiga were very hasty tempered and excitable, and a quarrel which among other people would end in words, often led to one man spearing another and perhaps killing him. If the death was instantaneous and the murderer was caught in the act, he was bound hand and foot, placed near the spot where the grave was dug, and tried by the elders of the village. The usual punishment was that the murderer was placed alive in the grave and buried beneath the body of his victim. Sometimes he was strangled and his body given to his relatives to bury; and there were also occasions when a murderer offered to pay a fine and his offer was accepted. In such a case the amount of the fine was settled by the head-man of the village, and might be three or four cows. The head-man met the relatives of the murderer and those of the murdered man at a place where there was a sacred *kirikiti* tree growing. There they killed a sheep, burning the skin and the entrails and eating the flesh. The head-man then produced a pot of purificatory medicine from which the murderer drank first, then the members of the dead man's family, and afterwards the others who were present as witnesses. The drinking of this signified that the quarrel was at an end, and that there would be no more attempt at vengeance.

Murders committed by members of other clans were common, and led to endless fighting between clans. If the clans did not go to war, the relatives of the murdered man would lie in wait and endeavour to catch either the murderer or a member of his clan, and kill him.

INHERITANCE

When a man died, all his property descended to his eldest son. The land which a man had cultivated became the property of his heir, and no one might dig there without the owner's sanction.

A man's heir also took all the childless widows to wife, unless there happened to be amongst them one who had looked after him as a child. In such a case that widow became the wife of some other member of the clan, but did not return to her own home. If a widow with children did not re-marry, she looked after her children until she was old, when they were expected to care for her. If a widow did not wish to become the wife of the heir, she might return to her father if he was willing to repay the marriage-fee which he had received for her.

Adoption was unknown, and should a man die without an heir, his relatives divided the property.

RELATIONSHIPS AND COUNTING

Father, tata.
Mother, mawe, but when speaking of her, nyina.
Husband, musaija.
Wife, mukazi.
Son, mutabane.
Daughter, muhala.
Father's father, muzukulu, swenkulu.
Father's mother, nyina nkulu.
Mother's father, muzukulu, swenkulu.
Mother's mother, nyina nkulu.
Father's brother, swento.
Father's sister, swenkazi.
Mother's brother, malumi.
Mother's sister, nyina ento.
Father's brother's wife, muka swento.
Father's sister's husband, ba swenkazi.
Mother's brother's wife, muka malumi.
Mother's sister's husband, iba nyina nto.
Father's brother's son, mukulu we sento *or* mulumunawe we sento.
Father's brother's daughter, munyanya we sento.
Father's sister's son, muzala wange.
Father's sister's daughter, muzala wange.

Mother's brother's son, muzala wange.
Mother's brother's daughter, muzala wange.
Mother's sister's son, mwana wa muzala.
Mother's sister's daughter, mwana wa muzala.
Son's son, muzukulu.
Son's daughter, muzukulu.
Daughter's son, muzukulu.
Daughter's daughter, muzukulu.
Brother's son, muzukulu.
Brother's daughter, muzukulu.
Sister's son, mwiwha.
Sister's daughter, mwiwha.
Wife's father, mukwhe.
Wife's mother, mukwhe.
Wife's brother, mulamu.
Wife's sister, mulamu.
Wife's sister's husband, mulamu.
Husband's father, tatazala.
Husband's mother, nyinazala.
Husband's brother, mulamu.
Husband's sister, omulamukazi.
Husband's brother's wife, mulamu.
Son's wife, ishezala.
Daughter's husband, ishezala.
Older brother, mukulu.
Younger brother, mulumunawe.
Older sister, munyanyaze.
Younger sister, munyanyaze.

Counting:

1. *Emu*, with the index-finger extended.
2. *Ibiri*, the two first fingers extended.
3. *Isatu*, the index-finger bent down and the other three extended.
4. *Enna*, the four fingers extended all close together and the thumb bent inwards.
5. *Etano*, fingers extended and thumb laid along index-finger.

6. *Mukaga*, right hand as for five and index-finger of left hand extended.
7. *Musanju*, right hand as for five and two first fingers of left extended.
8. *Munana*, all fingers extended with both thumbs bent in.
9. *Mwenda*, both hands extended with the thumb of right hand laid along the index-finger and left thumb bent inwards.
10. *Ikumi*, both hands extended with thumbs laid along index-fingers.
20. *Amakumi abiri.*
100. *Igana.*

After this they say one or more *igana* up to ten at which they stop as being the highest number.

Moon phases:

New moon, *mwezi abonekere.*
Full moon, *kucherana.*
Waning moon, *kwachwera.*

THE BATUSE OR BALYAN-WANDA OF RUANDA

CHAPTER XXVIII

THE TRIBE AND ITS GOVERNMENT

The clans—government—powers of the chiefs—taxation—murder—
homicide—death in battle—suicide—the chief priest

THOUGH much of the Ruanda country became Belgian
after the war, there is still a large part of Kigezi which is
British Ruanda. My information with regard to these people
was derived from two chiefs who were political prisoners in
Mbarara. One of them was a prince of Ruanda who had
fought against the British during the war and had been
captured, and both were exiles from their own country because their king regarded them as dangerous to him and
wished to kill them.

THE CLANS

The tribe was divided into clans which were totemic, having
both primary and secondary totems. Sub-divisions of several
clans were mentioned, but the information given was so imperfect as to be of little value. The names given were the same
as some of the main clans and details as to the totems were
lacking. The list, however, is given to show the existence of
such sub-divisions:

1. Abanyiginya, totem, *mpekhi* or *epu* and *efuti*, a calf born feet
foremost?
This was the royal clan and had three sub-divisions with the same
totems:
    (a) Abasindi.
    (b) Nabaganzo.
    (c) Abene, which had also a third totem, an unmarried girl
    with child.
2. Abega, totems, *mpekhi* and *efuti*.
Sub-divisions with the same totems:
    (a) Abakono.
    (b) Abaha.

PLATE XXXI

Chief of the Batuse, Ruanda

3. Abakono.
4. Abagisere, totem, *enyamanzi*, wagtail.
   Sub-divisions:
   (a) Abasinga, totems, *enyamanzi*, and *lubombo*, a cow.
   (b) Abazigaba,   ,,   ,,
   (c) Abatyaba,   ,,   ,,
5. Abazigaba.
6. Abasinga.
7. Abawungara.

The members of this clan intermarry and also marry people from outside tribes and from the clans Abakongole, Abaswere and Abasinga, but not from other clans, for these four clans were despised people and men of other clans would not marry girls from them.

8. Abatyaba, totem, *enyamanzi*. Abanyiginya and Abega clans refuse to marry girls from this clan.
9. Abasindi, totems, *mpekhi* and *efuti*.
10. Abakongole.
11. Abasambo, totems, *epu* and a house burned down and lightning. These came from Ankole.
12. Abaswere.

GOVERNMENT

The head of the country was the king, whose title was *Omwami* or *Mugabe*, and all important cases had to be brought to his court (*Kambera*) for trial. The king, however, did not appoint the great chiefs or *Abatwala*, for their offices were hereditary and they had been appointed by former kings, who divided the land into some forty districts and put a district chief over each. When, however, a district chief died leaving a son who was too young to manage the estate, the king appointed a guardian, often a brother of the dead chief, who administered the estate until the real chief was old enough. The new chief might then give his guardian a chieftainship under him and retain him as an advisor. If the guardian did not receive or accept such an office, he went to the king, who found him some post.

Each district chief was the magistrate in his own district; but appeal might be made from his jurisdiction to the court of the king, to which the chiefs were summoned by crier, for the district chiefs formed the council of the king. The court was under the direction of a special man, a kind of steward or *inhebe*.

The district chiefs were also responsible for building and other work for the king and the state; they had to find the necessary workmen and appoint overseers to direct them. Another man of the king acted as a kind of household steward to see that the buildings were kept in repair and properly attended to.

Each district chief appointed chiefs of the second rank or *Ibisonga* in his own district, and they in their turn appointed the chiefs of the third grade or *Abafragizu*. Each district chief also appointed a steward or *inhebe* who acted in his place when he had to be absent from his district. This man always possessed land near his chief so that he might be at hand when he was wanted. His special duty was to take charge of any building for the chief.

TAXATION

Every year a district chief had to bring two or three hundred large pots of honey, each holding some two gallons, and a supply of millet, peas, and beans to the king. This was brought to the district chief by the people on his estate, and he took a portion for himself before passing the required amount on to the king.

Twice in the year each person with cattle gave to the king a cow and a calf to supply him with milk and a fat animal to be killed for his meat. Milk was also sent daily to the court for the use of the king and his household.

MURDER

It was the duty of the relatives of a murdered man to hunt down and capture the murderer and put him to death; they rarely accepted any other settlement. If a murder was committed before witnesses, they would seize the murderer and hand him over to the relatives of the dead man. If, however, one man abused another before witnesses, the offended man might put the other to death without fear of punishment, for the witnesses would state the reason for his action and he would not suffer for it.

When a murder was committed secretly and the body was found without any trace of the murderer, it caused much difficulty. The relatives had to inform the chief of anything they knew concerning the relations of the dead man with the people of the district. Any person with whom the dead man had had a quarrel or disagreement was captured, and a priest killed a fowl and took an augury in order to find out whether he was guilty or not. Should the augury be in the suspected man's favour he was released, and some other magical means of finding the murderer were tried.

Sometimes a murderer would confess his deed to the king or chiefs and notify his desire to atone. The family of the murdered man were called to a meeting and the murderer had to supply a sheep. The king was present at the meeting and ordered the animal to be killed and cut open, after which the murderer and the head-man of the murdered man's clan placed their hands on the entrails. Portions of every kind of food used by the people were brought and placed in the sheep with purificatory herbs, and again the two men placed their hands in it. The sheep was then called *Maana* or god and was the pledge of peace. Some clans, however, refused to make peace with a murderer and awaited an opportunity of killing either the criminal or some member of his clan.

When a man killed another accidentally and succeeded in proving that there was no malice or intention about the act, he paid fourteen cows to the family of the dead man, with whom he remained on friendly terms. If a man wounded another he paid him eight cows as compensation.

When a warrior killed a man in battle, the king and chiefs honoured him and gave him presents of land and cattle. Sometimes when the king was specially pleased, he would give a warrior a princess to wife. The warrior had to be purified on his return from the battle, but observed no other taboo.

When a man committed suicide, he was buried as usual;
but a medicine-man was summoned to tell by augury whether
the house had to be deserted or was still fit to live in.

RELIGION

I received a statement respecting the religion of the Batuse
from Captain Phillips, the District Commissioner. They were,
he said, monotheistic and had a chief priest who was initiated
into his office by a journey up a certain mountain where there
was said to be a flock of sheep sacred to the god. This was a
dangerous exploit, but before a man was accepted as priest
he had to go there with a sheep, which he offered to the god.

This chief priest kept all the fetishes and carried out all
religious observances for the king, who kept neither fetishes
nor priests about him. When there was any illness or other
trouble, the king sent a bull, a sheep, or a fowl (in the case of
war, a bull, a ram, or a cock) to the priest, and an augury
was taken from the flow of blood and from the markings on
the lungs and intestines.

CHAPTER XXIX

THE KING

The kings of Ruanda—government and taxation by the king—food
of the king—wives of the king—heir to the king—death of the king—
mourning—burial—accession—the king's mother and her brother

THE list of the kings of Ruanda was given as follows: Kigwa,
who came from heaven—his son, Kimanuke, who begat
Randa — Merano — Kobo — Gihanga — Kalyaruanda —
Ruganza — Kirimu — Kigeri — Mutabazi — Gahima —
Ndahiru — Ndole — Muhenzi — Namuhesera — Sekalongoro
— Huhi — Kirima — Ndabalasa — Mubamwhe — Gahiridirwa
— Lwogera — Lwabugiri — Lutariridwa, who was killed by
his brother Musinga, who still reigns.

The king's court was the court of appeal for all his subjects and his council was composed of the high chiefs. He imposed taxation of honey, millet, peas, beans, cattle, and milk, and the chiefs were responsible for any building or other state work he required.

The king's first meal in the morning was of milk, which he took either fresh or clotted as he preferred. At noon he generally drank beer, but he took no other food until evening, when he had meat with peas, beans, or millet porridge, but he might never eat sweet potatoes. After this meal he drank either beer or milk, which shows that the people were abandoning the strict rules of the milk diet which would have forbidden his drinking milk immediately after eating meat and vegetables. During the night he was roused and offered milk to drink. The favourite wife waited upon him and ate with him, and special boy attendants ate any meat that was left over from his meal.

The king married as many wives as he wished, suitable girls being added to his harem as they were found. The favourite of the moment was treated as the chief wife. These women were continually consulting medicine-men and priests, who told them whether they were going to bear children and took auguries to decide who would be the mother of the future king. The king often chose a prince to succeed him, and when he grew up informed him of his future and made him a partner with him on the throne. The other princes were sent to govern different parts of the country as chiefs.

When the king felt that he was seriously ill, he ended his life by taking poison. When he died the news was circulated over the country. There was no rule against naming the king after his death nor against saying that he was dead. The whole tribe shaved their heads and all men kept apart from women during the two months of mourning. The males of cows, goats, and sheep were also separated from their females for this time, and the udders of cows, after milking, were smeared with ashes instead of with white clay as was usual at other times. One cow was killed when the king died.

A certain district was reserved for the burial of the kings, and each king had a hill kept for his grave alone. On this a large house was built and the grave was dug inside it; servants were selected to look after the tomb, and cows were dedicated to the dead king. The hill was thereafter looked upon as sacred and no king would walk upon the hill where a predecessor lay buried. Though only one cow was killed for the king at his death, two or three hundred were sacrificed at the end of the mourning.

The king usually stated which son was to reign in his stead and if possible his wishes were respected; but if he had made no appointment, the chiefs chose a prince to be their new king. If in this case any brother prince objected, the two princes went to war until one or the other was killed.

The king's mother and her brother acted as advisors to the king. A special district about four miles from the tombs of the kings was reserved for the burial place of the kings' mothers.

CHAPTER XXX

LIFE AND OCCUPATIONS OF THE PEOPLE

Food—serving meat—entertainment of visitors—fire—the cattle—care of the cows—value of cows—birth of calves—goats, sheep, and bees—agriculture—growing millet—drums—dances—adoption—slaves and servants

FOOD

THE Batuse were not so dependent upon milk as were the cow-people of Ankole, but it formed an important part of their diet. When a man rose in the morning, his wives or servants brought butter and anointed him, rubbing it well into the skin. They then gave him as much milk as he could drink and he took no solid food till evening. At noon he might drink beer or milk, after which he usually slept for a time. In the evening, however, he had a meal of meat and plantain or millet porridge, and after it he might drink milk again.

Meat was always cut from the bones before being served, and the bones were given to the servants or to peasants. Men sometimes ate with their families, but almost always they ate alone and in secret, and even the food that was left over from their meal might not be seen, for should there chance to be bones amongst it, the man was laughed at and made fun of by those who saw it. It was the duty of a man's wife to cut up the meat and remove all bones. If a friend paid a visit he might partake of a meal only if he was with his host from the beginning of it; if he arrived during the meal he was not permitted to approach. The rules of hospitality were very strict, and even a poor person of the same clan would be invited to share a man's meal, while the richest member of one of the despised clans would never be allowed to do so. Among the better classes the cooks were men, but among poor people women cooked for their husbands.

There were no special rules about fire; but it was always preferable to obtain it from some other fire, and only if this was impossible would they use fire-sticks to kindle it.

The Cattle

The people were largely agricultural, but cows were looked upon as their wealth and they kept large herds, some running even into thousands; while a man who was considered only moderately rich would have four or five hundred.

The people, because of their agricultural pursuits, had fixed dwellings, but the herdsmen wandered about with the cows for pasture. The cattle were of mixed types, some short-horned and some long-horned; they were divided into herds of two to four hundred, each herd being under the care of a head-man and twelve or more others. They roamed the pasture lands two or three months at a time without returning home, sleeping in grass huts hastily erected, while the cattle were left in the open without fences. The calves were kept in the huts and their presence prevented the cows from straying, while a watch was kept to protect them from wild animals. The men stayed only a few days in each place. The wives of the herdsmen lived in the villages near their fields; but they had to bring food daily to the place where their husbands were, for even the herdsmen did not live entirely upon milk. Cattle were never kept inside the fences enclosing the dwellings of the king or other owners, but the herdsmen had to bring milk after each milking to the owner of the herd even if the cattle were at some distance.

The men regarded their cows as their own and might sell or exchange them as they thought fit, but the king claimed all the cattle in the country and might take any he wanted from any herd. The value of a cow was twenty goats and of a bull fifteen goats, while a goat was valued at five hoes. A woman who had been captured in war might be restored to her tribe for a payment of three cows for a woman of the better class and six goats for a peasant.

When a cow was thought to be about to calve at an inconvenient time during a journey or while grazing at such a distance that the calf would have to be carried home, the herdsmen tied a little grass round its horns close to the head and this was said to retard the birth. When a cow which had calved did not cast the after-birth, the first milk was placed upon a stool for a time and then poured away. If the cow recovered without parting with the after-birth, the owner might not drink the milk from it but left it to the herdsmen until the cow had another calf and the placenta came away. For fourteen days after a cow calved, the milk was drunk by the herdsmen or by children and not by the owner of the cow. No taboo was attached to the navel cord of calves.

Goats were preferred to sheep, but both were reared in large numbers, not so much for meat as in order to exchange them for cows and other necessary articles. Most men also kept bees, for honey was demanded as a tax by the king and was an article of food among all classes. A large pot of honey with the comb was sold for a goat, and a small pot of refined honey for two hoes.

Agriculture

Each wife possessed a plot of land on which she raised crops to supply the family with food. Among the better classes the wife did not go out to work herself but left it to the servants and slaves. Among the poorer people, however, both husband and wife worked in the field.

They grew millet, both the large kind and the small millet called *bulo*, peas, beans, maize, sweet potatoes and various other roots, and kassava.

For the millet crop the ground was dug over with the common short hoe; and before the seed was sown, a small basket of it was taken to the medicine-man, who gave it his blessing and mixed some medicine with it or placed a fetish in it. Some of this seed was mixed with that which was to be sown, and the basket with the remainder was kept in the field during the sowing and afterwards taken home and kept in a safe place to ensure good crops.

As the grain ripened, guards were placed to scare off birds and wild animals. The firstfruits of the crop had to be eaten by the owner and his wife, and the grain was stored in granaries near the houses. For use the millet was ground and boiled to a stiff porridge which formed the principal food of the people.

DRUMS AND DANCES

Drums were in common use in the country and were beaten morning and evening. Drums were beaten before the king's house at the noon hour and all the people clapped their hands. It was thought that if these drums did not sound, disorder would prevail and the people would not know what time of day it was. Even when the king was dead these drums were sounded. Special drums were also beaten at new moon, and were the signal for a fresh relay of monthly workers to take up their posts and relieve those on duty about the king.

The chief drums were *Kalinga, Kiragutu, Kirimugezi*, and *Basibihugo*. Kalinga was given to the king on his accession by the people and he accepted it by taking the stick, beating the drum, and then clapping his hands. The people were never again permitted to see this drum. When the skin wore out a new skin was put on over the old, and each month a bull was killed and the blood smeared over the drum.

A chief wore two beads on each side of his head, but he did not possess a drum and only used one when it was necessary to propitiate some ghost which was troubling him. A drum was given to him for this special purpose, and he took it to his kraal, where he beat it for the benefit of the ghost.

When saluting the king, the people knelt and clapped their hands.

There was always dancing at new moon, which was accompanied by singing, by the music of the royal band, and by bells. The musical instruments consisted of drums and the horns of animals through which the musicians blew, while some members of the band had bells on their legs which sounded as they stamped to mark the rhythm.

ADOPTION

A man who had no son might adopt the child of some relative without any ceremony, but, as a man might take as many wives as he wished, it was not often that a husband was left without a son. If a boy who had been adopted committed some misdeed for which he was cast off by his new parents, his own parents would not take him back. He had to find means of atoning for his fault and gaining the forgiveness of his adopted parents.

If a man adopted a boy from a clan other than his own, he took him to the fireplace, dropped some millet into the fire and said, "This is my own son and when I am dead he will attend to my needs." A woman naturally did not welcome an adopted son, for he was a standing rebuke to her.

SLAVES

There were several classes of slaves:

(1) The conquered aborigines of the land who were really free but were regarded by the upper classes as slaves inasmuch as they did menial work for them.

(2) Household slaves. These were mostly women from among the free people who engaged of their own will in this

PLATE XXXII

Wife of a Prince of the Batuse of Ruanda

kind of service. They could not be sold and might leave service and marry when they wished.

(3) Slaves who had been purchased or captured during wars or raids. These were also women and were seldom sold; when once a slave entered a family she remained there for life. Such slaves were often taken by their owners to wife, and their sons were regarded as legitimate and might inherit property.

CHAPTER XXXI

MARRIAGE, ILLNESS, AND DEATH

Forbidden relationships—initiation—arranging marriages—marriage ceremonies—taking home a bride—polygamy—entertainment of visitors—treatment of illness—death—burial—mourning—the heir—the widows

MARRIAGE between the descendants of a brother and sister was forbidden until they reached the fourth generation, that is, the great-grandchildren of a brother and sister might marry.

There were no initiation ceremonies, but before the sons of princes or chiefs were considered to be of marriageable age, they had to prove that they were capable of settling some quarrel or lawsuit between men. The chief instruction given to a youth was how to manage cattle, but he was also taught to cultivate the land.

Infant betrothals were common, and the parents of a boy might agree with those of a baby girl for their children to marry when of a suitable age. The boy's parents gave the others a cow as a pledge of the betrothal, and as long as they kept the cow the engagement was binding. If, however, the parents of the girl discovered any cause for breaking the pledge, they returned the cow with a message that the engagement was at an end. When a boy thus engaged came to a reasonable age, he was told of the arrangement and took presents of beer to his prospective father-in-law. When a boy grew up without anything being arranged for his marriage, he asked his father's brother to find a wife for him.

When the day of the marriage came, the bridegroom took a cow and, accompanied by some friends, went to the kraal of the bride's parents, timing his visit to arrive at sunset when the cattle returned from pasture. The friends and relatives of the bride received the young man outside the kraal and they drank beer together. Then a sister of the bride came, and conducted the young man, leaving his friends outside, to a hut in the kraal where the bride was sitting. The bridegroom carried with him a runner of wild gourd which he twisted into a wreath and put on the bride's head. A pot of milk was given to him and he drank a mouthful which he puffed over the bride. He and the bride then placed their hands on the stones of the fire-place on which the pots stood while cooking; they churned a little butter together; a pot with water was put on the fire and together they sprinkled in flour, stirred it with one stick, and made porridge. Then the bridegroom returned to his friends outside the kraal gate and there they danced and drank beer all night, for none of them might sleep.

In the morning a mat was spread outside the kraal gate and the bride's father and some friends sat on it with the bridegroom. A cow was given to the friends of the bridegroom when they left to go home, and later in the day, after the bride's friends had discussed matters, the bridegroom also went home to prepare things for his bride's arrival.

The party which conducted the bride to her new home included her father, her brother's wife, her sister, and her young brother. The bride was carried in a litter and veiled, and the party arrived at the bridegroom's kraal when the cows were returning from the pasture. The bride was received by women relatives of the bridegroom, who took her into a house which they had prepared for her.

In the evening the bride joined her husband, but her young brother slept between her husband and herself that night and sometimes for two or three nights and the marriage might not be consummated until he had gone. The rest of the bride's party left on the second day, after receiving presents.

A son-in-law did not fear his wife's parents, but was regarded and treated by them as a son.

A man might marry as many as five wives, but he brought only one of them to live in his own village; for the others he built houses in their villages and visited them there. If he was wealthy, which was usually the condition of a man who married more than one wife, he gave each of them cows to supply her with milk, a man to herd them, men to dig her field, and also maids to wait upon her and work in her field.

A wife was usually restricted to her husband in sexual intercourse, but when a great friend of the husband paid him a visit he might permit him to live with one of his wives who acted as the visitor's wife for the time. It was, however, more usual for a guest to go to another house with his own wife, or for the host and his wife to sleep on a mat on the floor and leave the bed to the guest and his wife.

ILLNESS AND DEATH

When a man fell ill, his wife informed his relatives and a medicine-man was summoned to discover by augury whether magic was being used or whether the illness was the work of some ghost. If magic was found to be the cause of the illness, the name of the person using it had also to be discovered by augury, and he was accused and brought before the king or some chief to be tried. Invariably a man who had been discovered by augury to be guilty was condemned without question; he might appeal to the poison ordeal, but he had very little chance of escape, and was always put to death. If the augury showed the illness to be due to a ghost, a bull was offered to the ghost and it was begged to stop troubling the man.

Before a man died he generally named his heir, who was usually one of his sons, though not necessarily so and not always the eldest son. If a man died without having named his heir, the king or his clan appointed someone to inherit his property.

When a man died, all ornaments and clothing, with the exception of a loin-cloth, were removed, his legs were bent up into the squatting posture, and his head was shaved. A cow was brought to the bedside, a little hair from it was put in the right hand of the dead man and a little milk milked over it. This hand with the hair in it was then placed under the head.

In the case of an ordinary man, the grave was dug by the relatives or servants in the garden near, or, should he have no land, in some secluded spot, and the body was buried there. Should he, however, be a wealthy man, the grave was dug big enough for a bedstead to be placed in it. This was covered with skins, on which the body, wrapped in mats, was laid and covered with skins of wild animals and cows. A second bedstead was placed on top of the first to keep the earth from the body, and the grave was filled up with earth, which was piled into a mound over it. The weapons of a dead man were put on his grave, and in the case of a woman her flour basket was buried with her.

A hut without any doorway was built over the grave and a growing fence planted round it. There was always the fear that someone might disturb the dead by digging up the body for the purpose of working magic, and the heir was therefore responsible for keeping this fence in repair until it had grown big enough to keep off people and cattle, after which no further attention was paid to it. After the burial all the people who took part in it were given hot water to wash their hands before leaving for their own homes.

A cow was brought and killed by the grave after the burial and was cooked and eaten by the mourners. The skin was dressed and worn as mourning by the heir, or by some favourite child of the dead man, for two months, during which time he might not come into the presence of the king. The mourners might neither wash nor shave. They lived together in one house, avoided all other people, and had to be strictly chaste lest they should incur the ghost's displeasure.

After the mourning the heir was purified by an elder of the clan, and he then took the mourning garment and buried it in some secret place. The mourners shaved their heads and hid the hair. A medicine-man decided whether the house of the dead man might still be inhabited or not. If the people were permitted to remain there, they, the place, and the pots had to be purified; but if they had to go they gave the pots and furniture away and left the house to fall down.

The heir was purified again by an elder of the clan and then went to buy a cow, which he took to the king, whom he was not on this occasion allowed to see. The next day he visited the king, taking a present of a young bull, and informed him of the death. This reception constituted his acknowledgment by the king as the dead man's heir, but if he proved unsatisfactory he might later be dismissed from the chieftainship.

The heir took all his father's widows except old women and his own mother. He even took widows with children, and the children regarded him as their father.

When a married man lost his father he lived apart from his wife for two months, and on the death of his mother he avoided his wife for one month.

INDEX

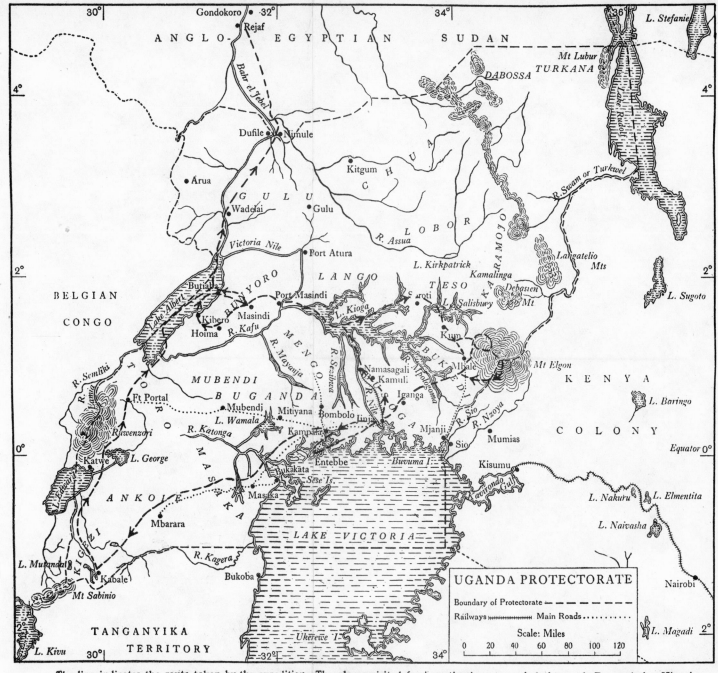

The line indicates the route taken by the expedition—The places visited for investigation were: Ankole people Banyankole—Kigezi people Bakyiga—Bakunta on shore of L. Edward—Katwe and Fort Portal people Bambwa and Bakonjo—Bunyoro people Banyoro—Soroti and L. Salisbury people Bateso—Mt Elgon people Bagesu and Basabei—Busoga people Basoga.

THE LIBRARY
ST. MARY'S COLLEGE OF MARYLAND
ST. MARY'S CITY, MARYLAND 20686

087009